BIG BAD CITY

BIG BAD CITY

Slinkachu

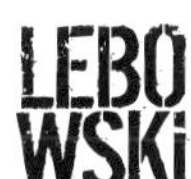

Big Bad City is the not so literal translation of Slinkachu's book *Little People in the City*. We – Lebowski Publishers in collaboration with the artist known as Slinkachu – made a painstaking selection of photographs that appeared in the original edition, but also added work Slink has made since the publication of *Little People in the City* and – happily for you and us – some photographs he made in Amsterdam and Rotterdam especially for this Dutch edition. We admire Slinkachu and we hope you will enjoy this bilingual edition (which took ages to translate) as well as the brand new afterword Slink wrote for all us aficionados of little people in the city.

The Publisher, 2010

Eerste druk, september 2010
Tweede druk, december 2010

Oorspronkelijke titel: *Little People in the City*
Oorspronkelijk uitgegeven door: Boxtree (imprint van Pan Macmillan Ltd), 2008

Dank aan Fishy Eve & Jopkop

Omslagontwerp en typografie: DPS Design & Prepress Services, Amsterdam

ISBN 978 488 0190 9
NUR 640

www.slinkachu.com
www.little-people.blogspot.com
www.lebowskipublishers.nl
www.andipamodern.com

Lebowski Publishers is een imprint van Dutch Media Uitgevers bv

INTRODUCTIE DOOR SLINKACHU

Politieman Neemt u mij niet kwalijk, mijnheer. Kunt u mij vertellen waar u mee bezig bent?

Slinkachu O, eh… Ik was net bezig dit plastic figuurtje vast te plakken.

Politieman U zegt?

Slinkachu Kijk, hier. Het is een… eh… kunstding. Soort van. Ik neem foto's van deze poppetjes, en dan laat ik ze achter.

Politieman O, ha! Wat leuk! Neem me niet kwalijk, ik dacht dat u lijm aan het snuiven was, dat zien we veel in deze buurt, dat mensen van die superlijm snuiven.

Slinkachu Ja, ha.

Politieman Ja, dit is leuk. En ook een klein speelgoedautootje! Wat lief. Mijn kinderen zouden dit prachtig vinden!

Slinkachu Ja… het is een… eh… klein prostitueetje. En haar klant zit in de auto.

Politieman …o… nou, ja… eh… zet 'm op.

Slinkachu Eh, yep. Bedankt…

INTRODUCTION BY SLINKACHU

Policeman	Excuse me Sir. Would you mind telling me what you are doing?
Slinkachu	Oh. Er… I was just gluing down this little plastic person.
Policeman	Eh?
Slinkachu	Here, look. It's an… er… an art thing. Kind of. I take photos of these little people. Then leave them.
Policeman	Oh, ha! Cute! Sorry, I thought you were sniffing glue, what with that super glue. We get a lot of that around here.
Slinkachu	Yeah. Ha…
Policeman	Yeah, this is cute. Ha, a little car too! Sweet. My kids would love this!
Slinkachu	Yeah… It's, er… a little prostitute. And a punter. In the car.
Policeman	…oh… oh, well, er… carry on.
Slinkachu	Er, yeah. Thanks…

BIG BAD CITY

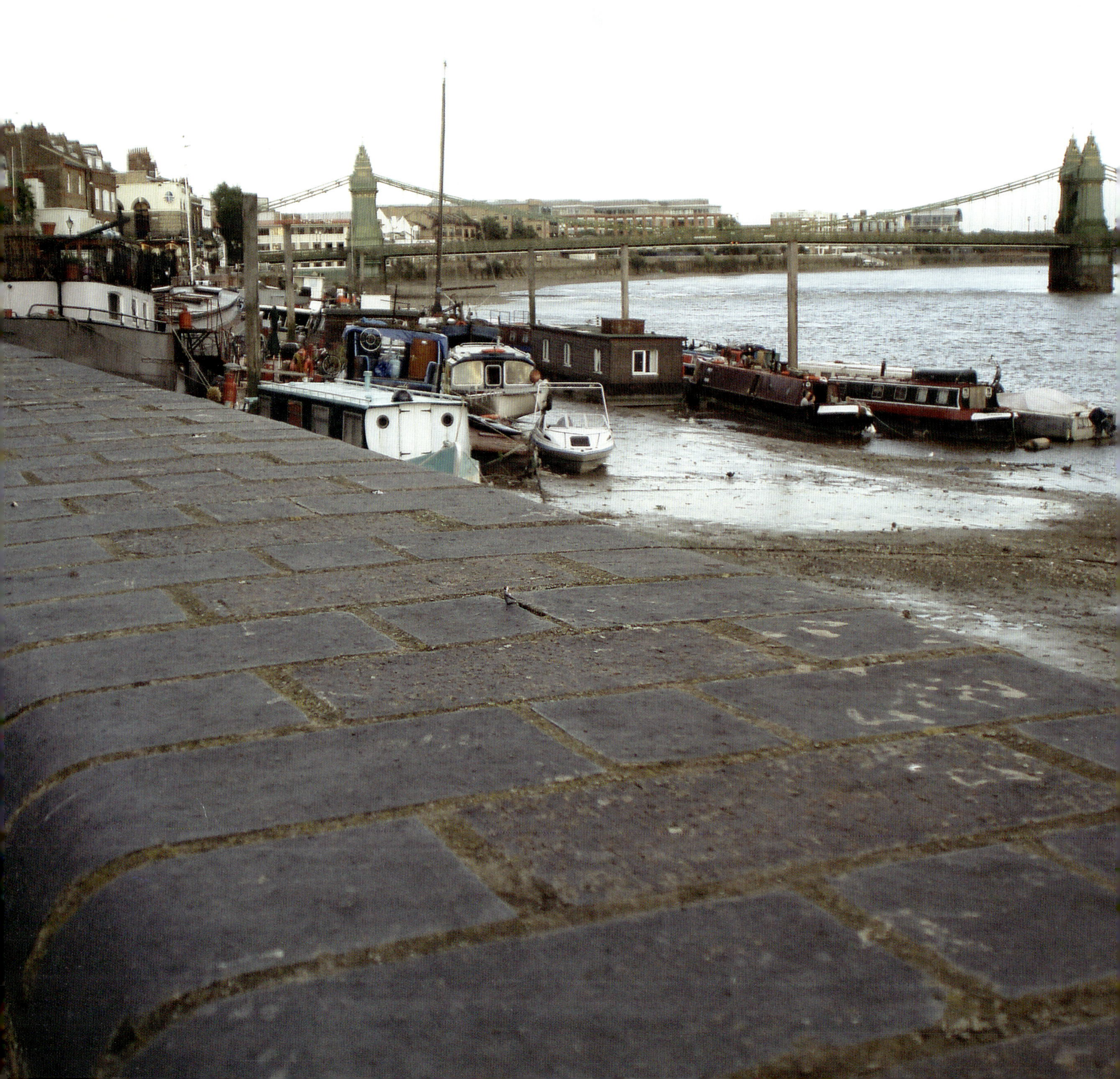

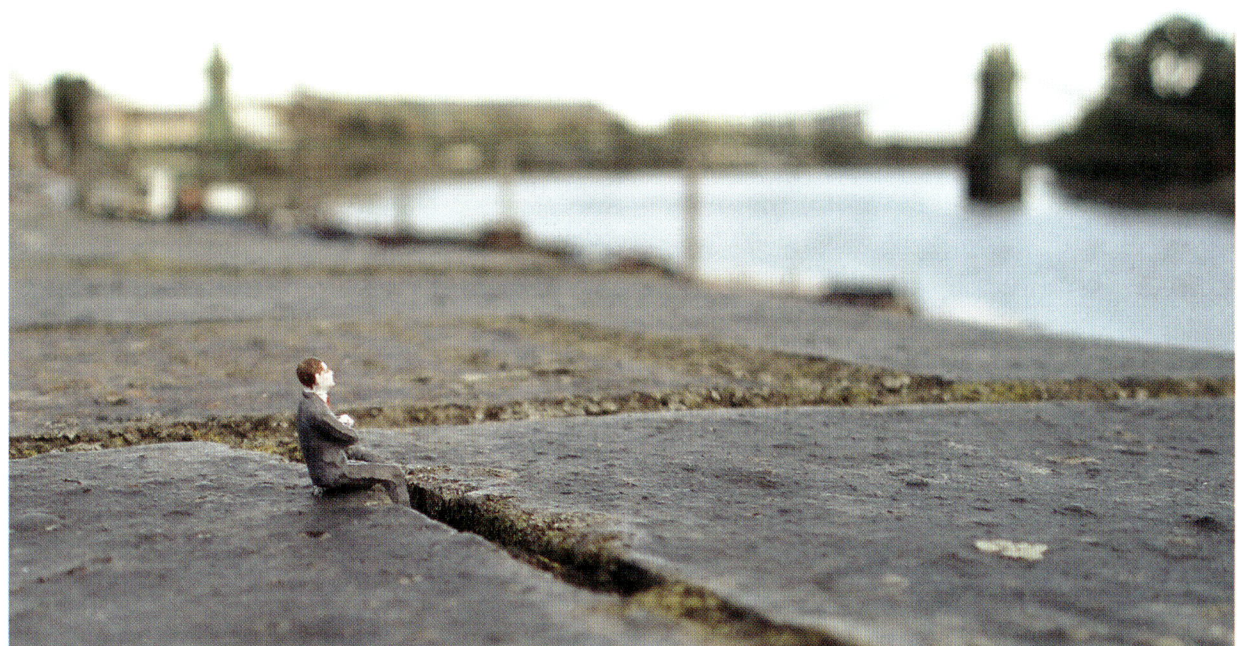

Dreams of Packing it All In

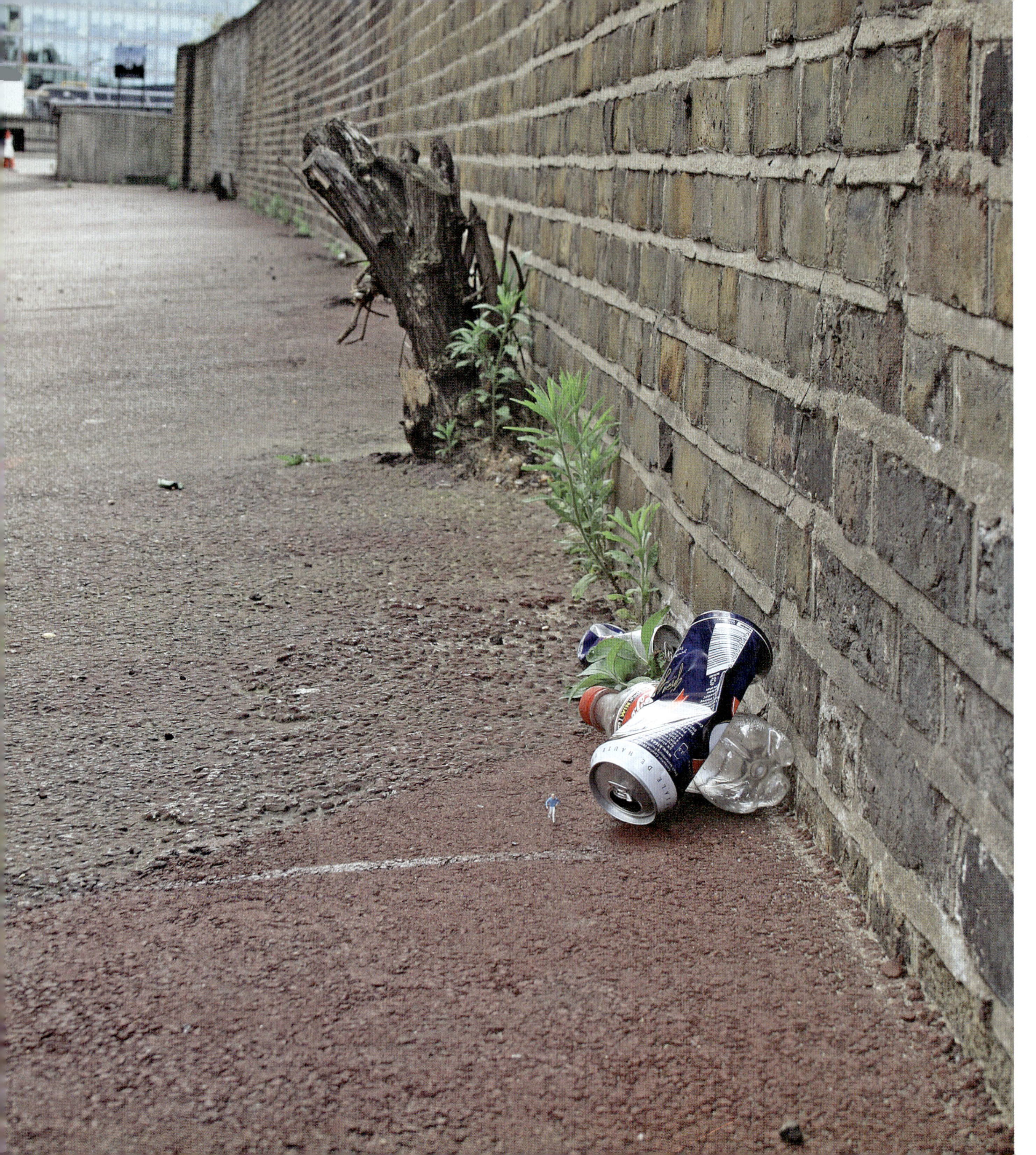

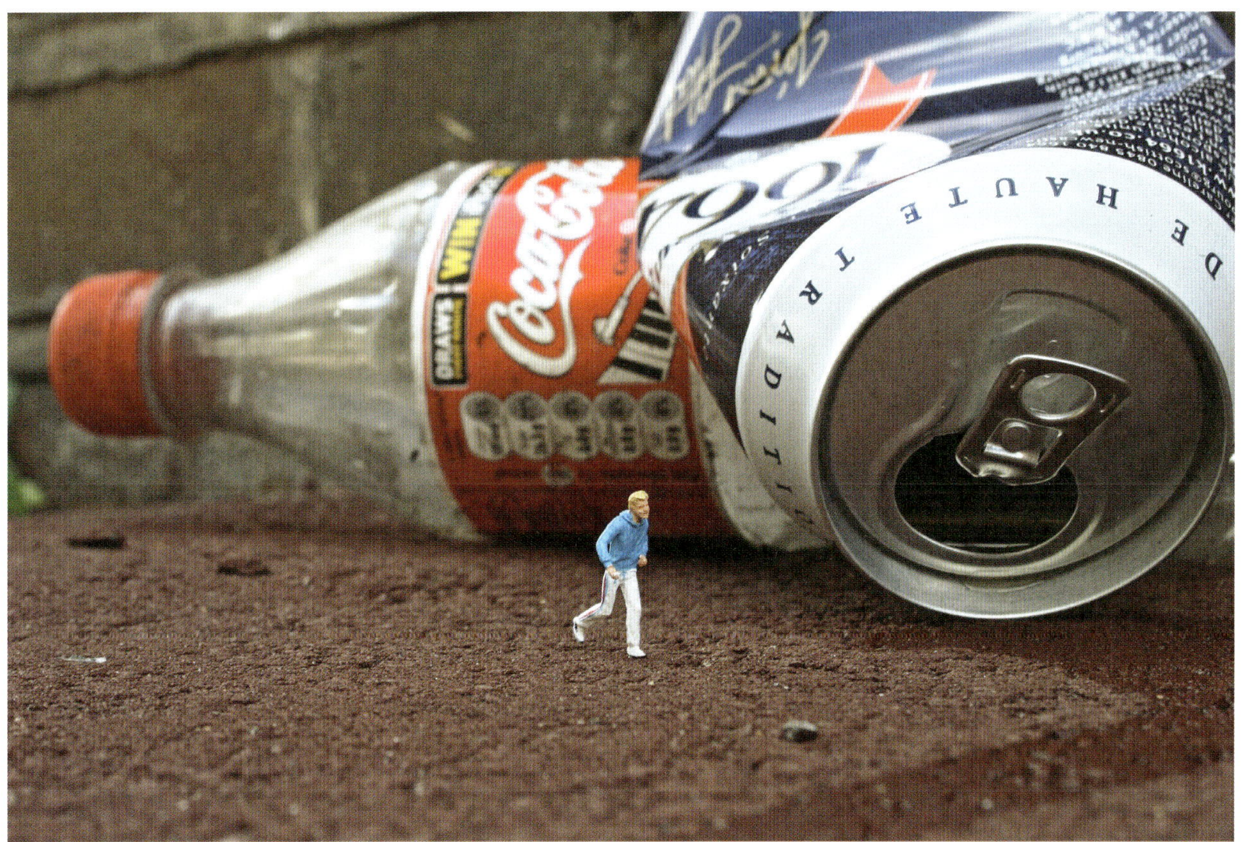

Scenic Route

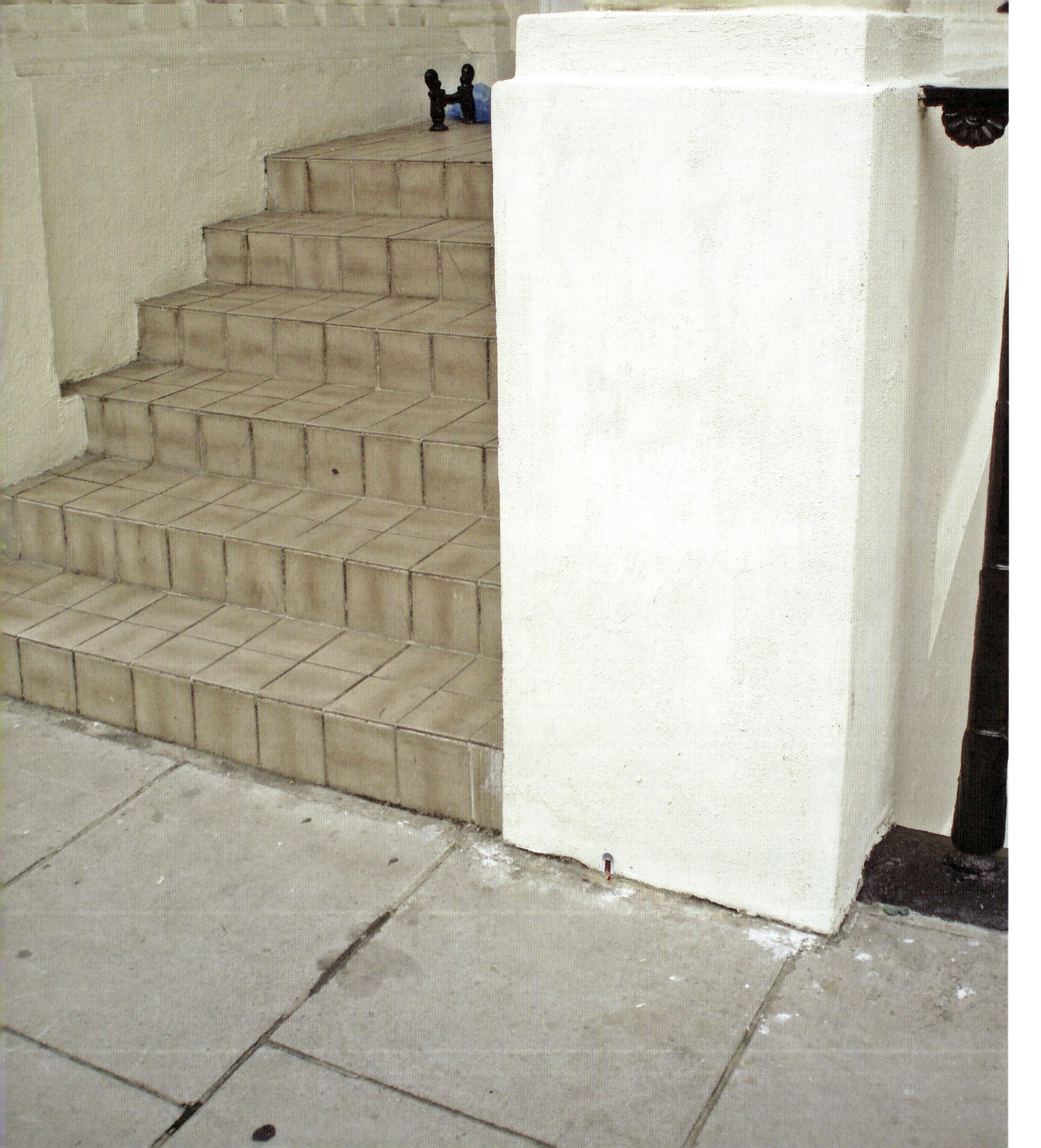

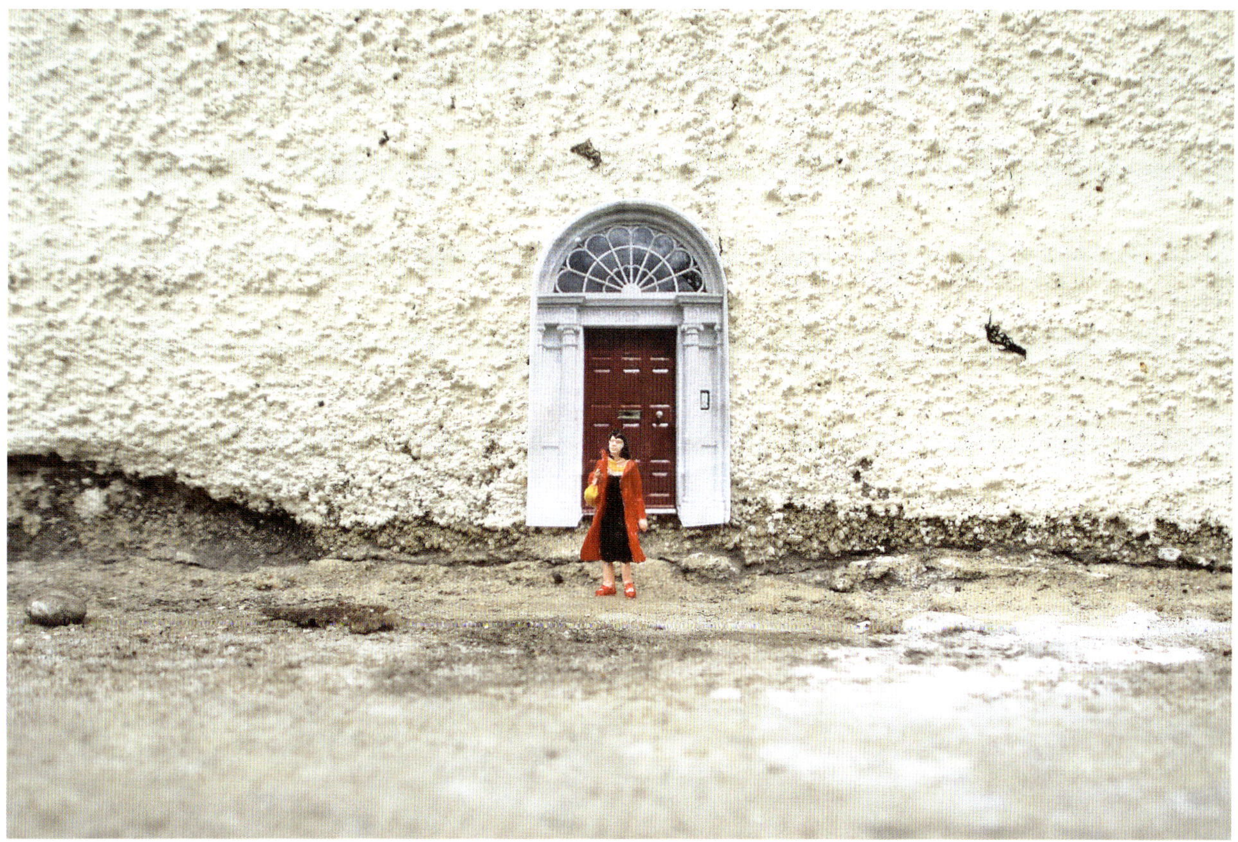

Paddington Doorway

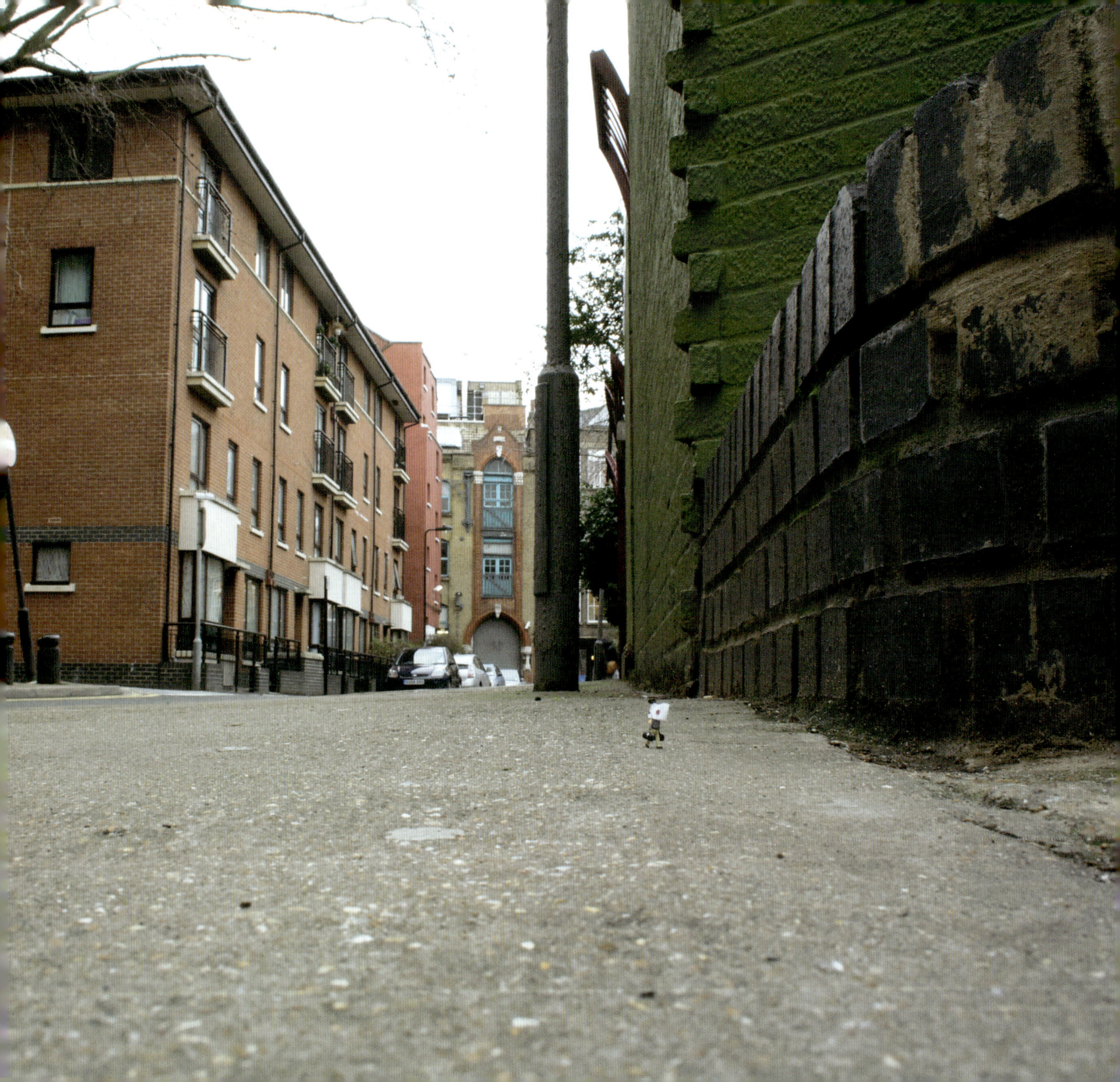

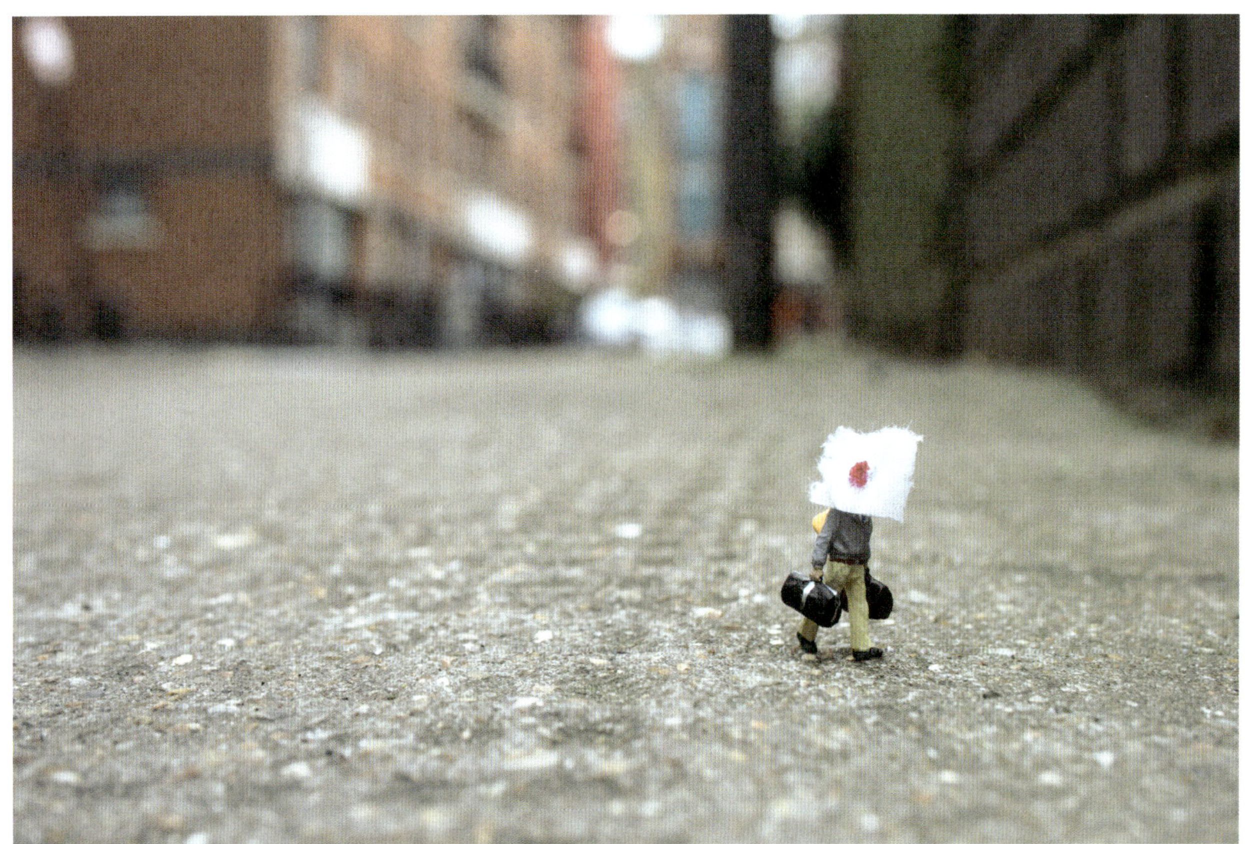

Close Shave

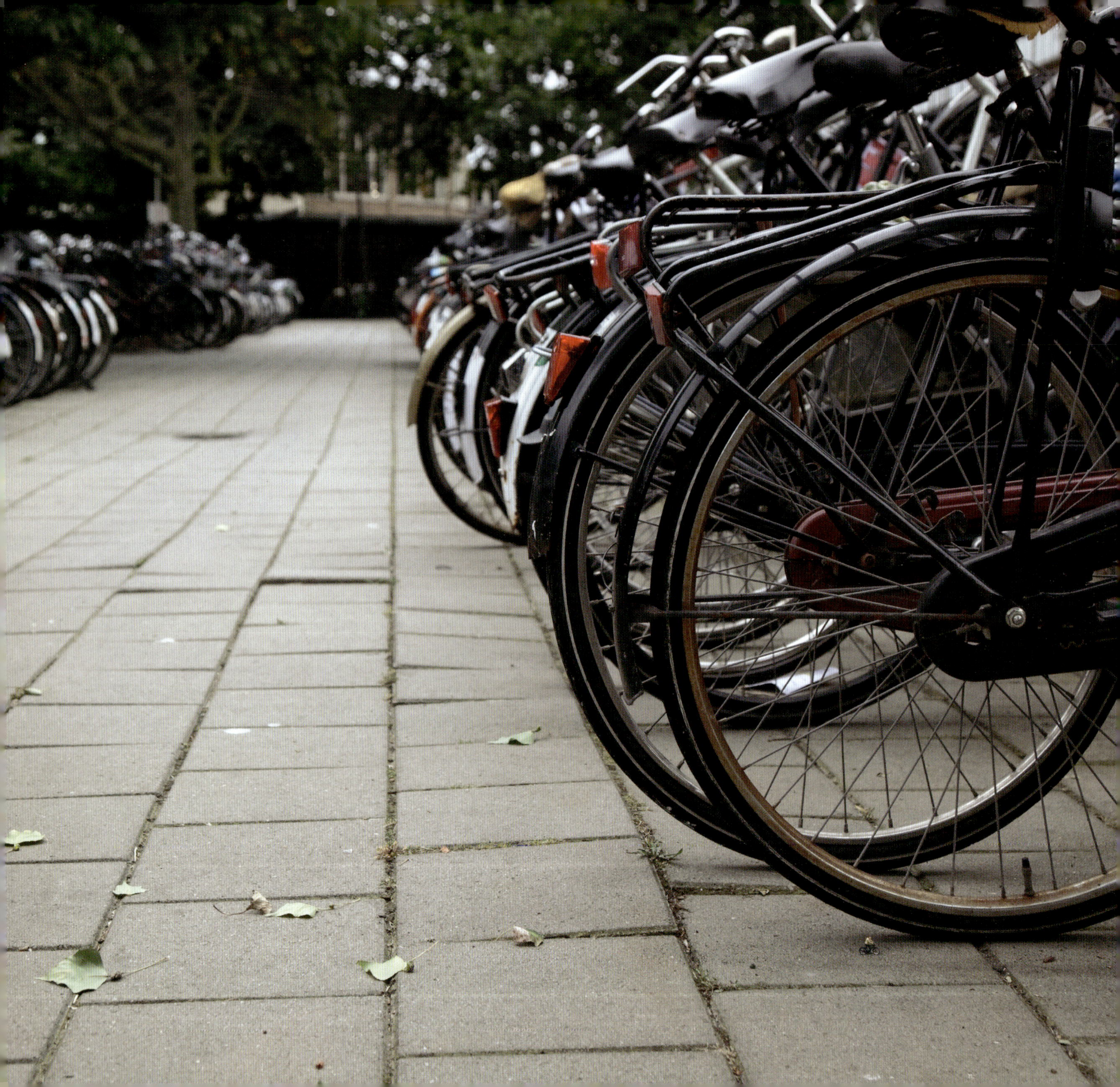

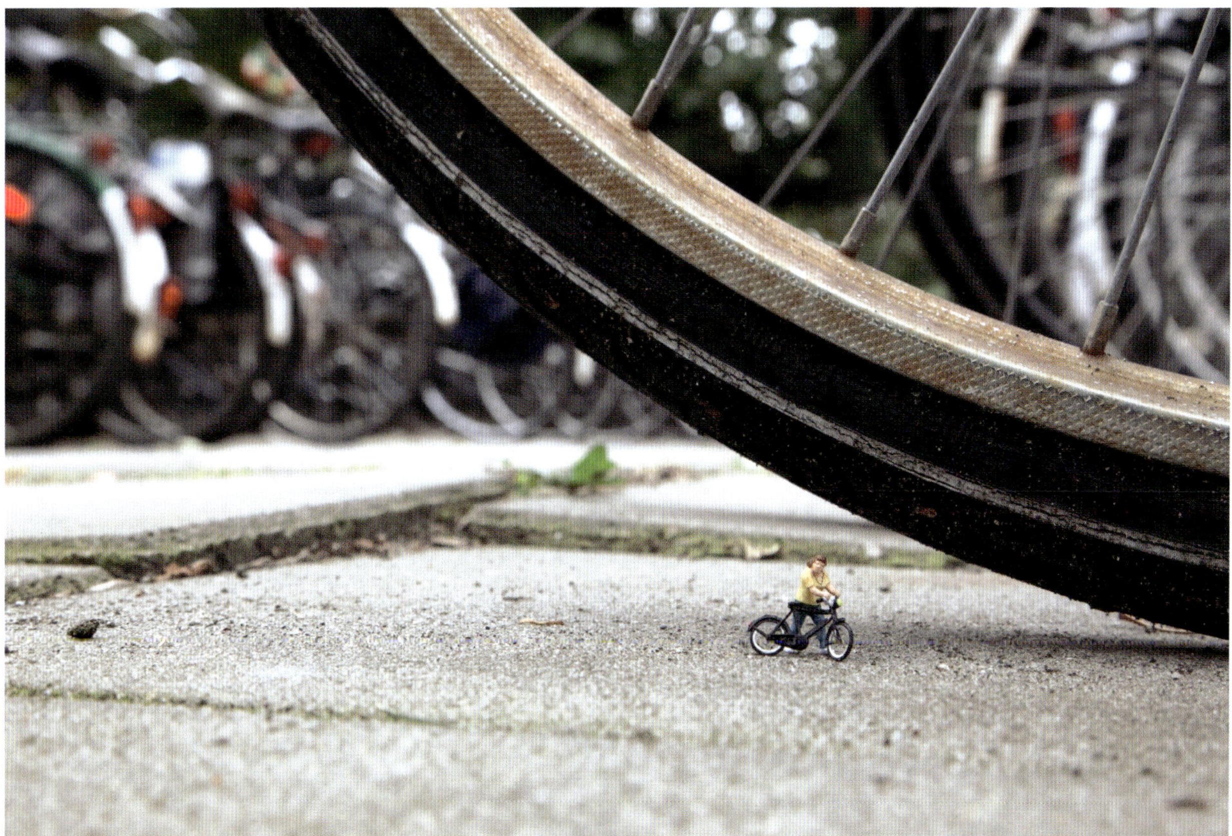

Living Life in the Cycle Lane

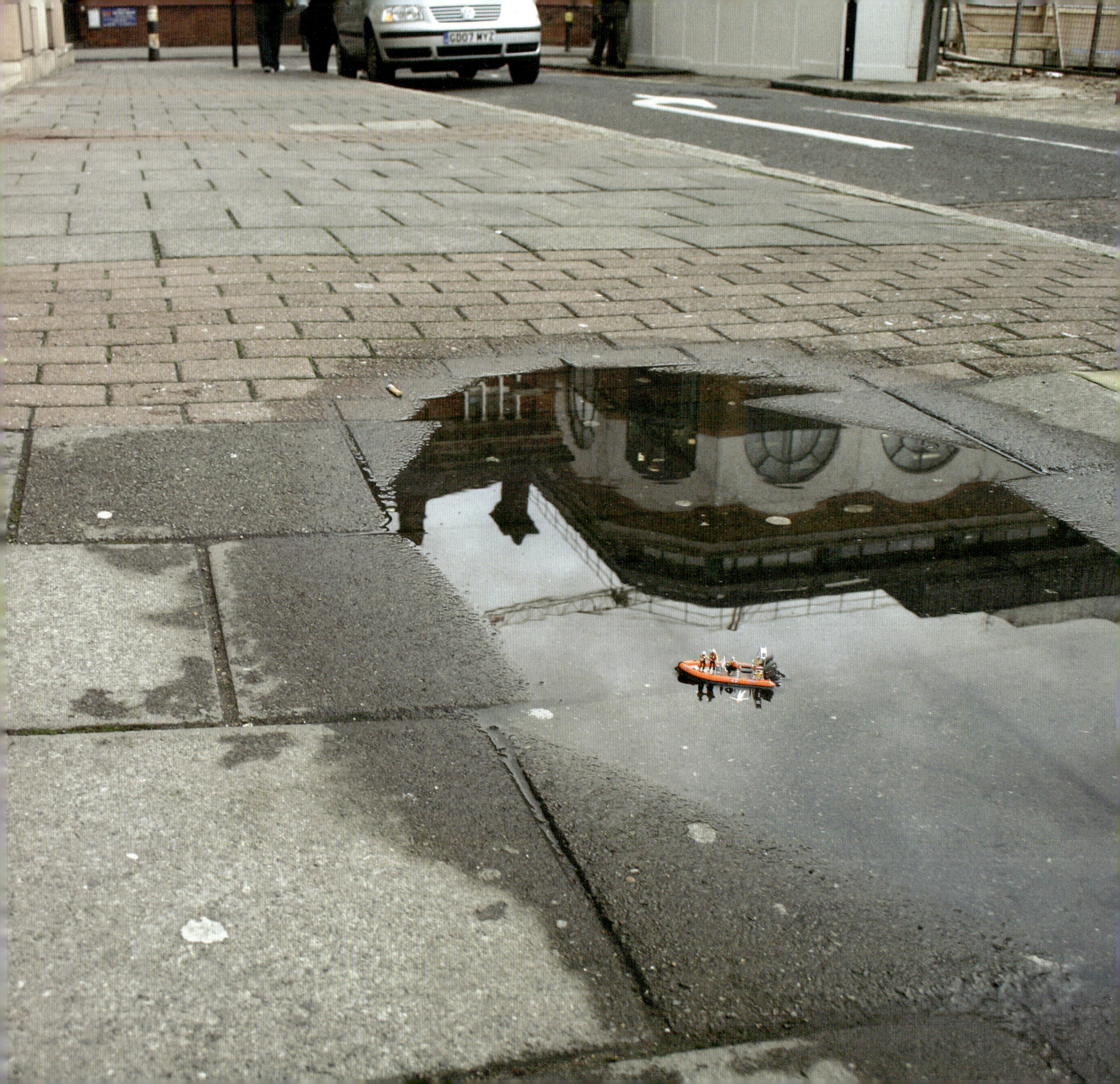
GD07 MYZ

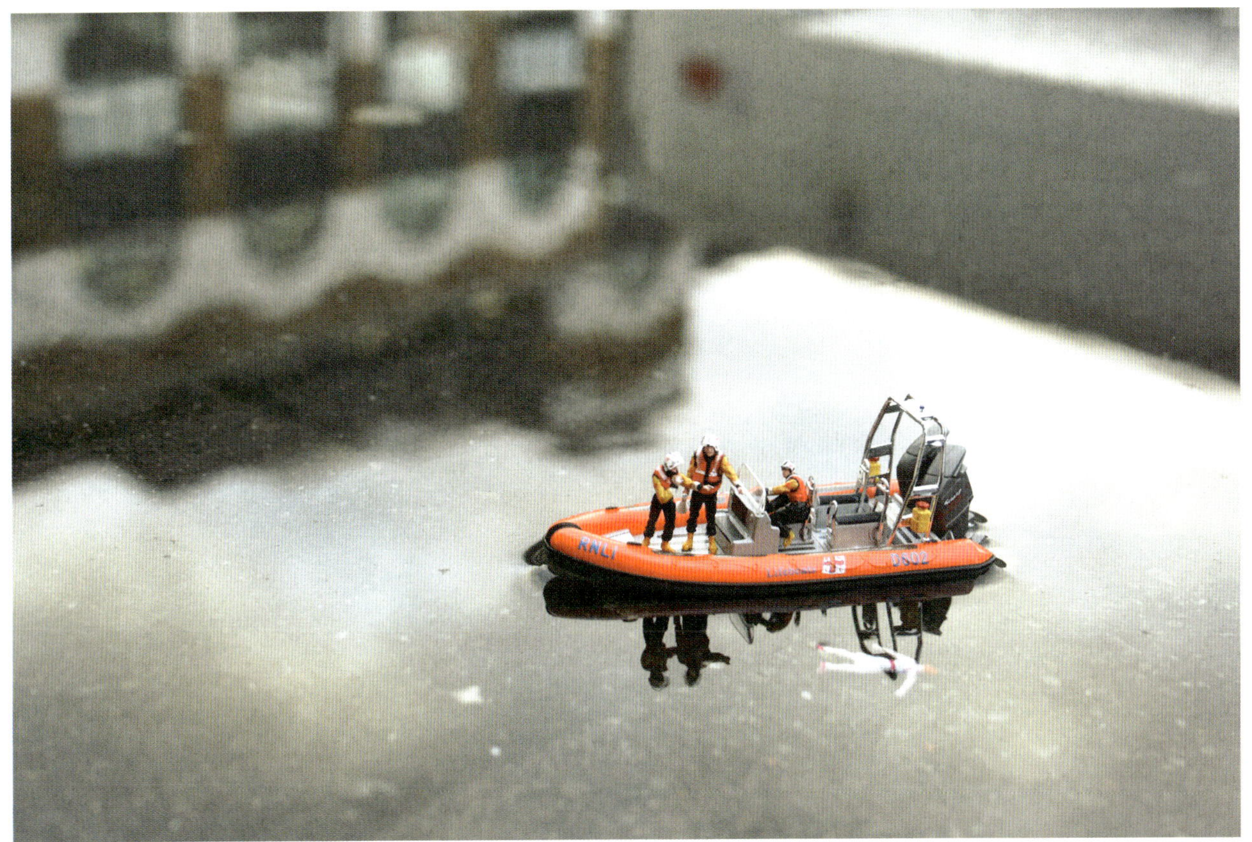

After the Storm

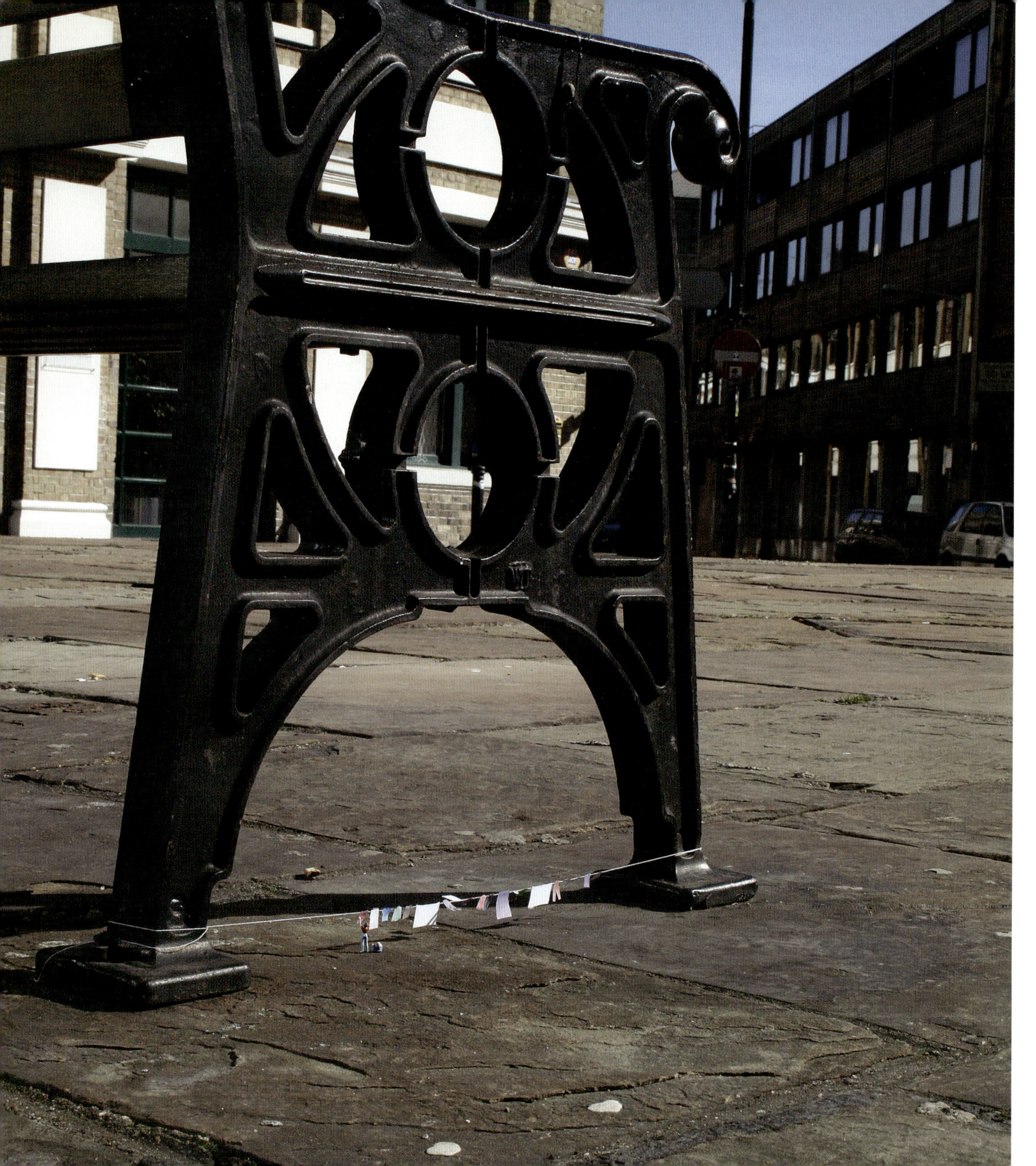

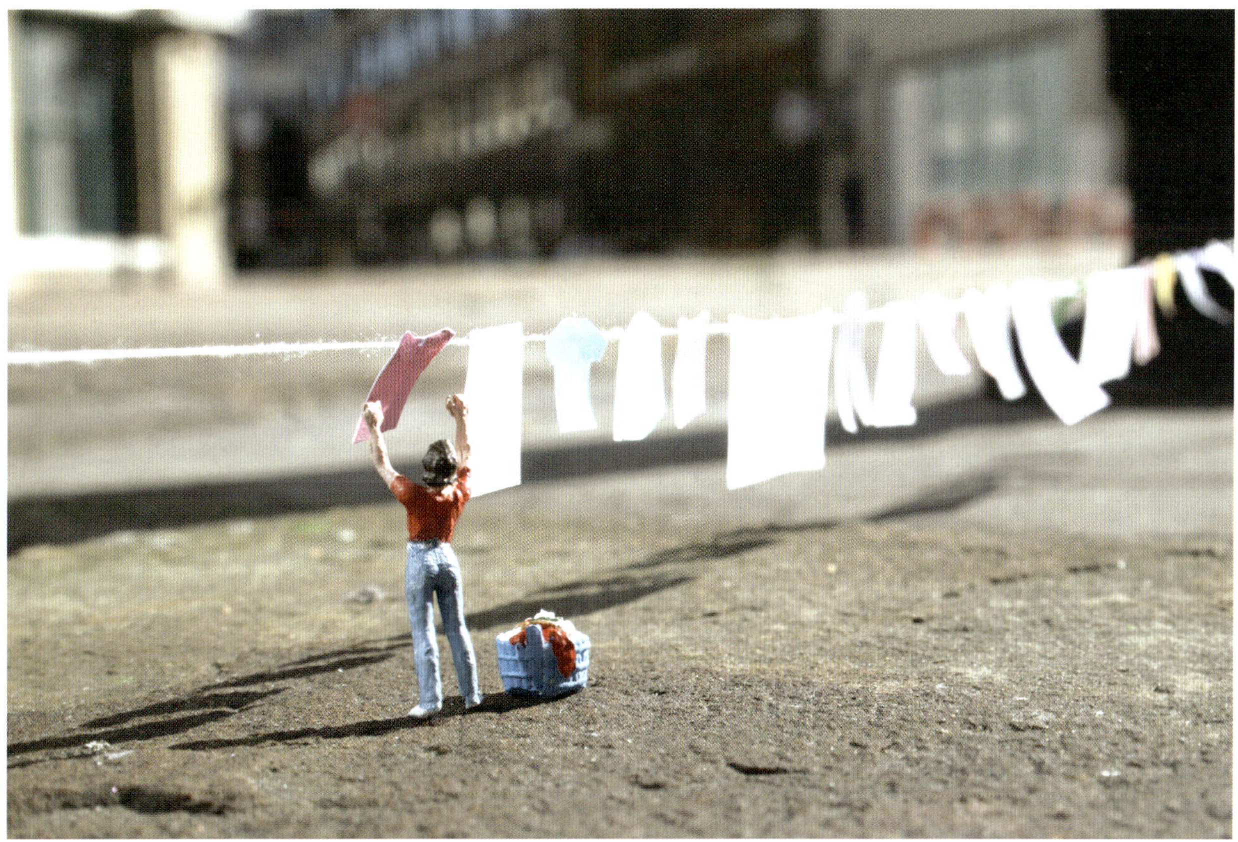

Hung Up

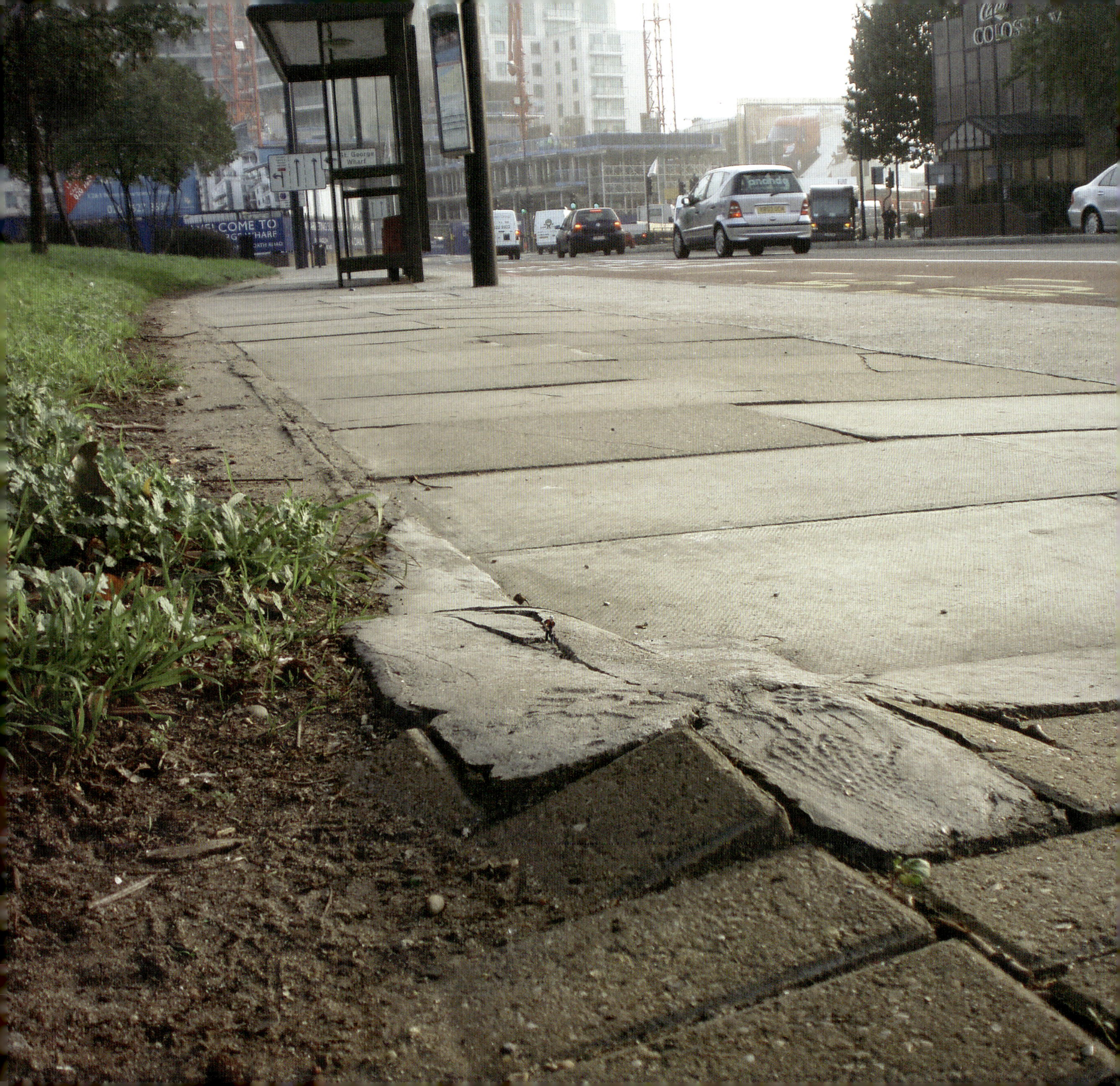
St George
Wharf
COME TO

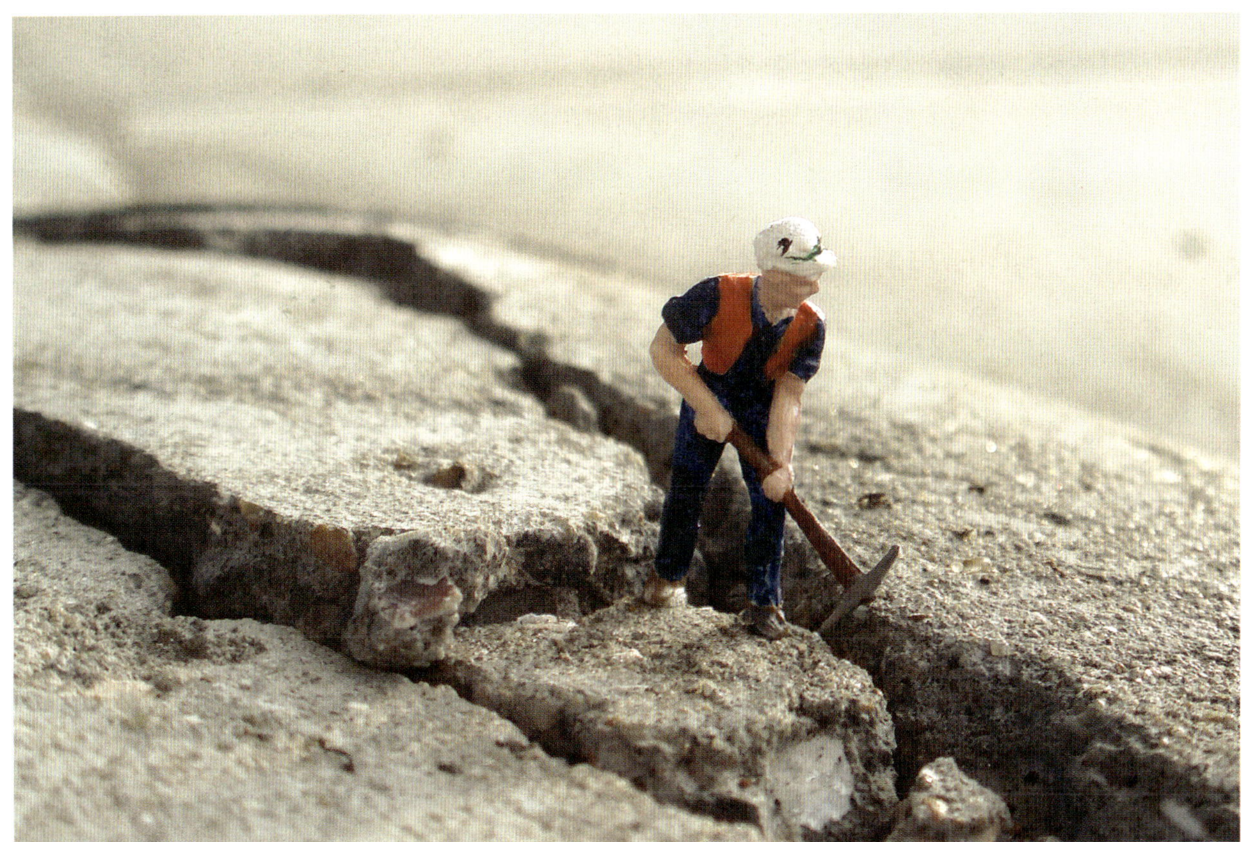

Roadworks

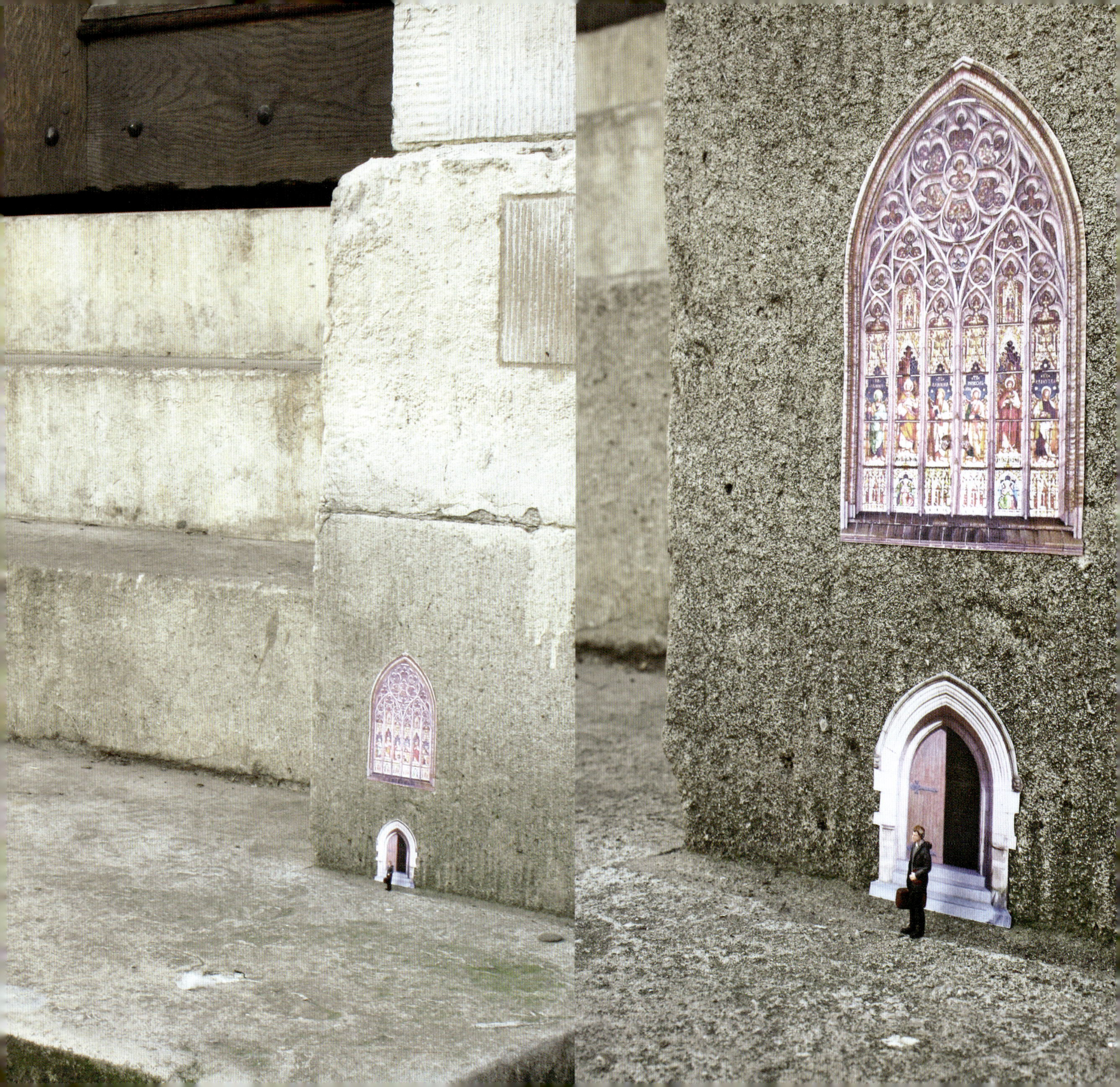

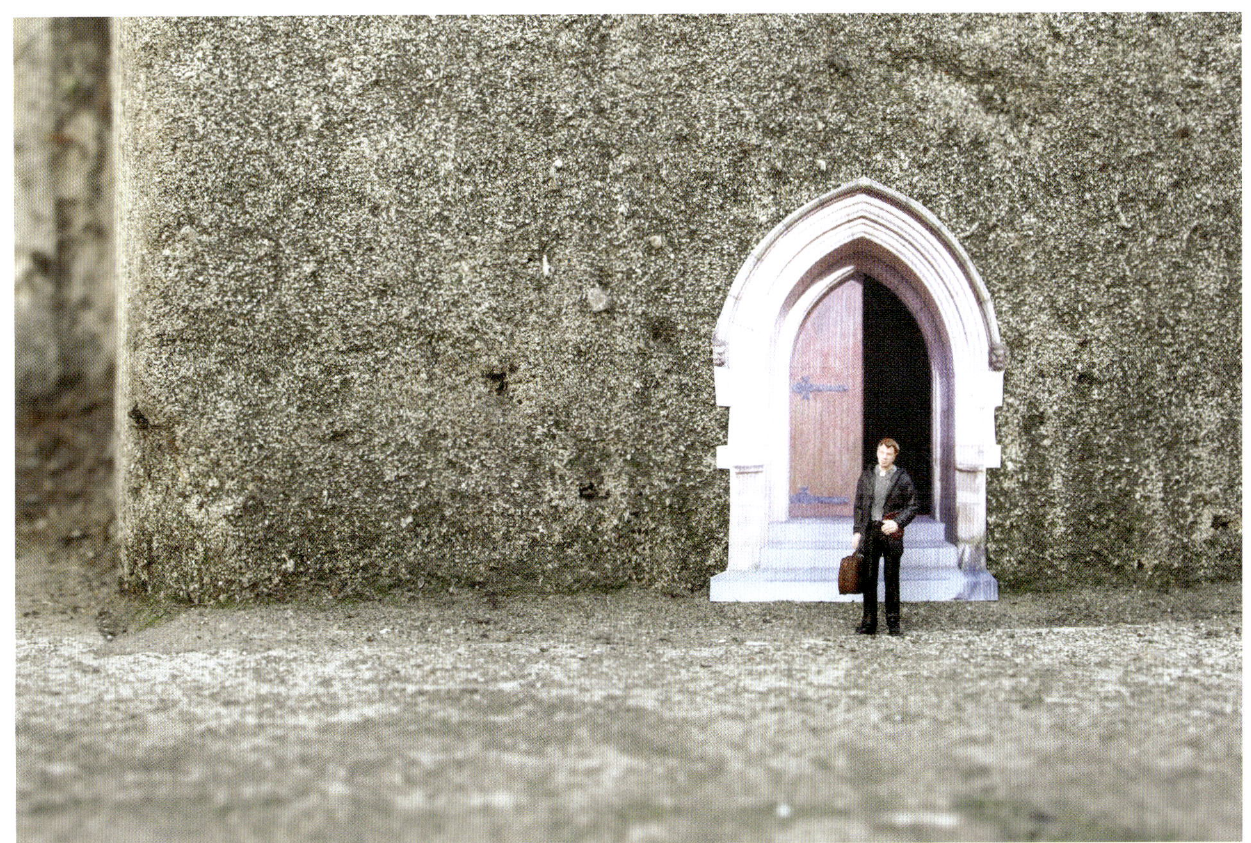

Quiet Sunday

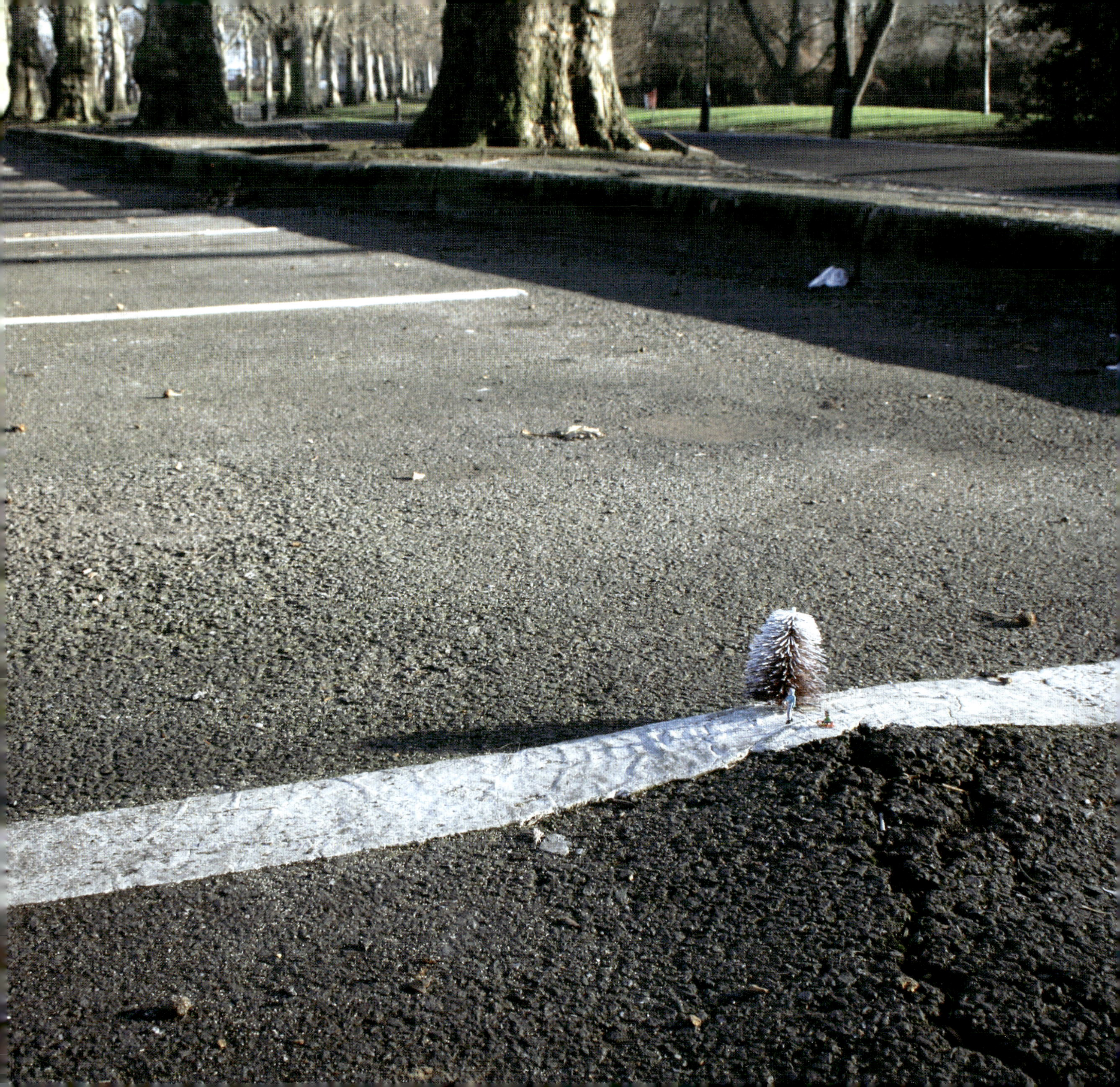

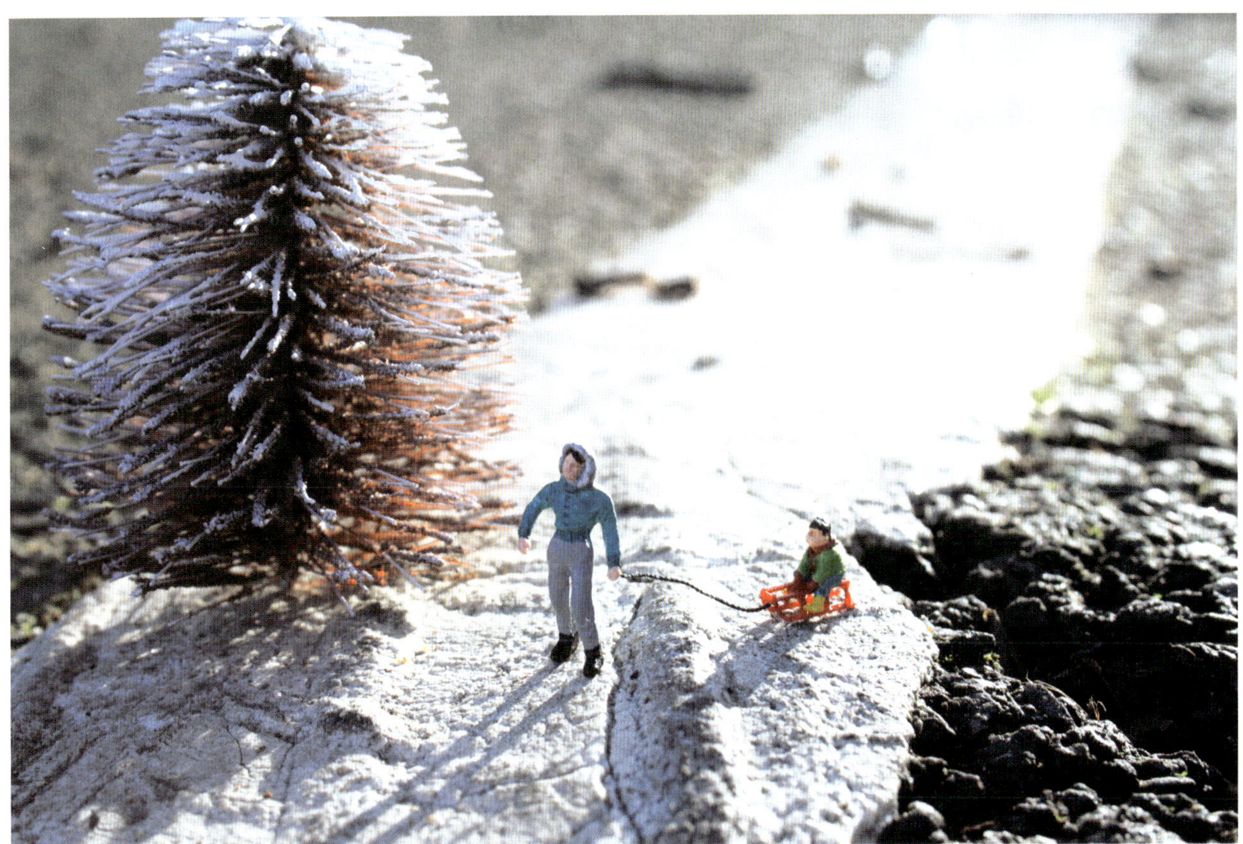

Wonderland

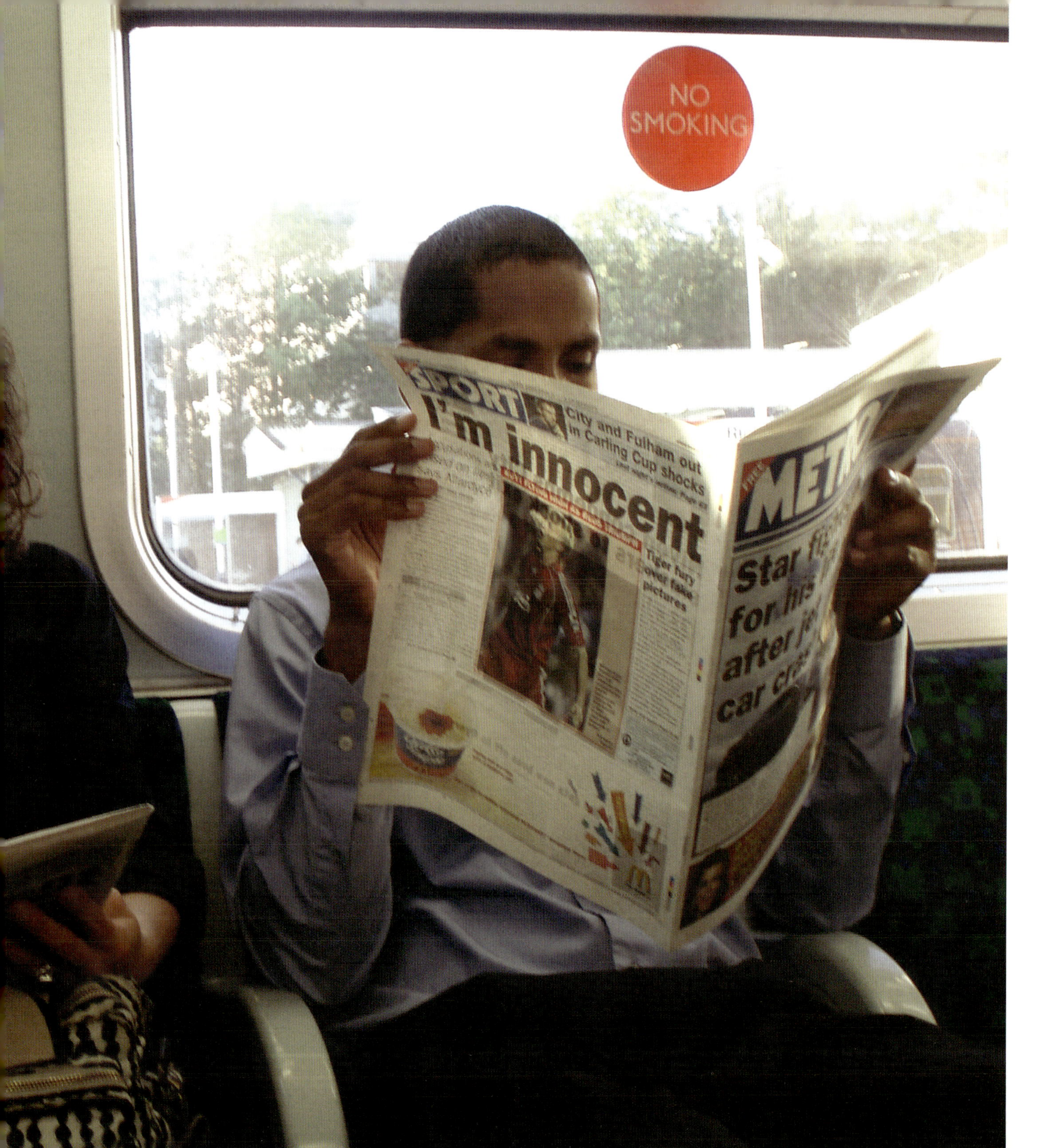
NO SMOKING
SPORT
I'm innocent
City and Fulham out in Carling Cup shocks
Tiger fury over fake pictures
METRO

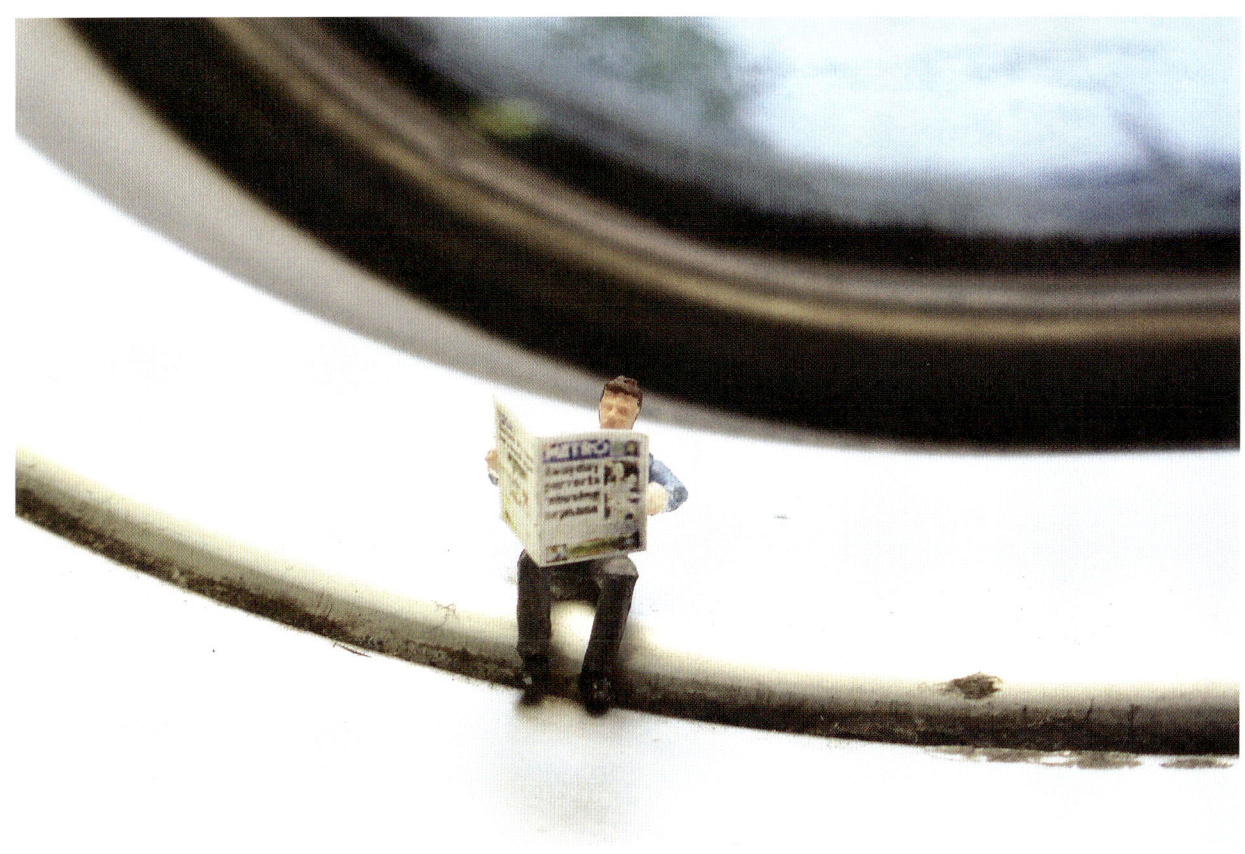

Commuting

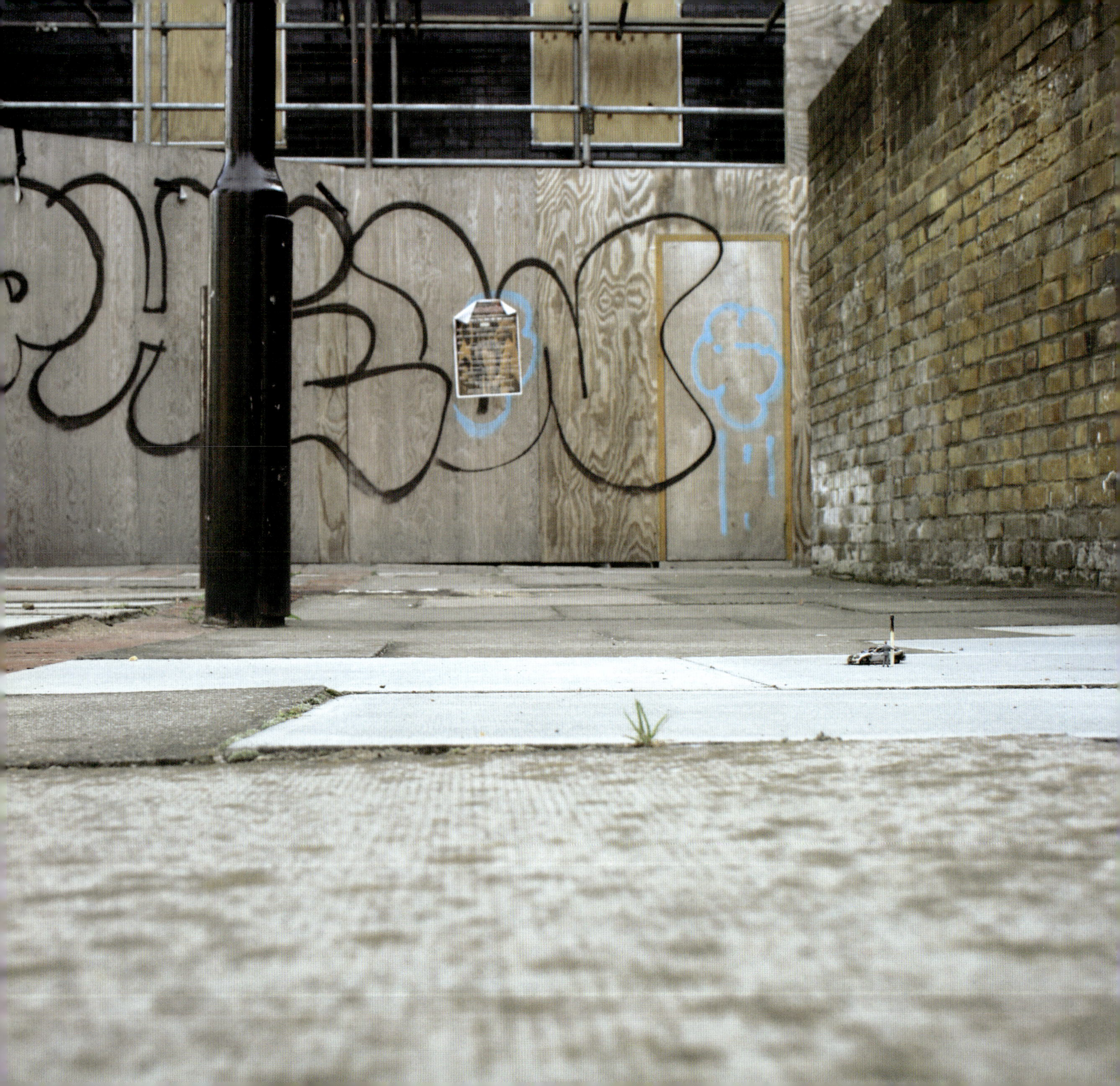

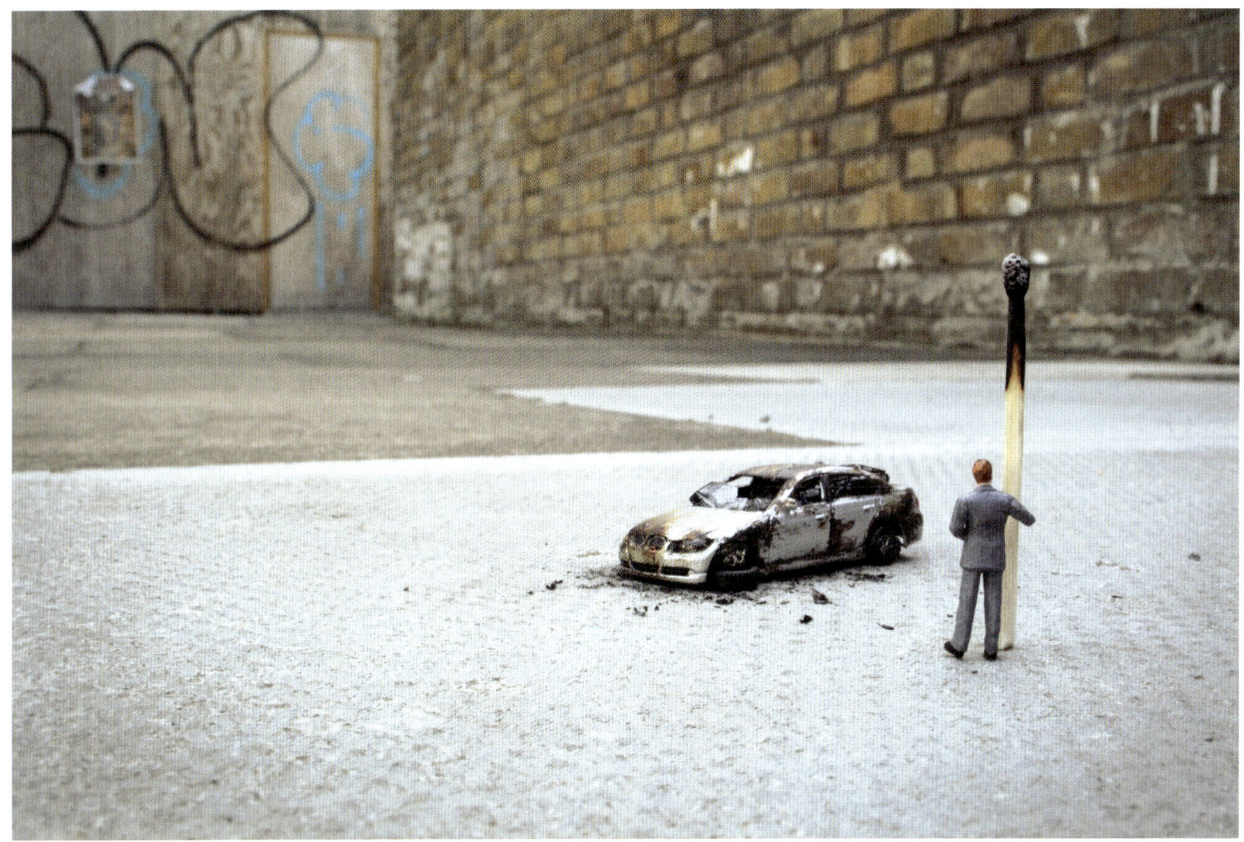

Company Car

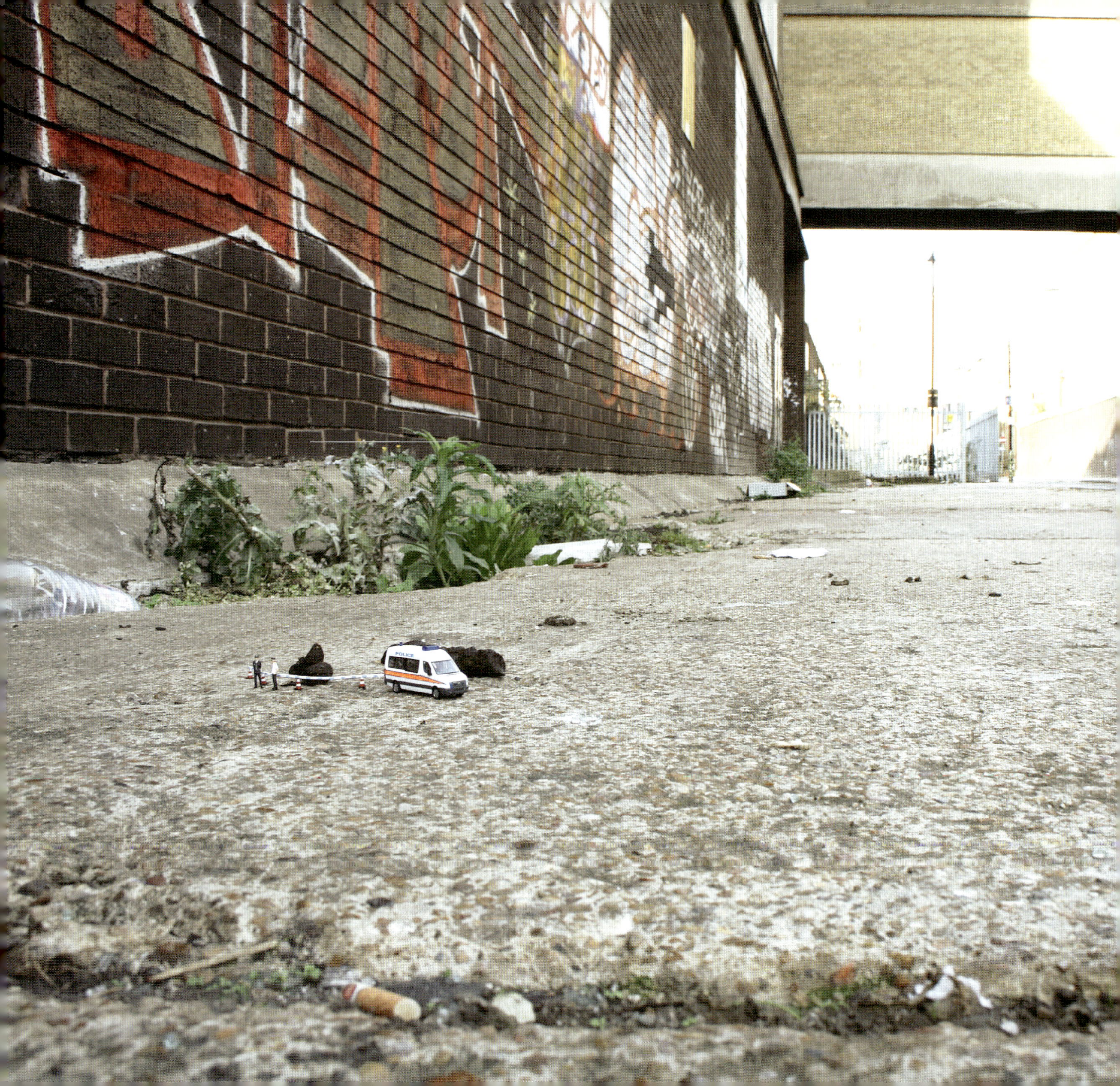
POLICE

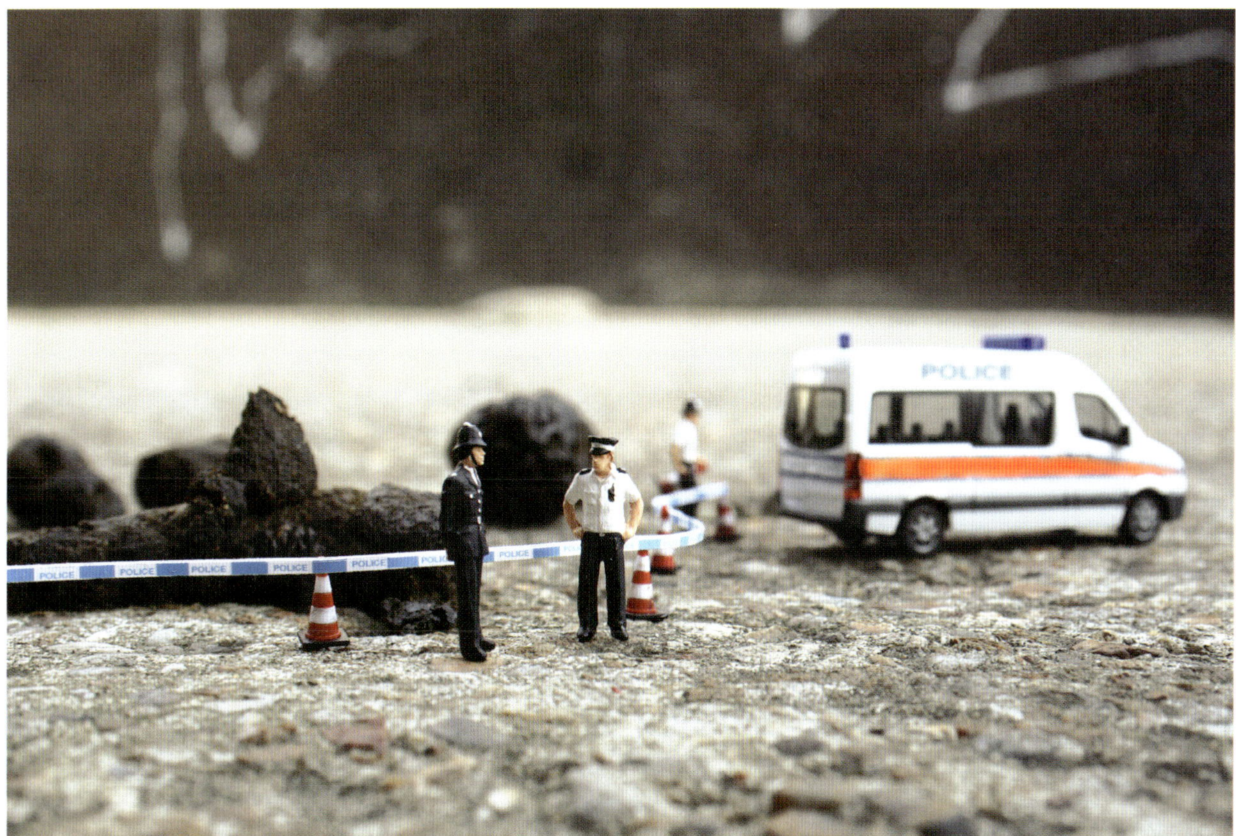

Terror Alert

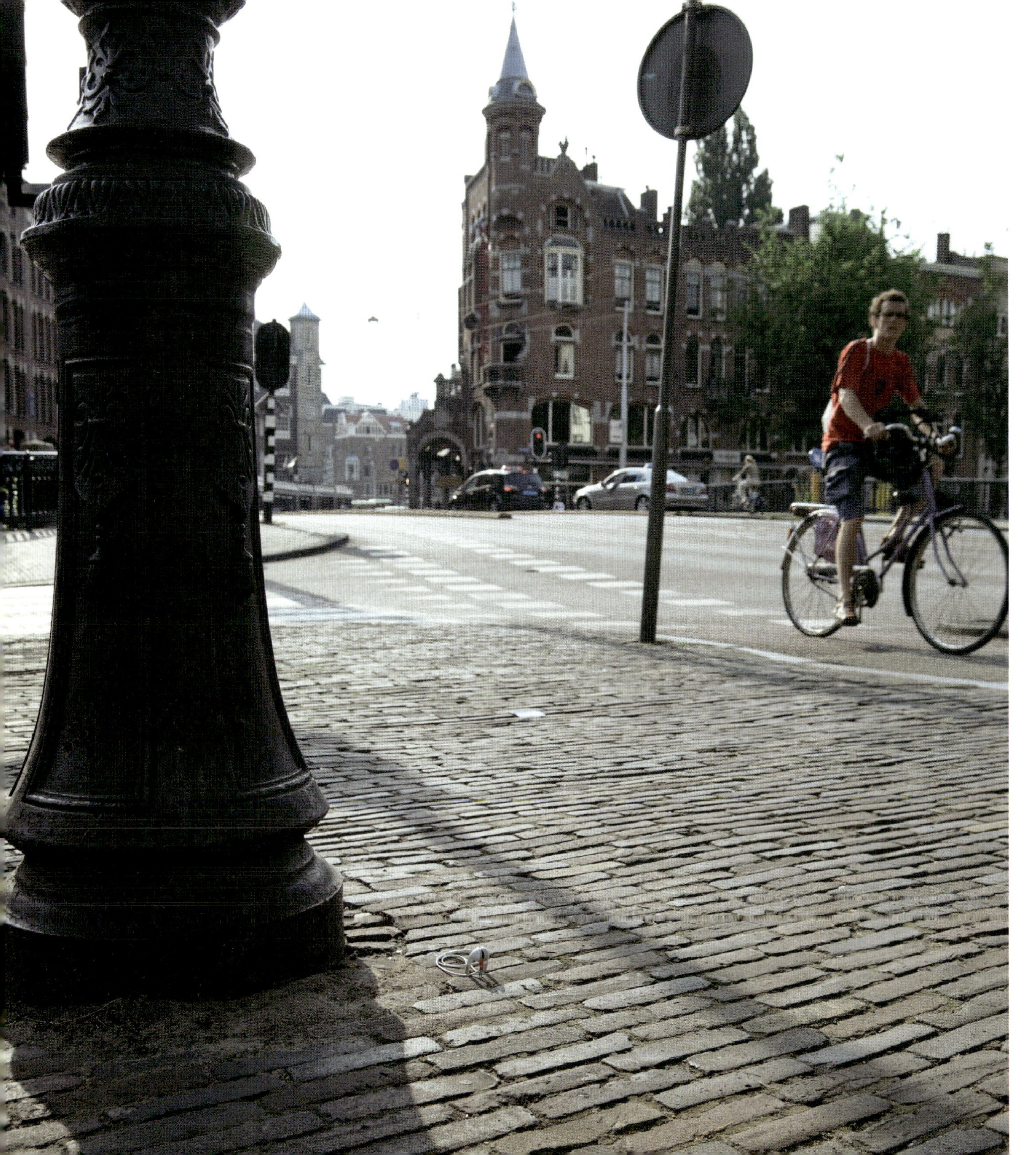

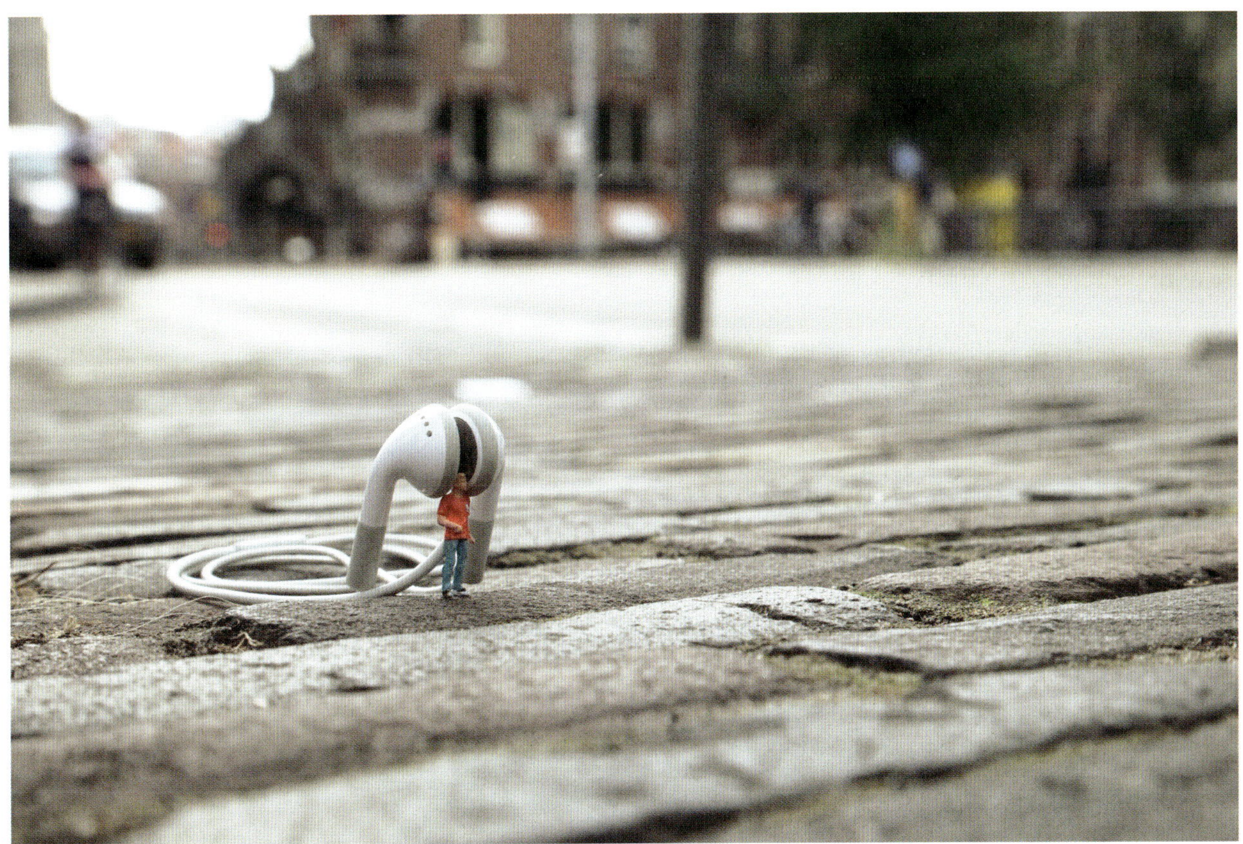

Background Noise

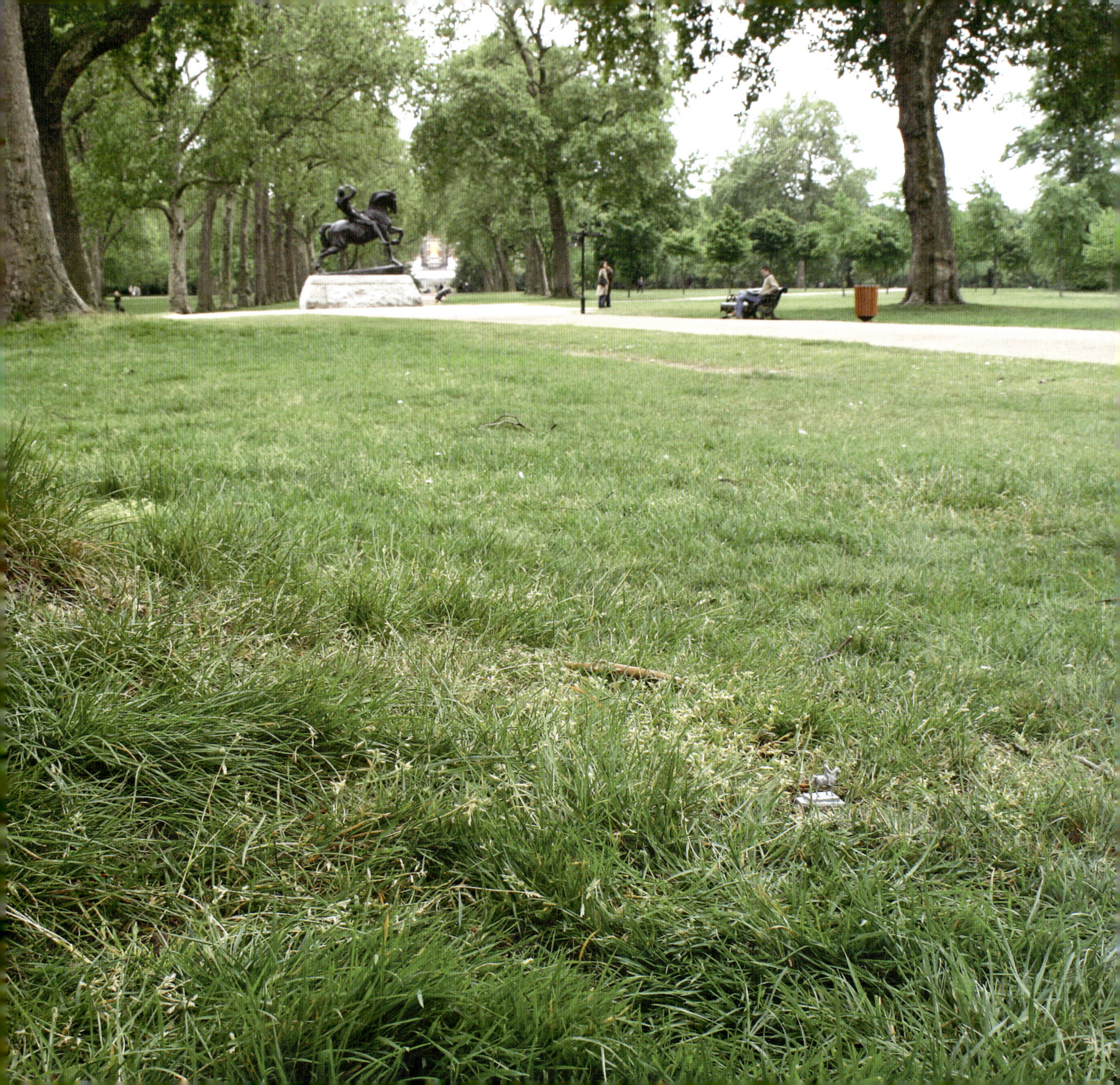

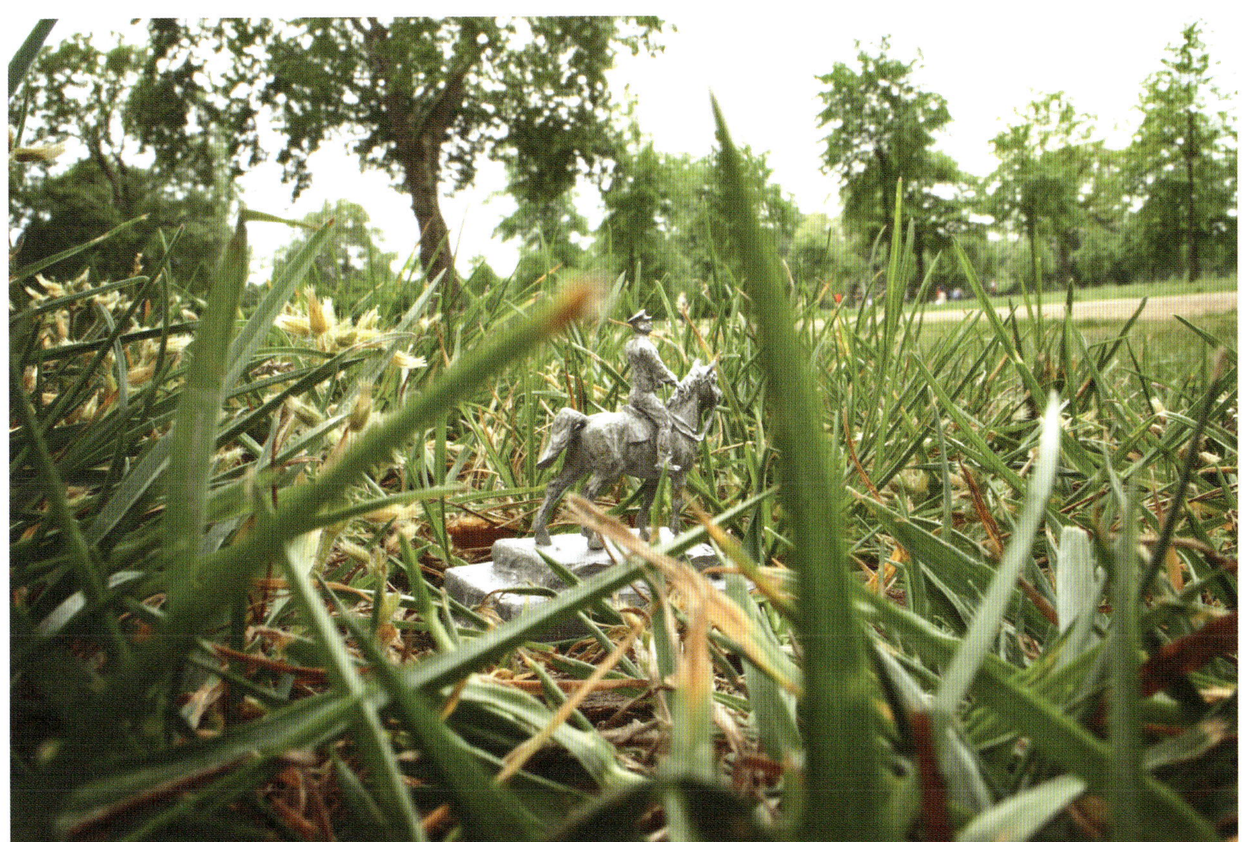

The Forgotten Soldier

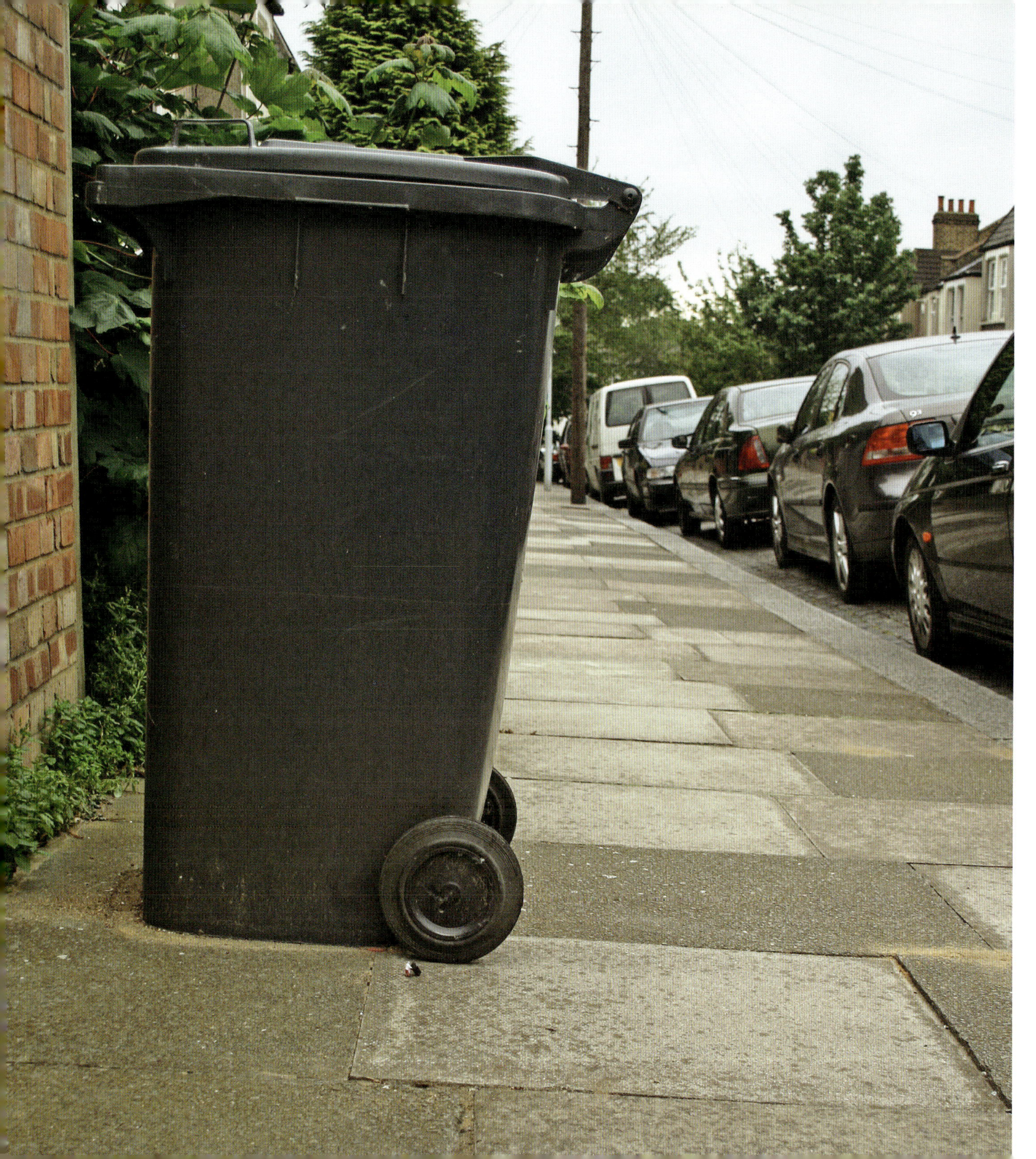

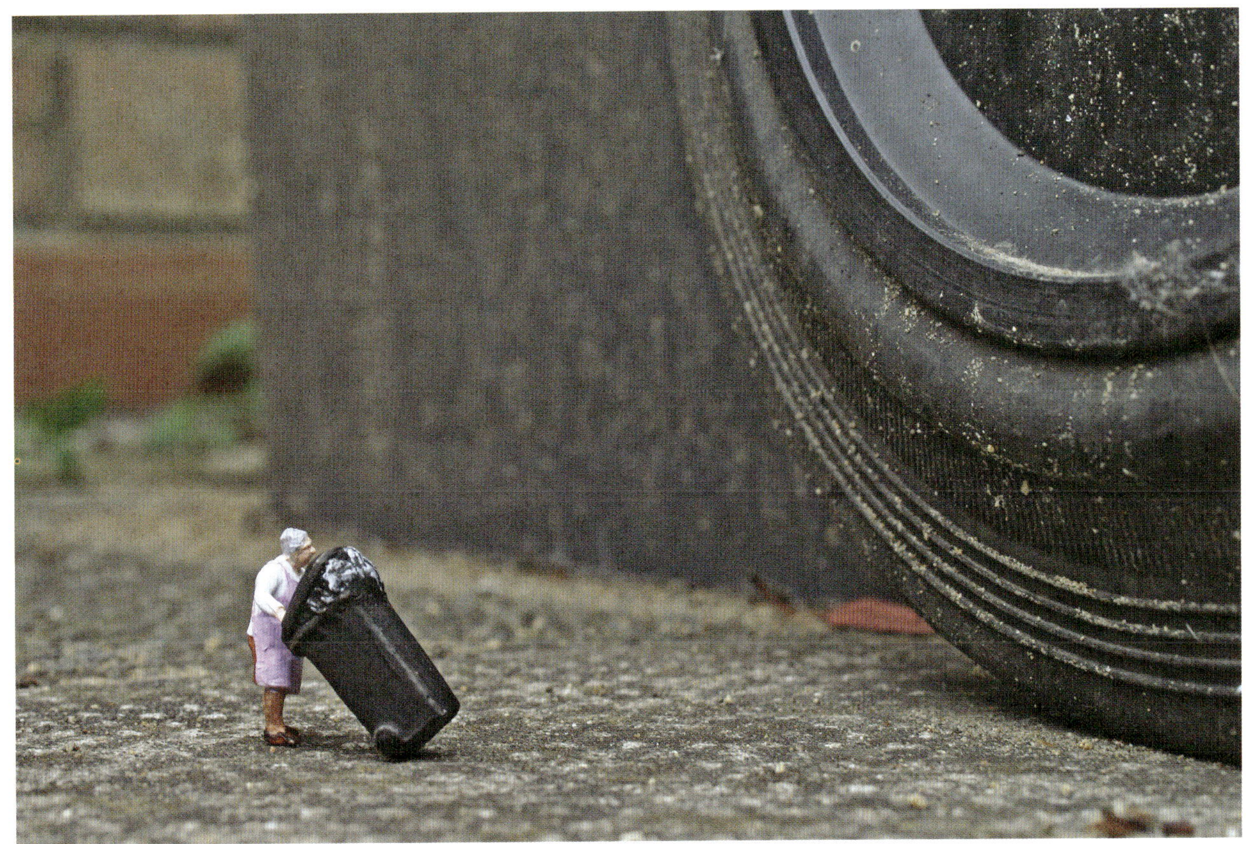

Bin Day

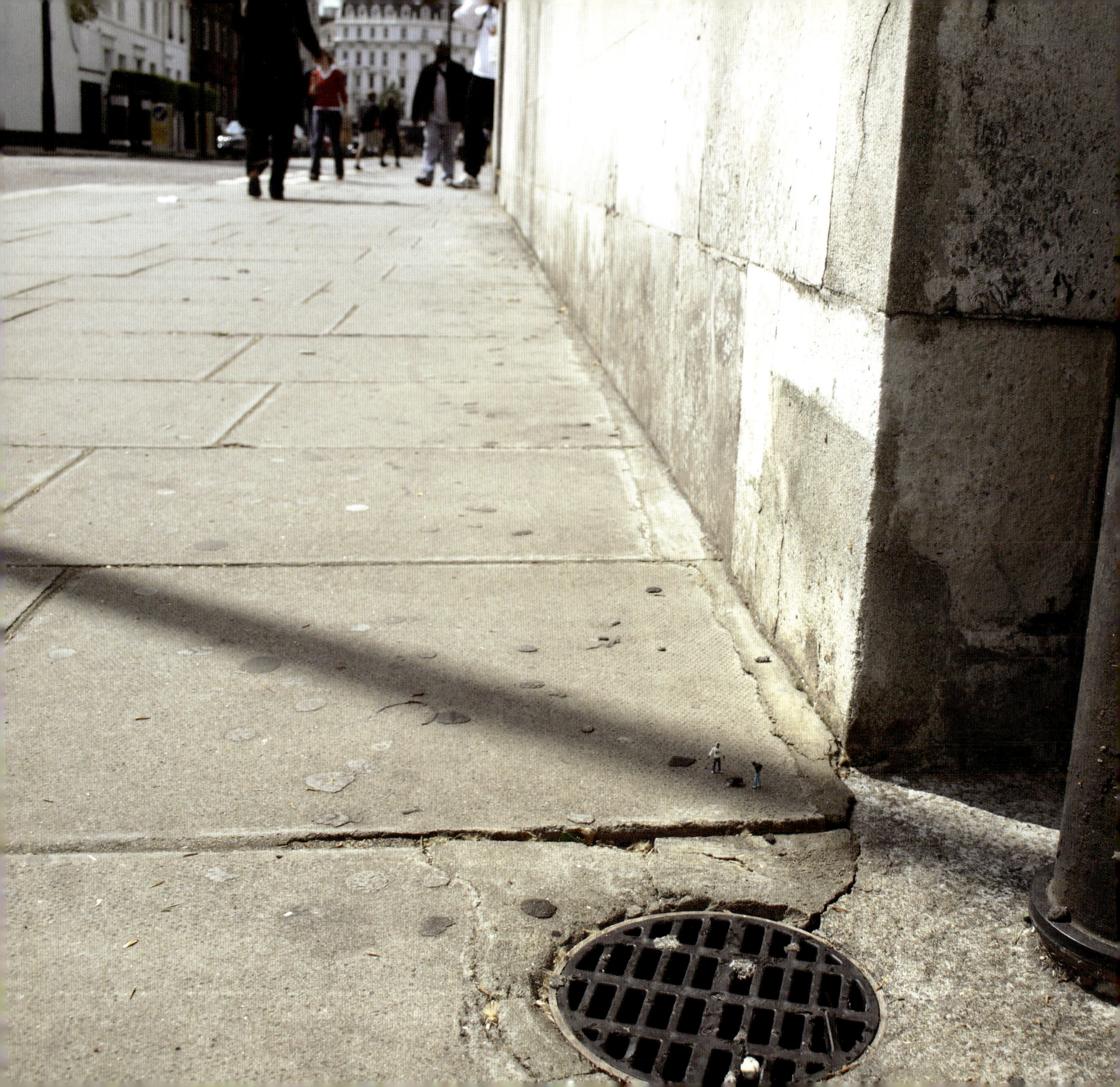

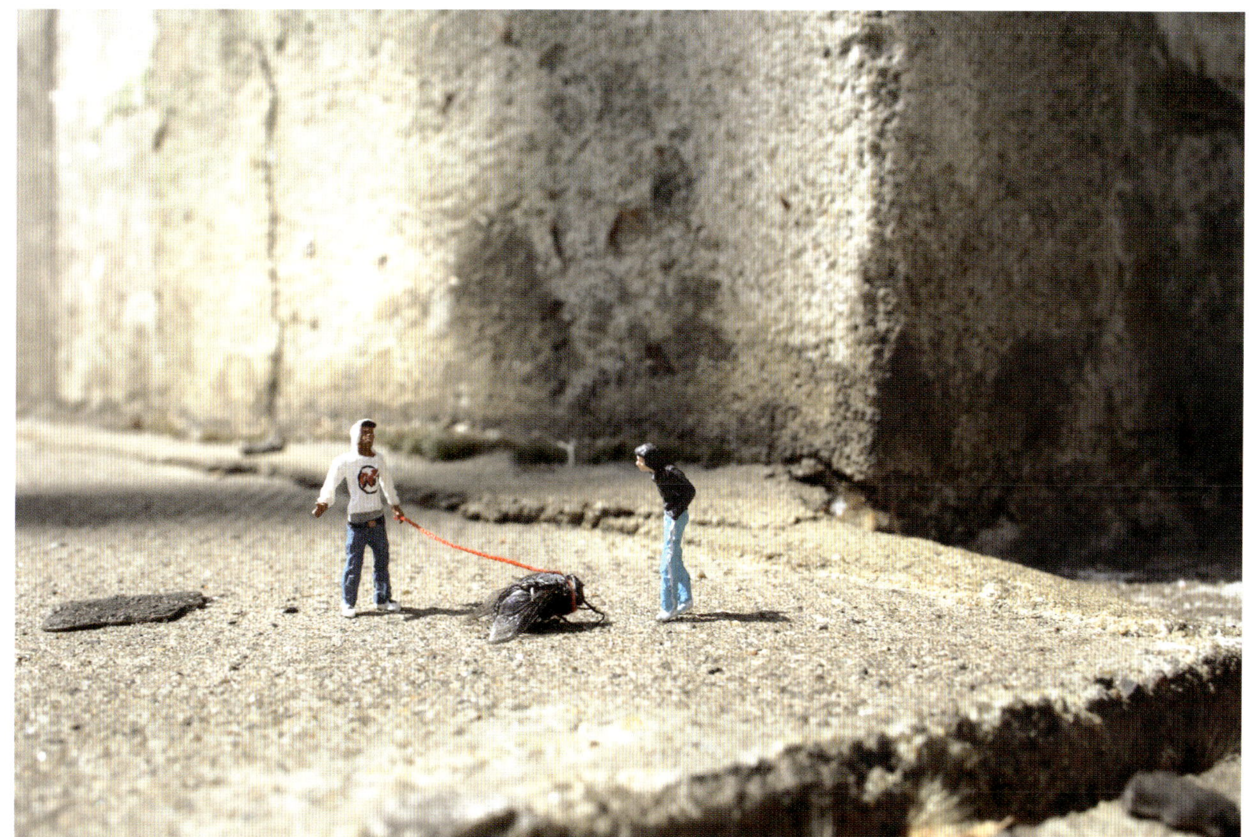

Banned Breed

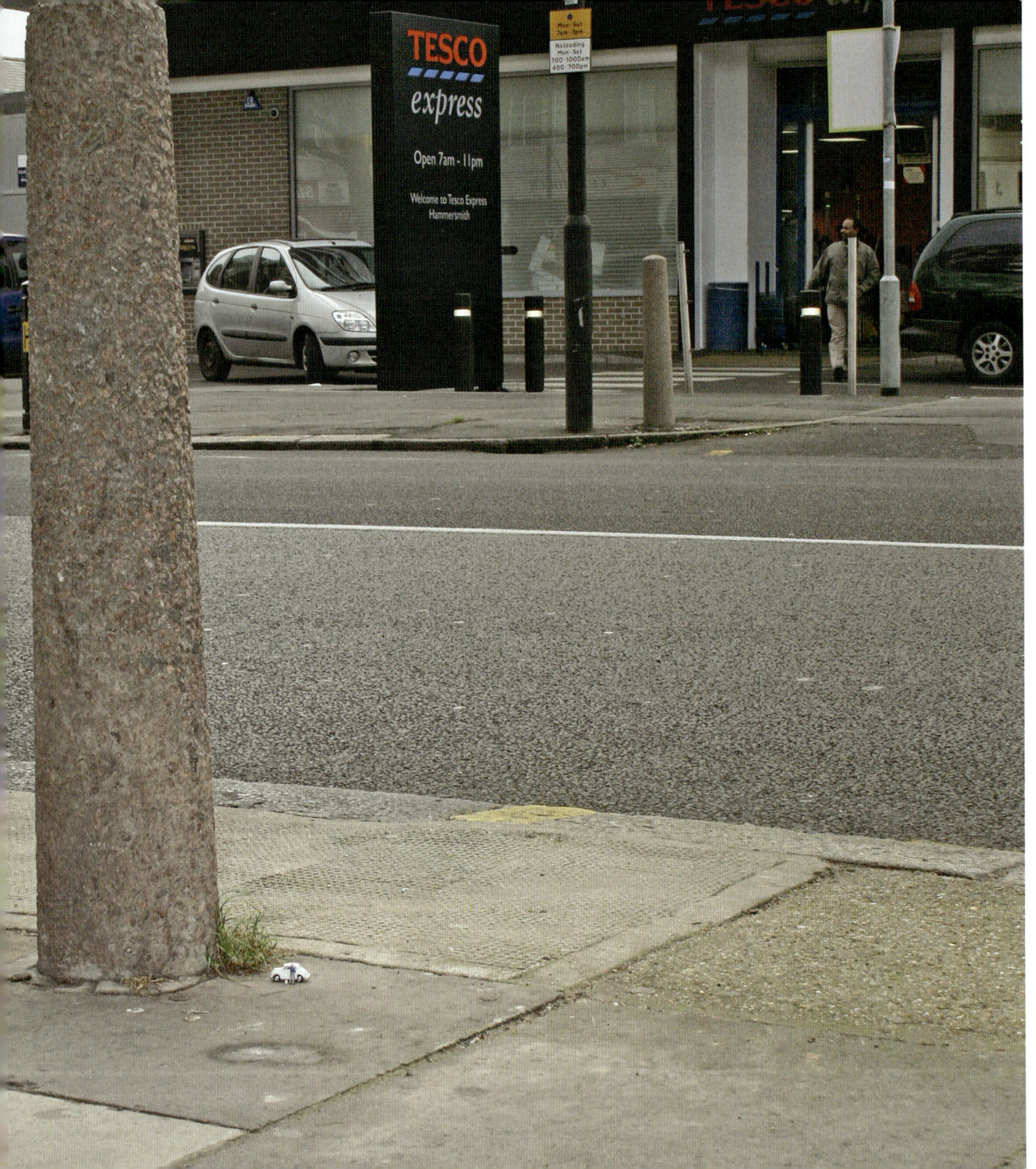
TESCO
express
Open 7am - 11pm
Welcome to Tesco Express
Hammersmith

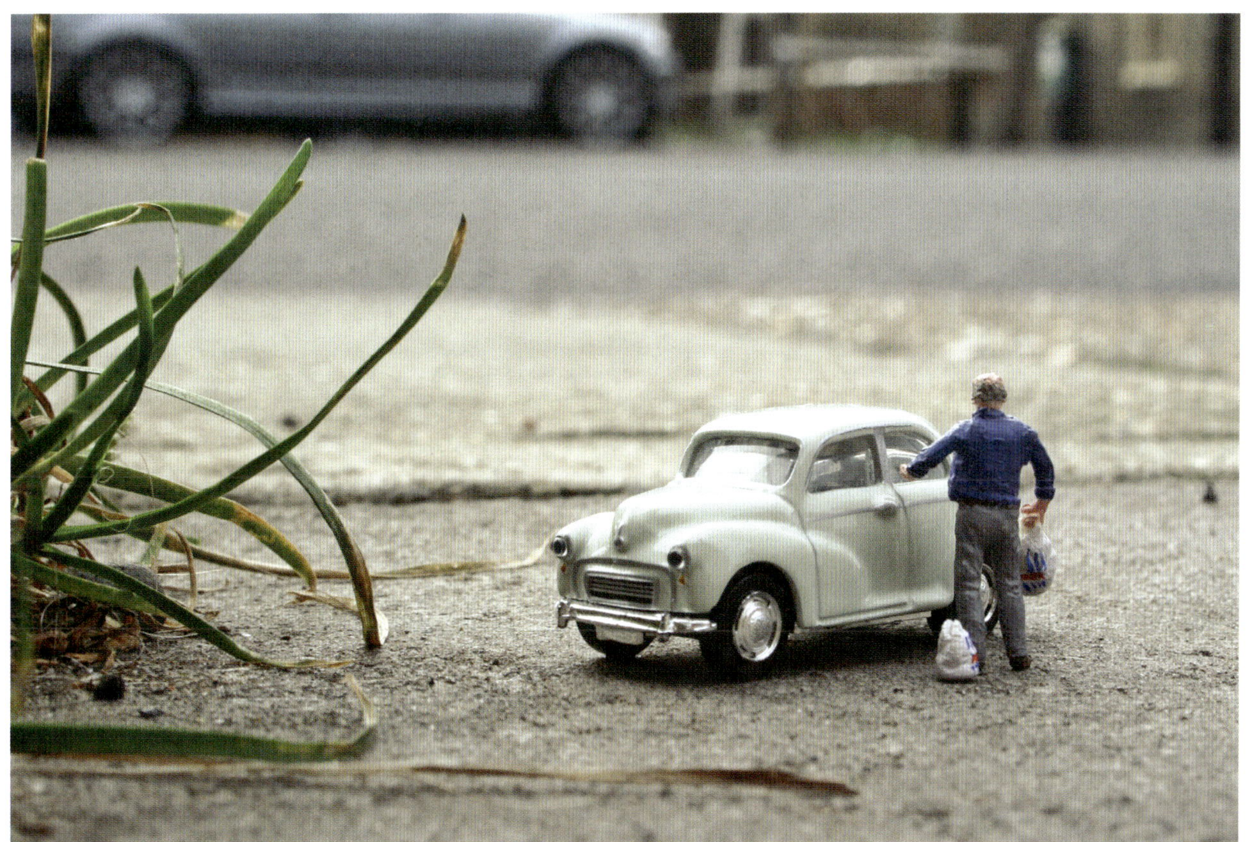

Shopping for One Again

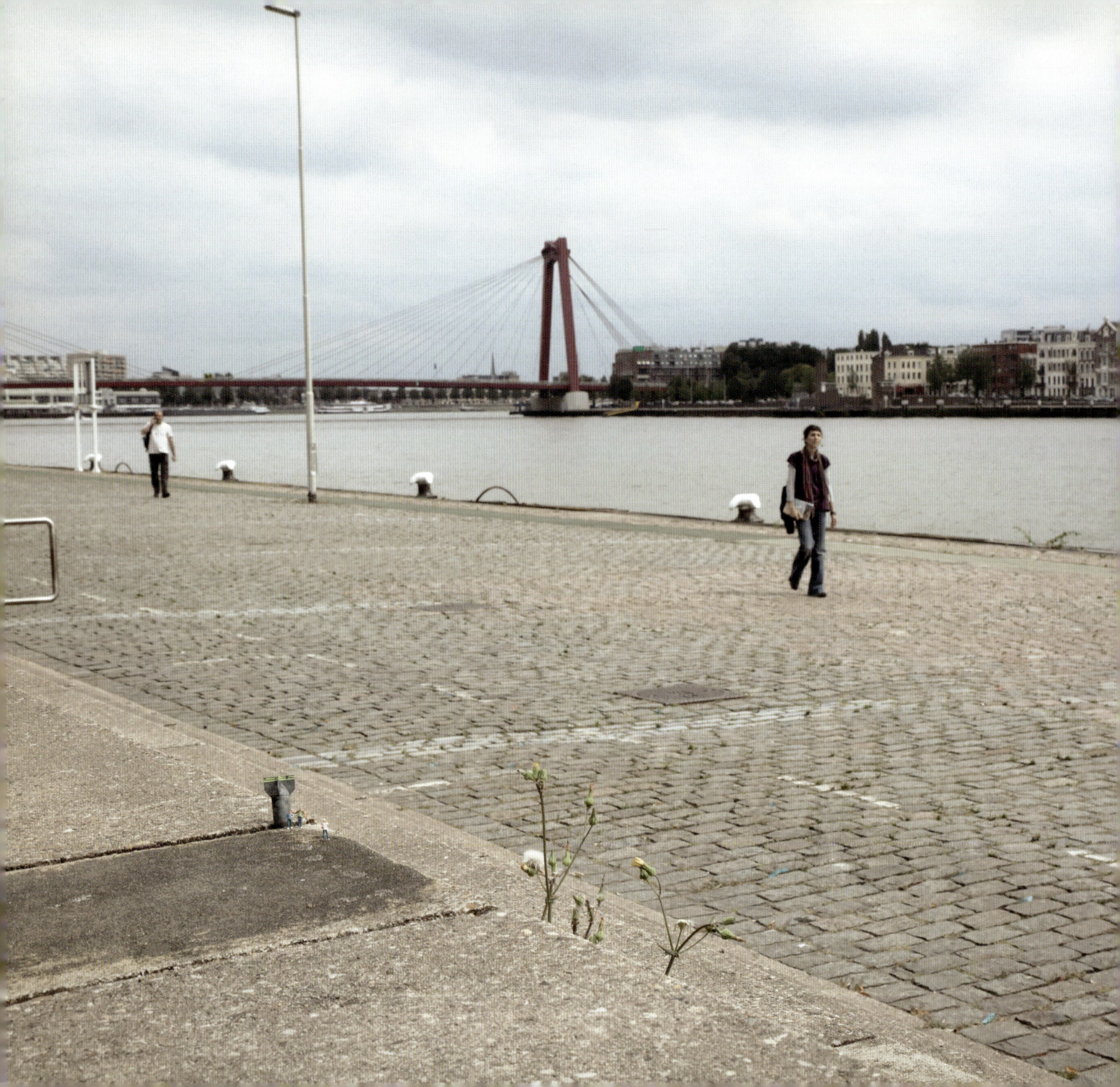

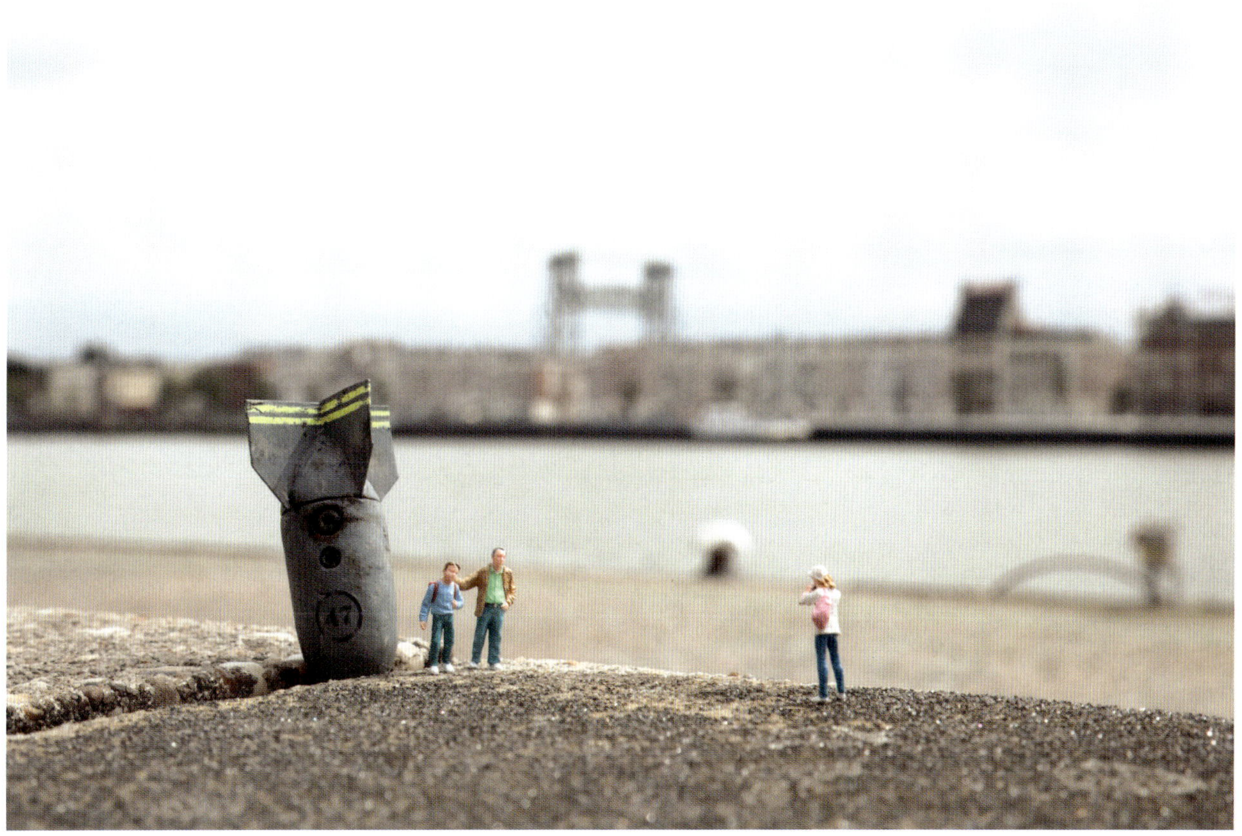

The Spoils of War

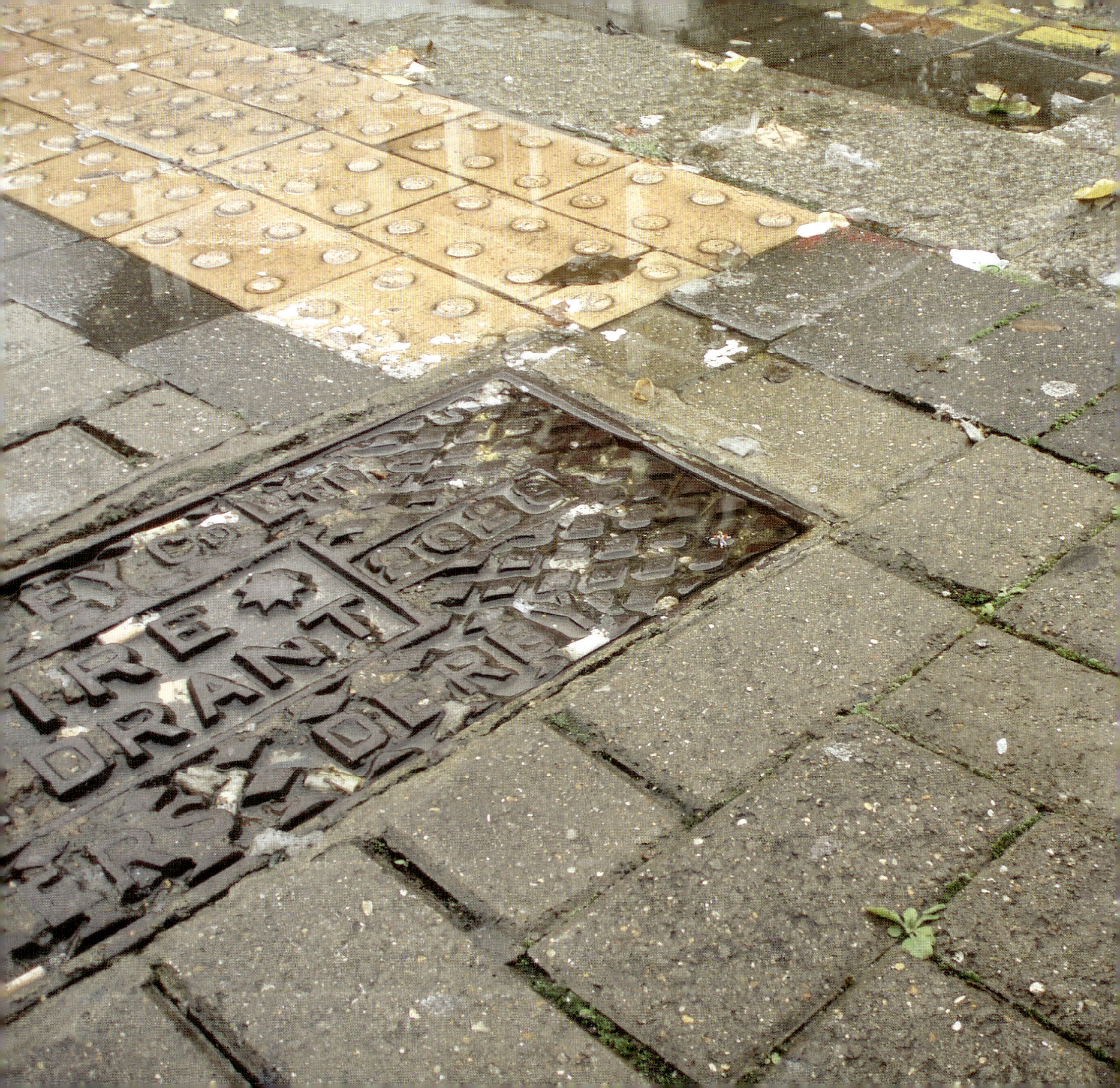
IRE
DRANT

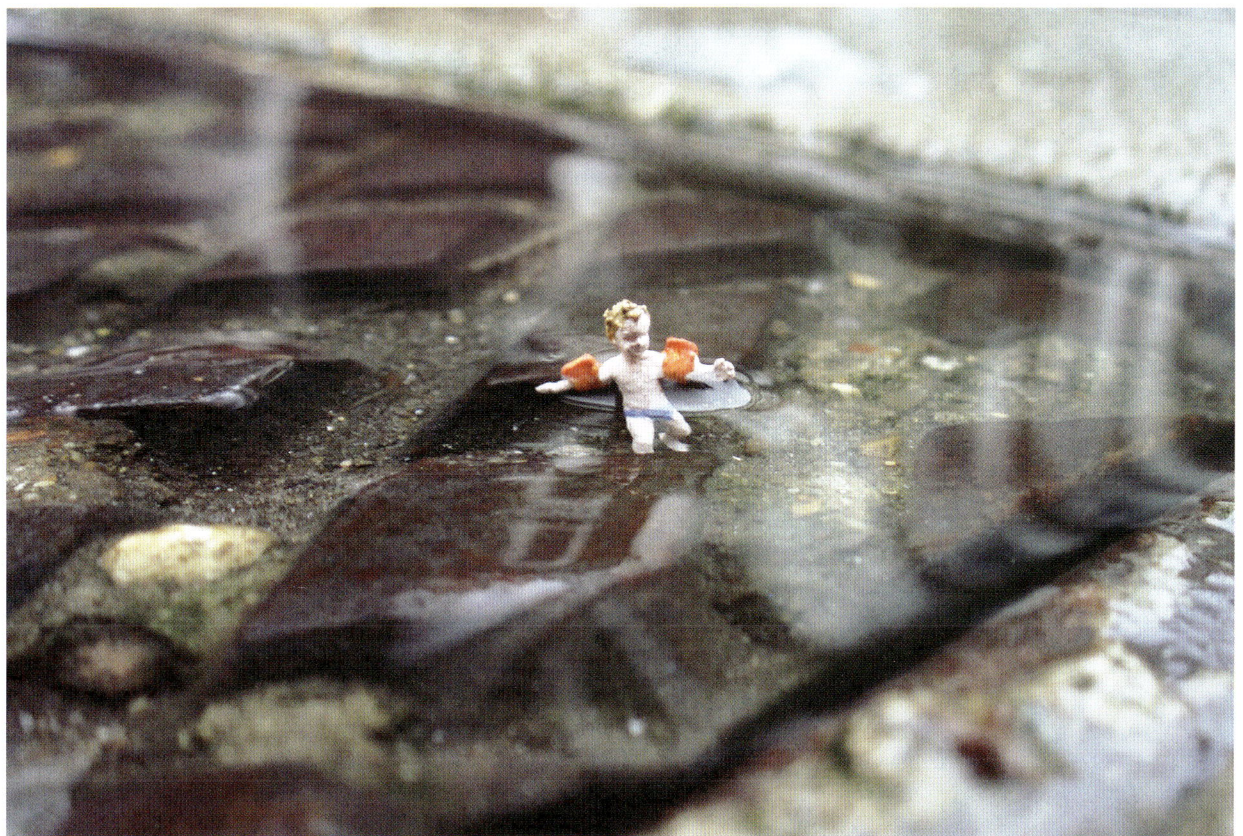

Manhole Swimming

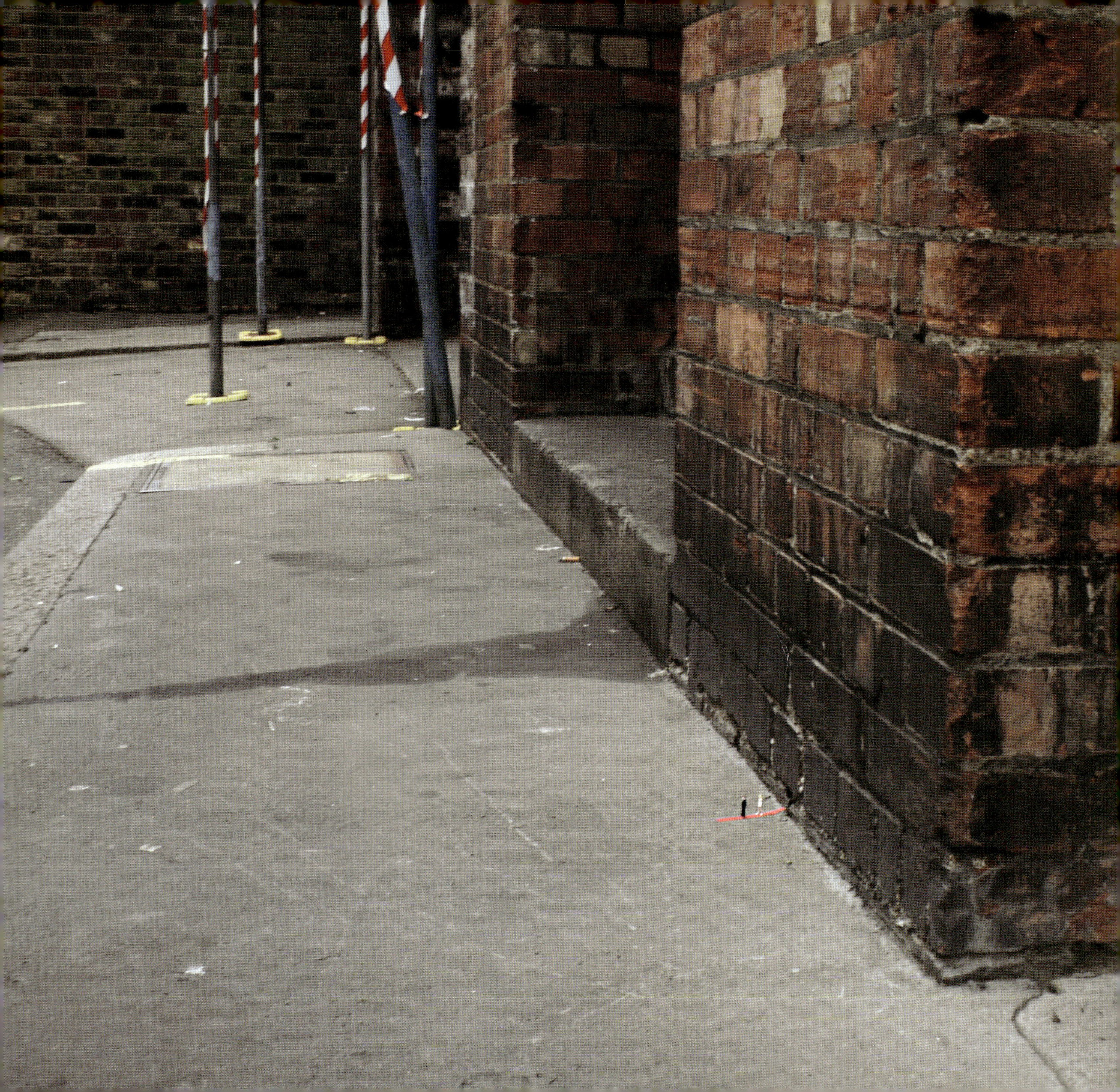

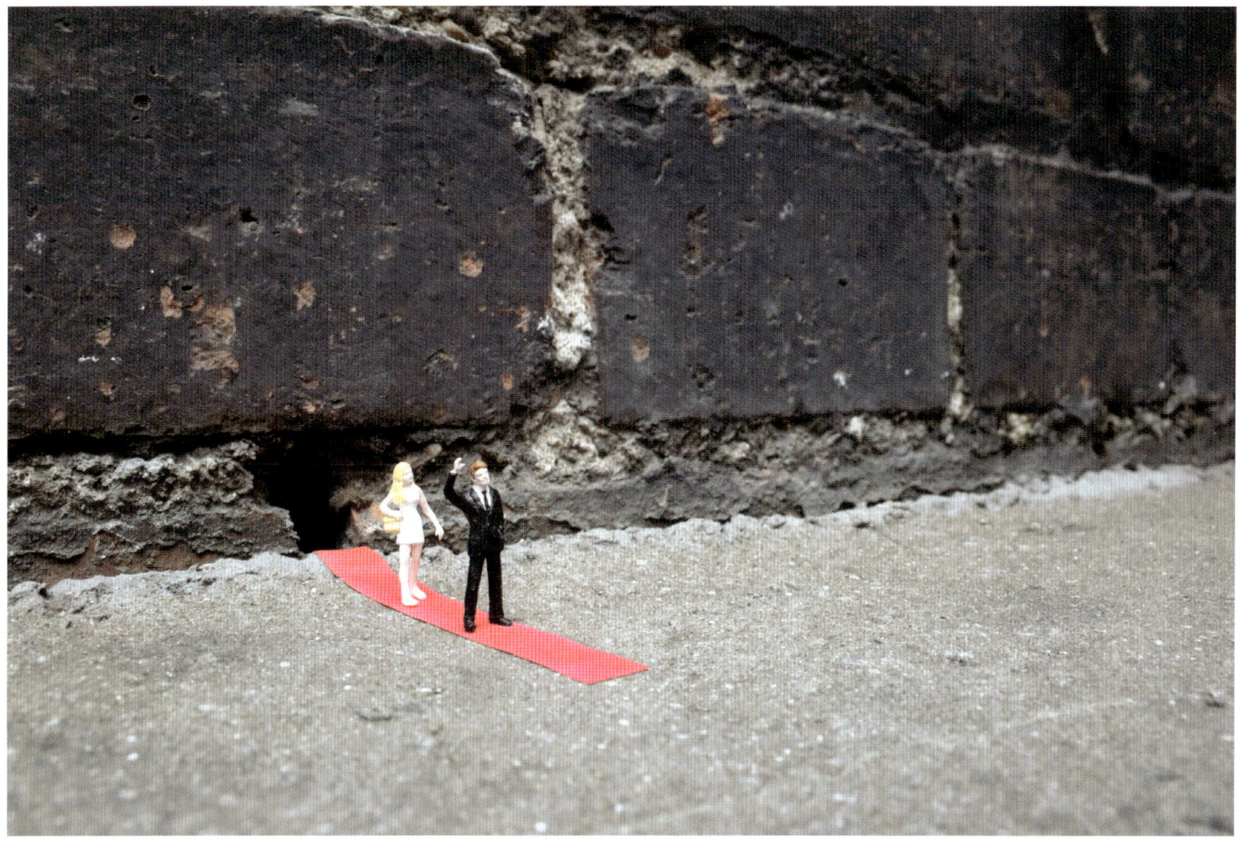

D-List

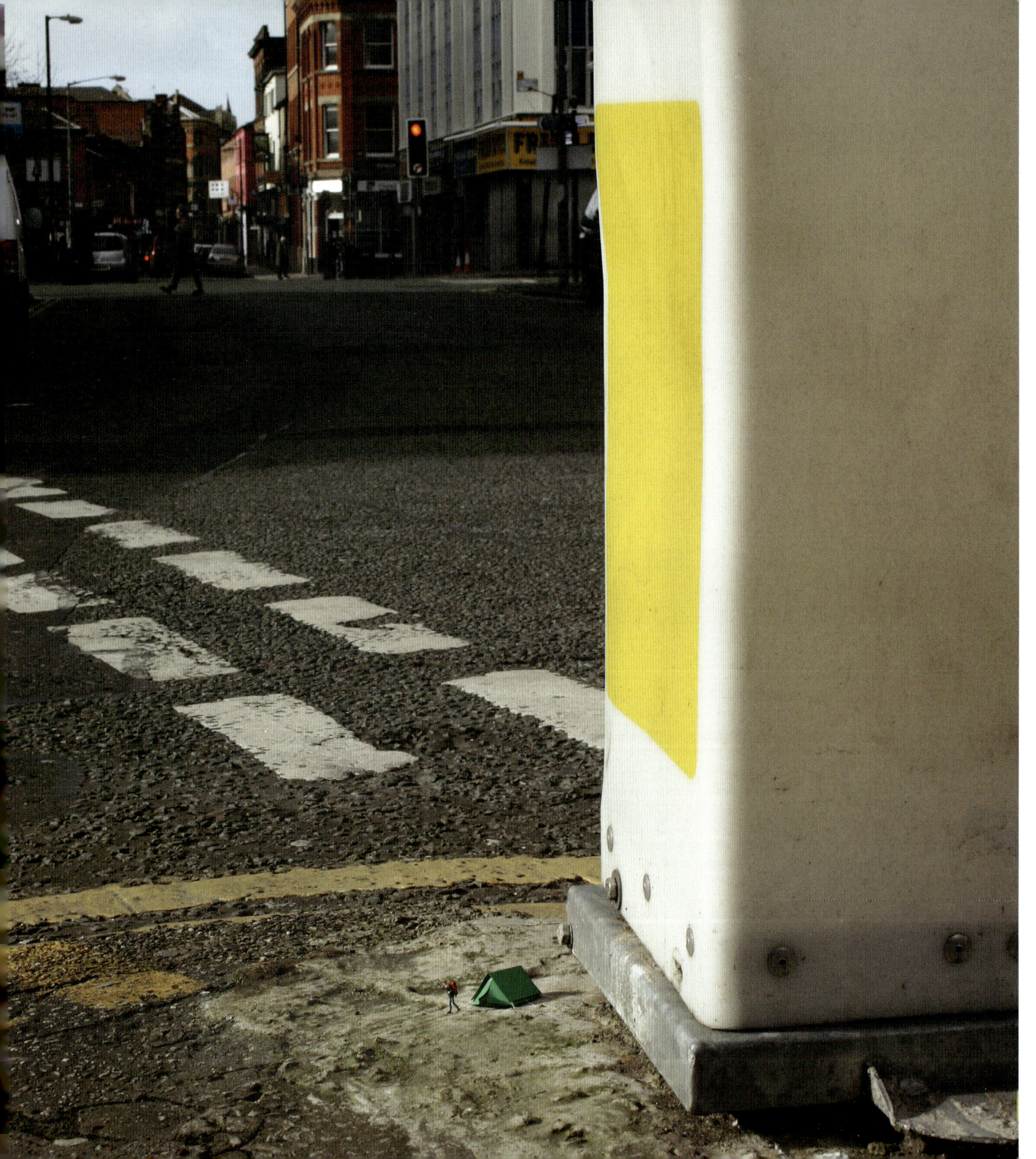

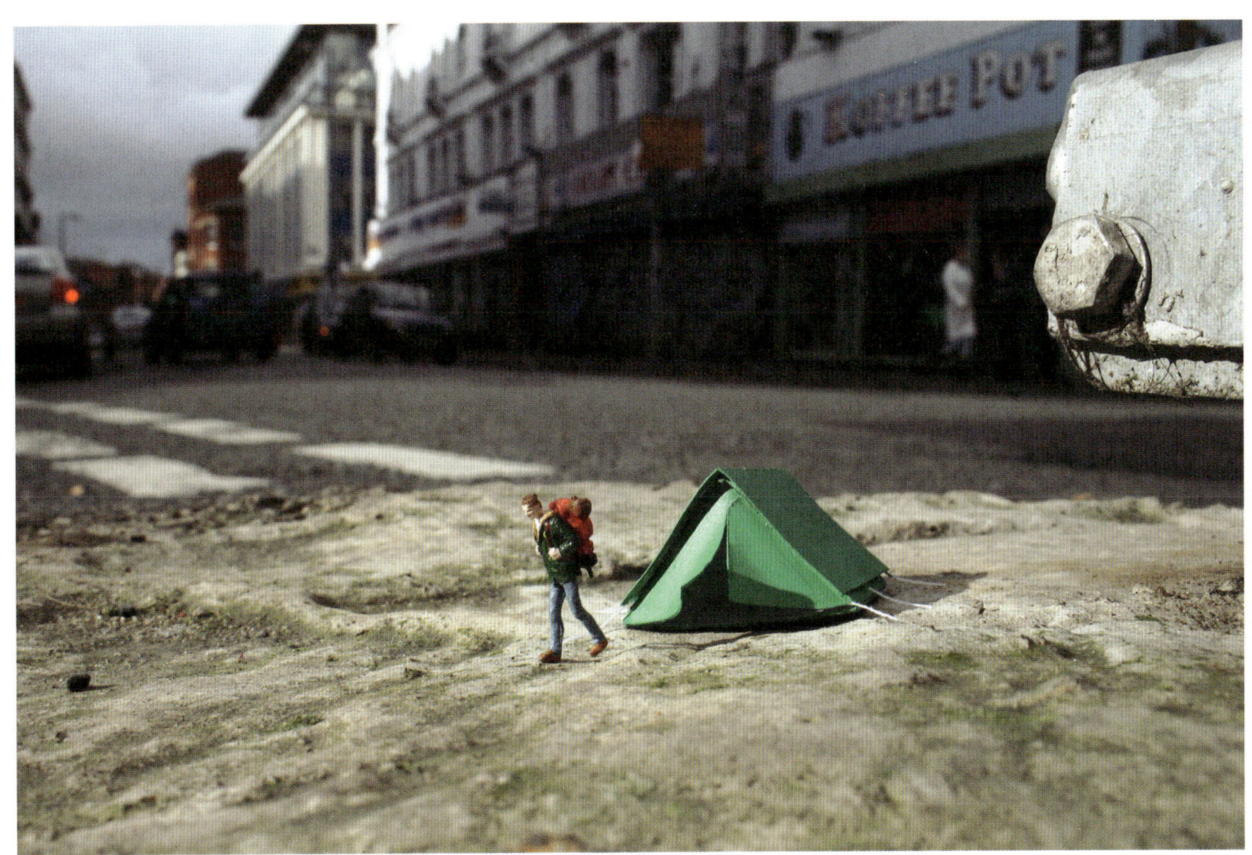

Urban Camping

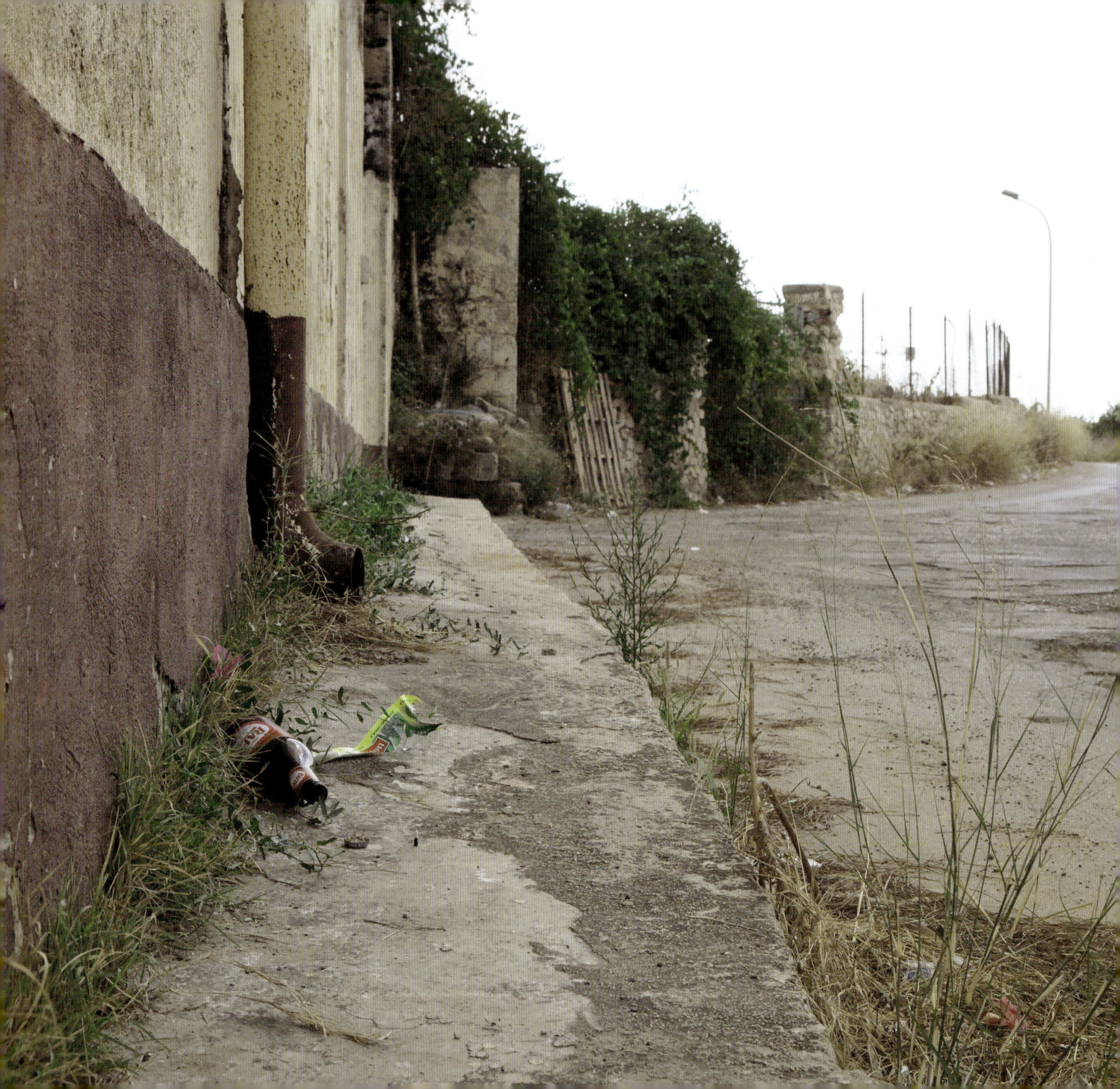

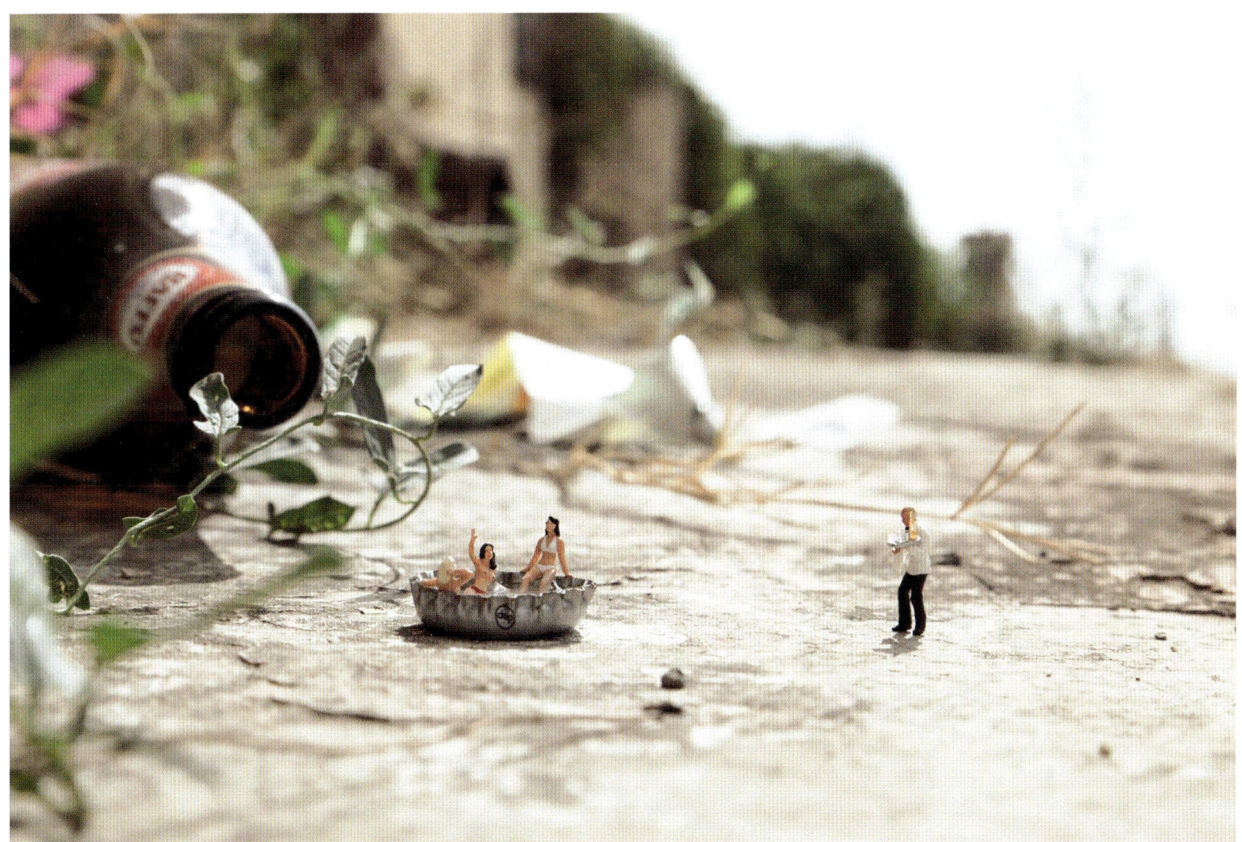

The High Life

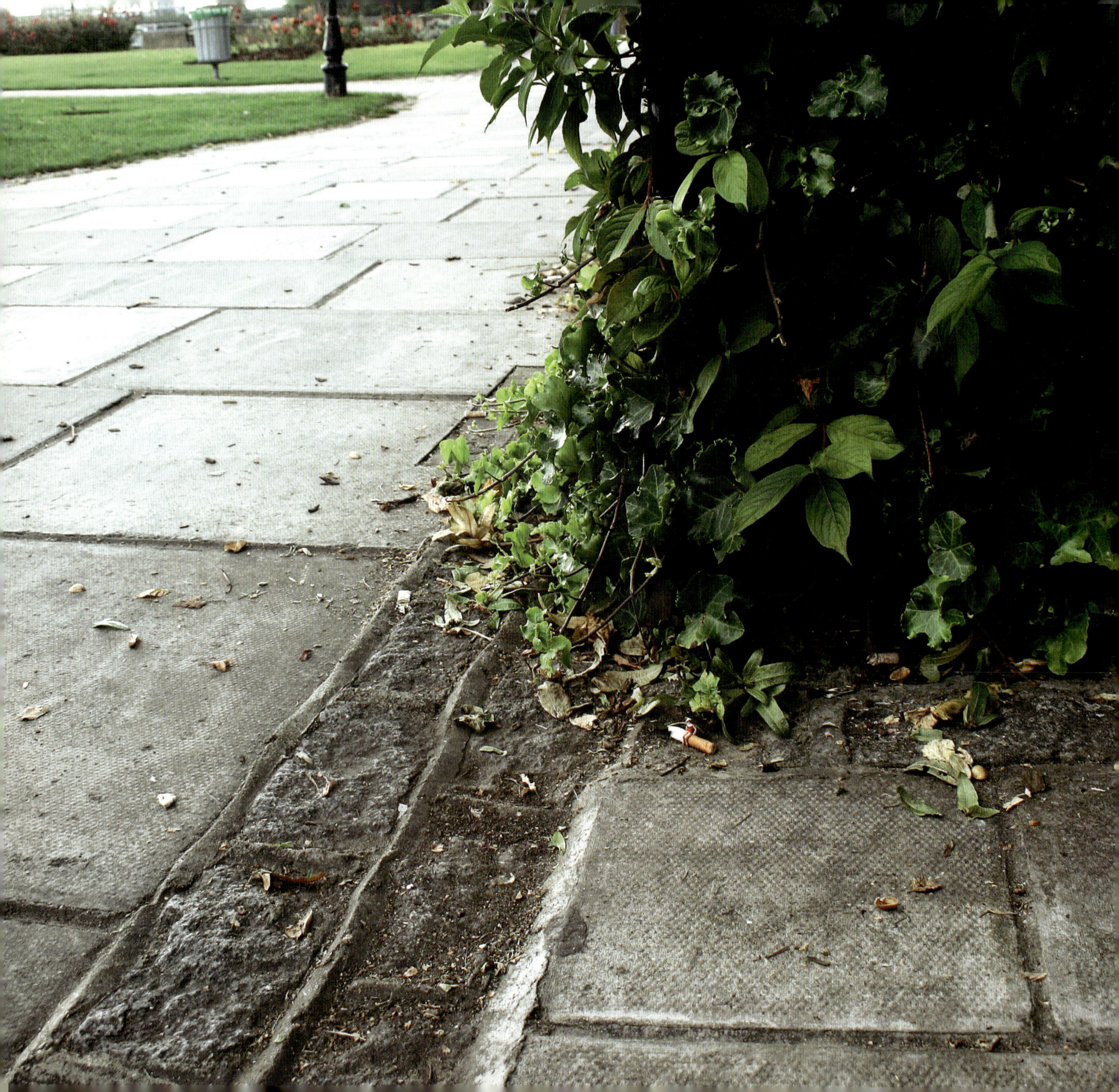

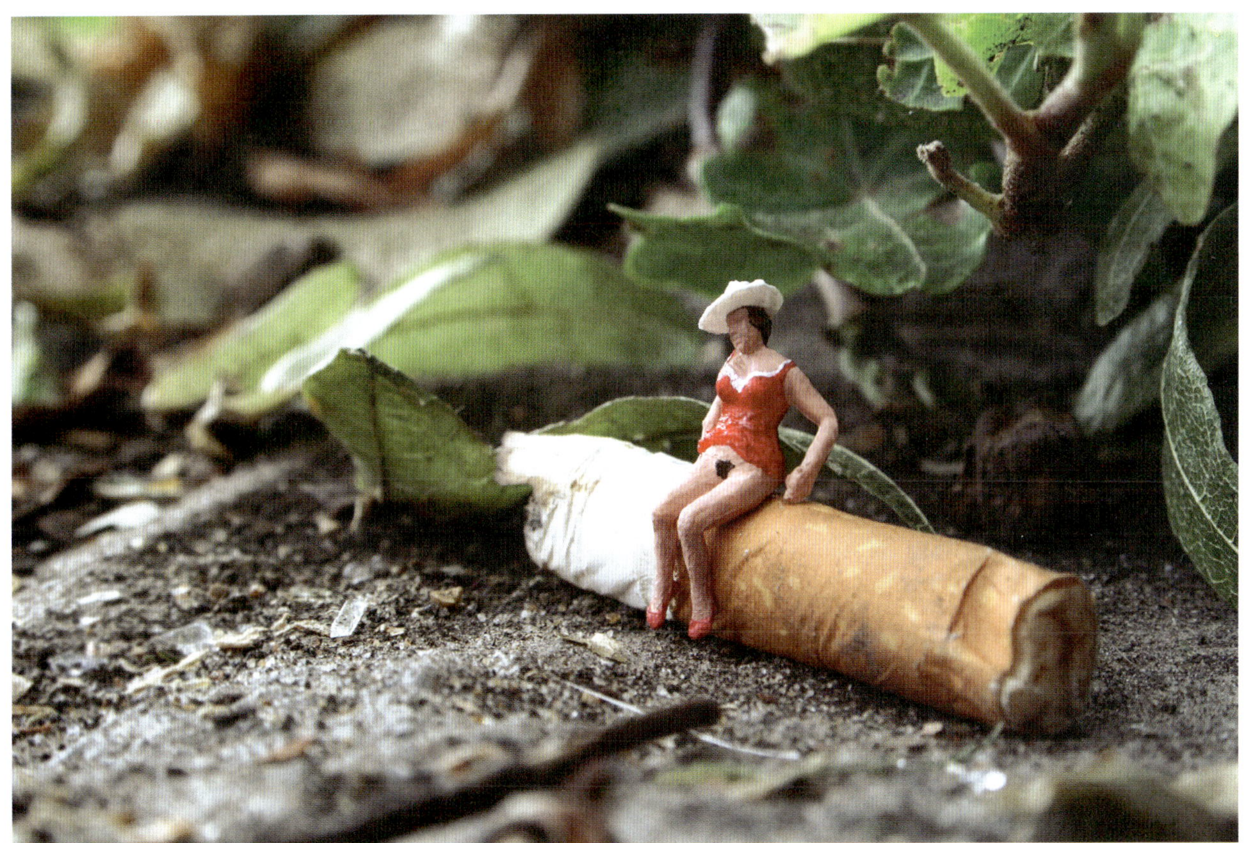

Exhibitionism

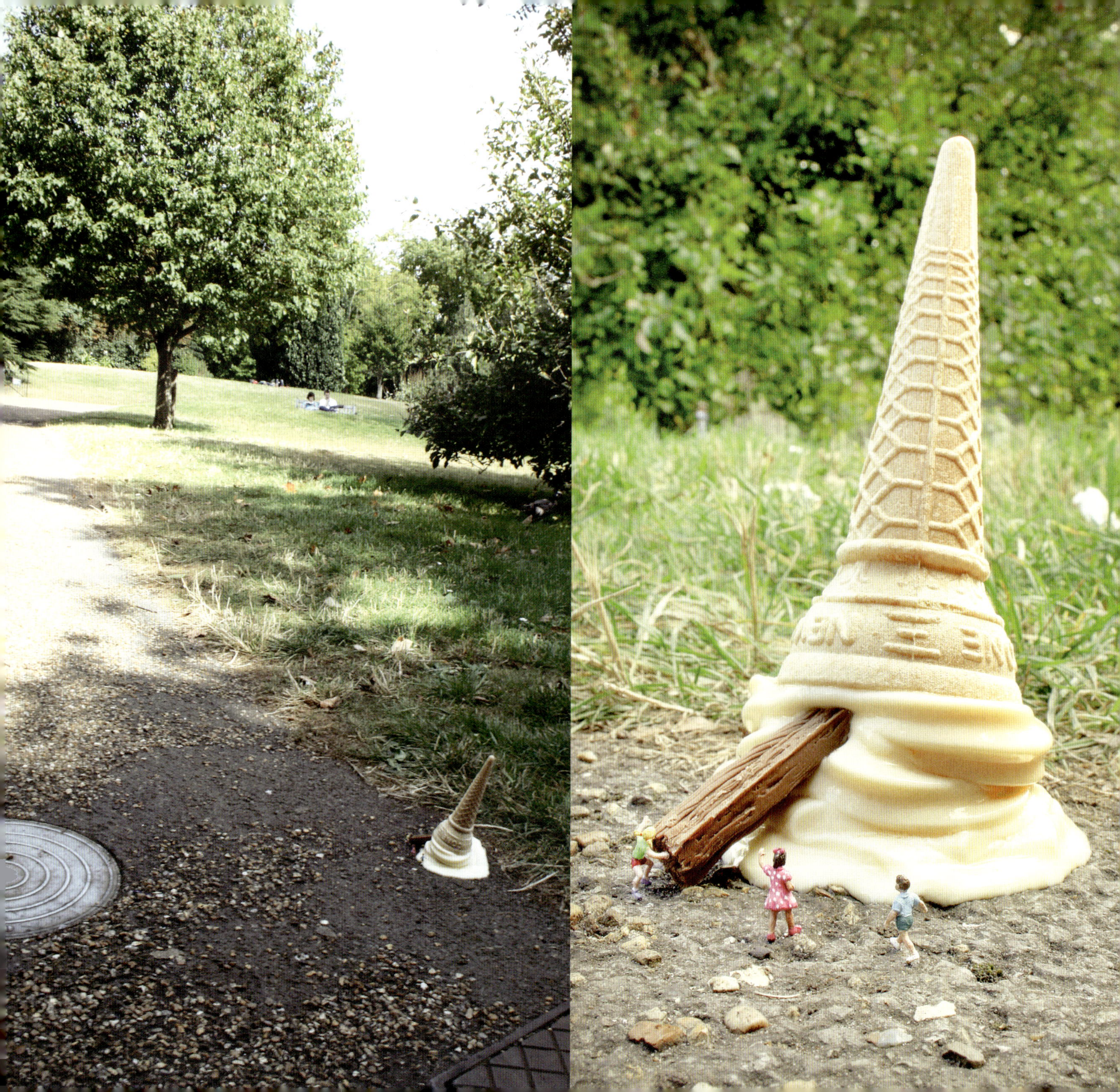

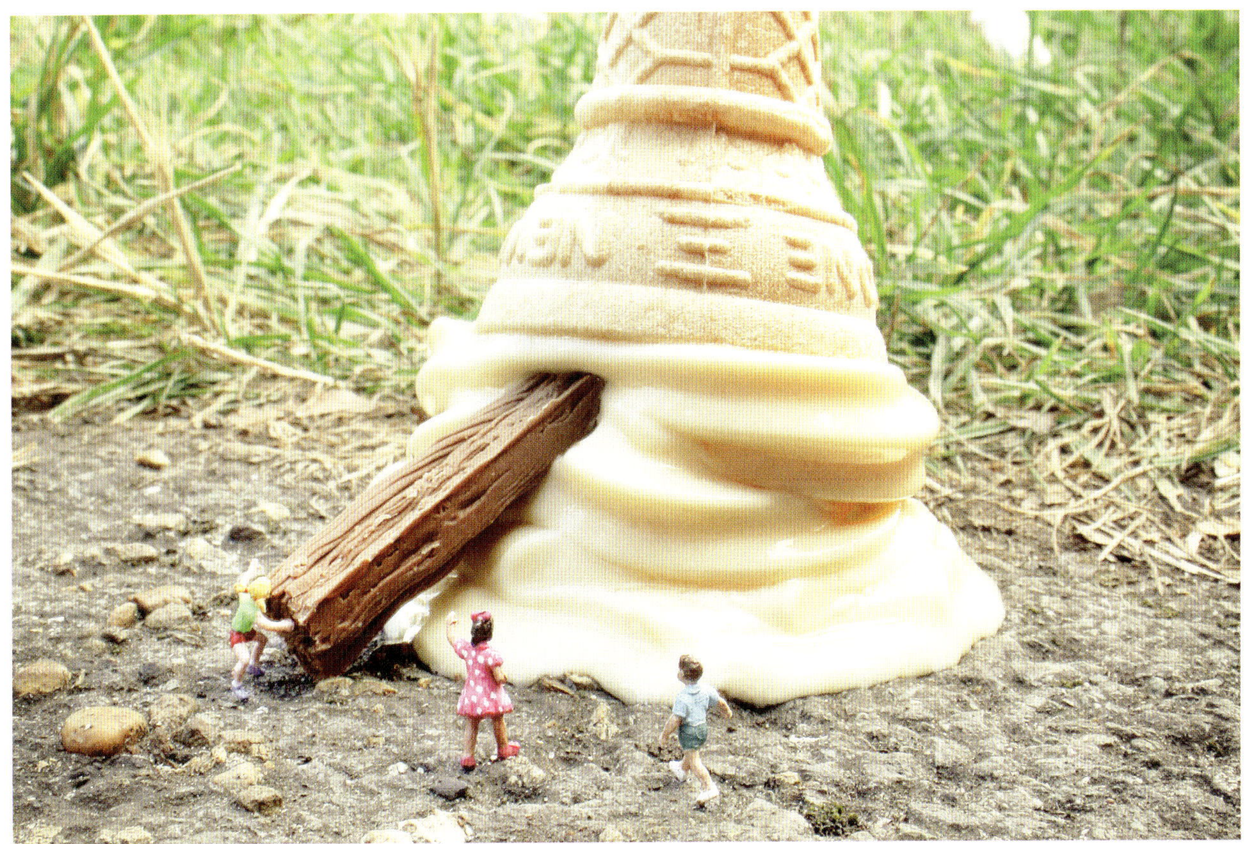

The Mother Lode

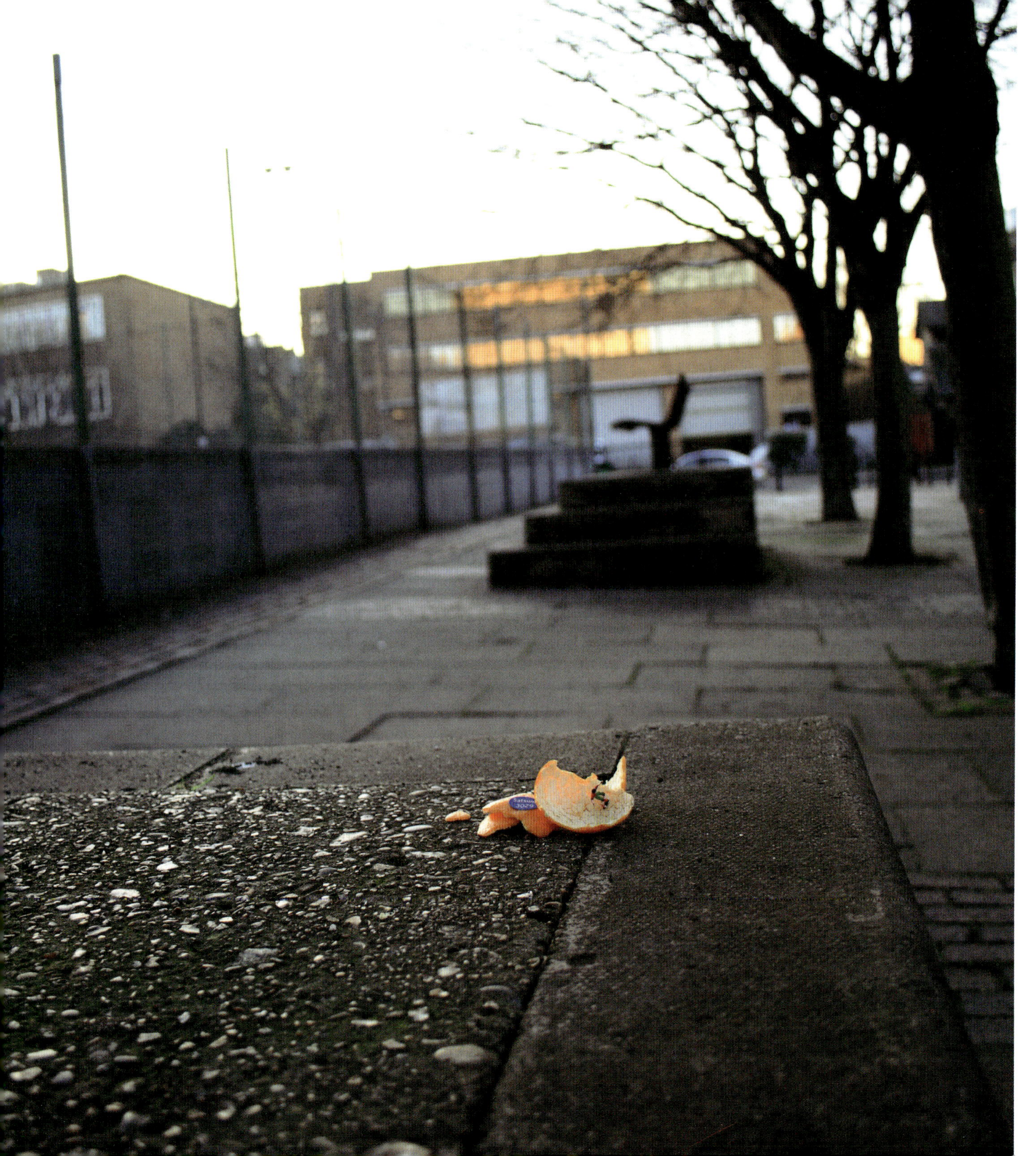

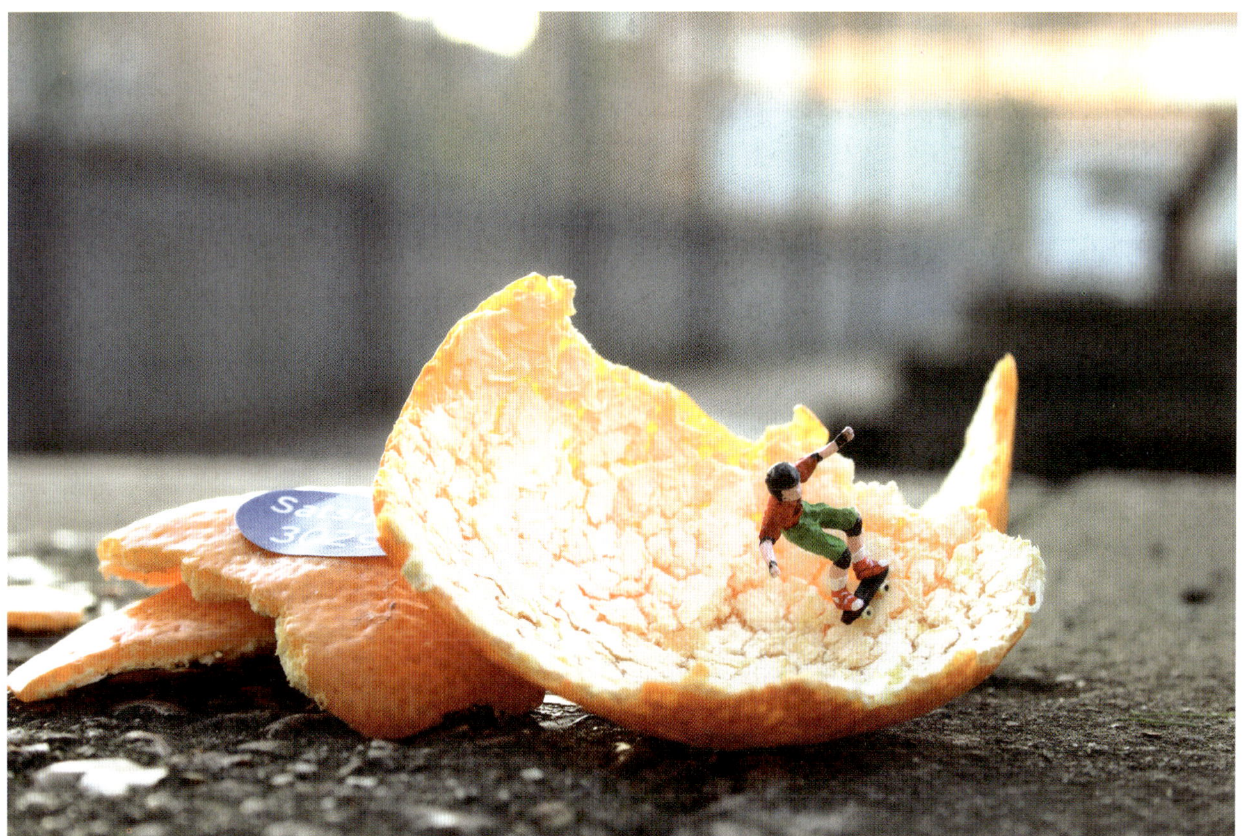

Local Amenities for Children

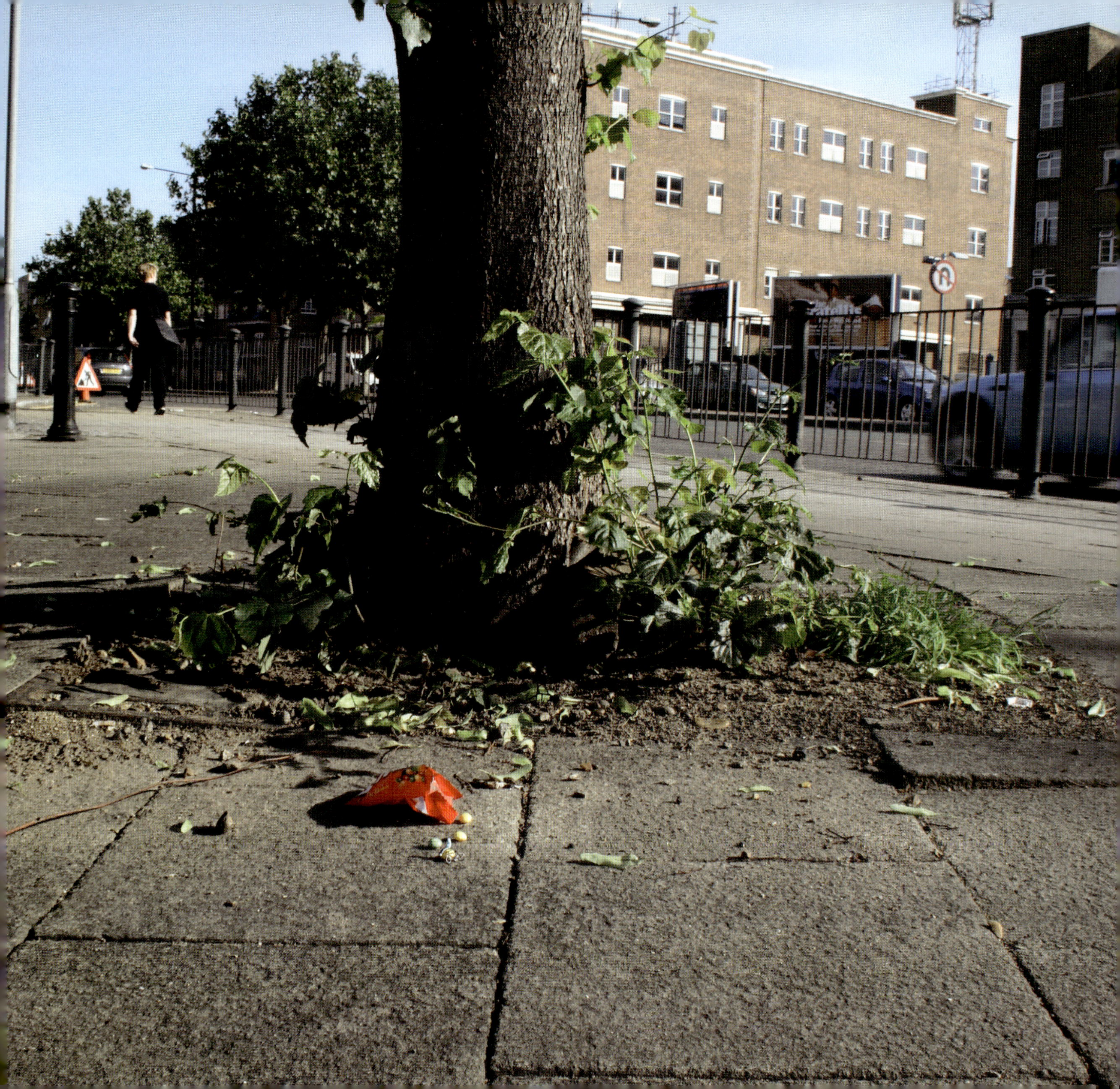

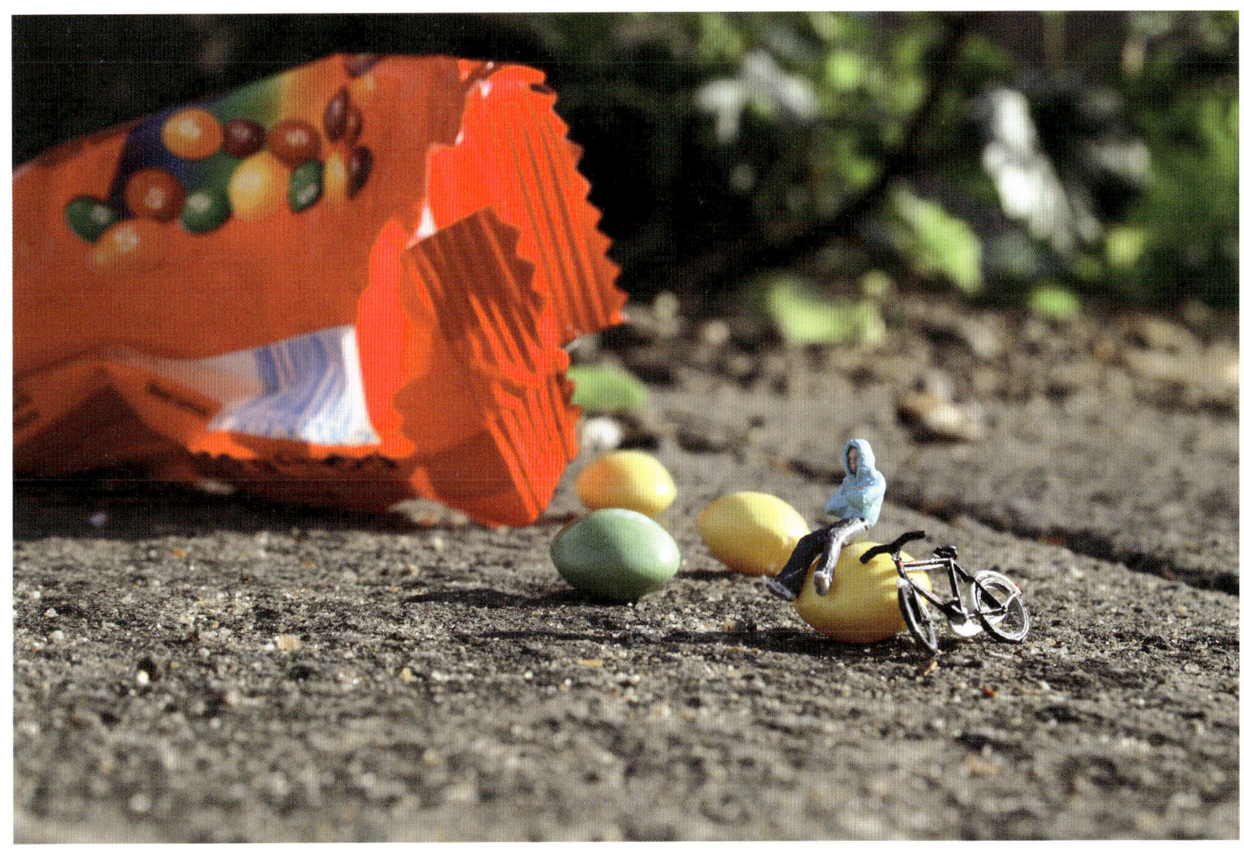

Unwanted Ones

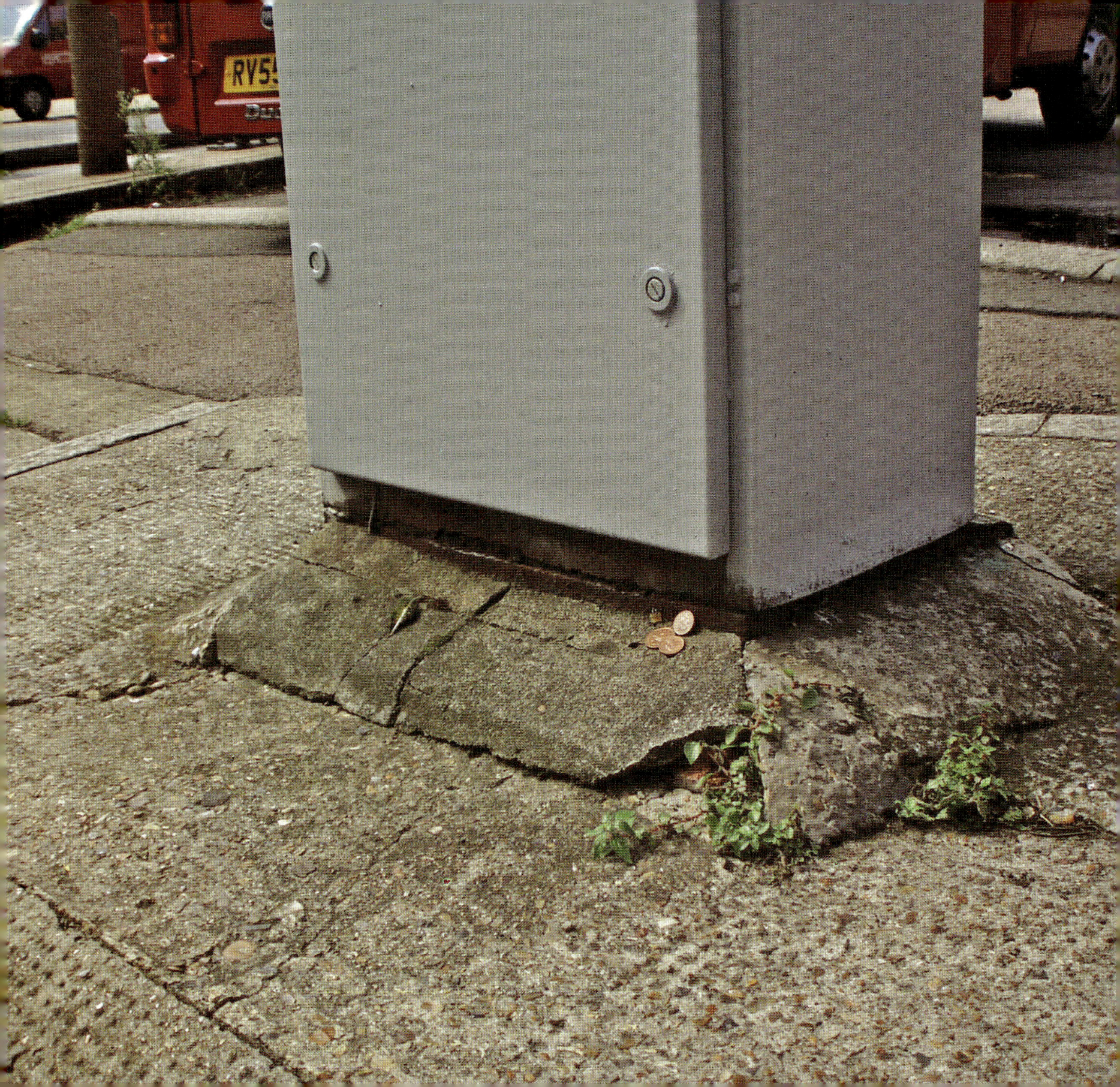

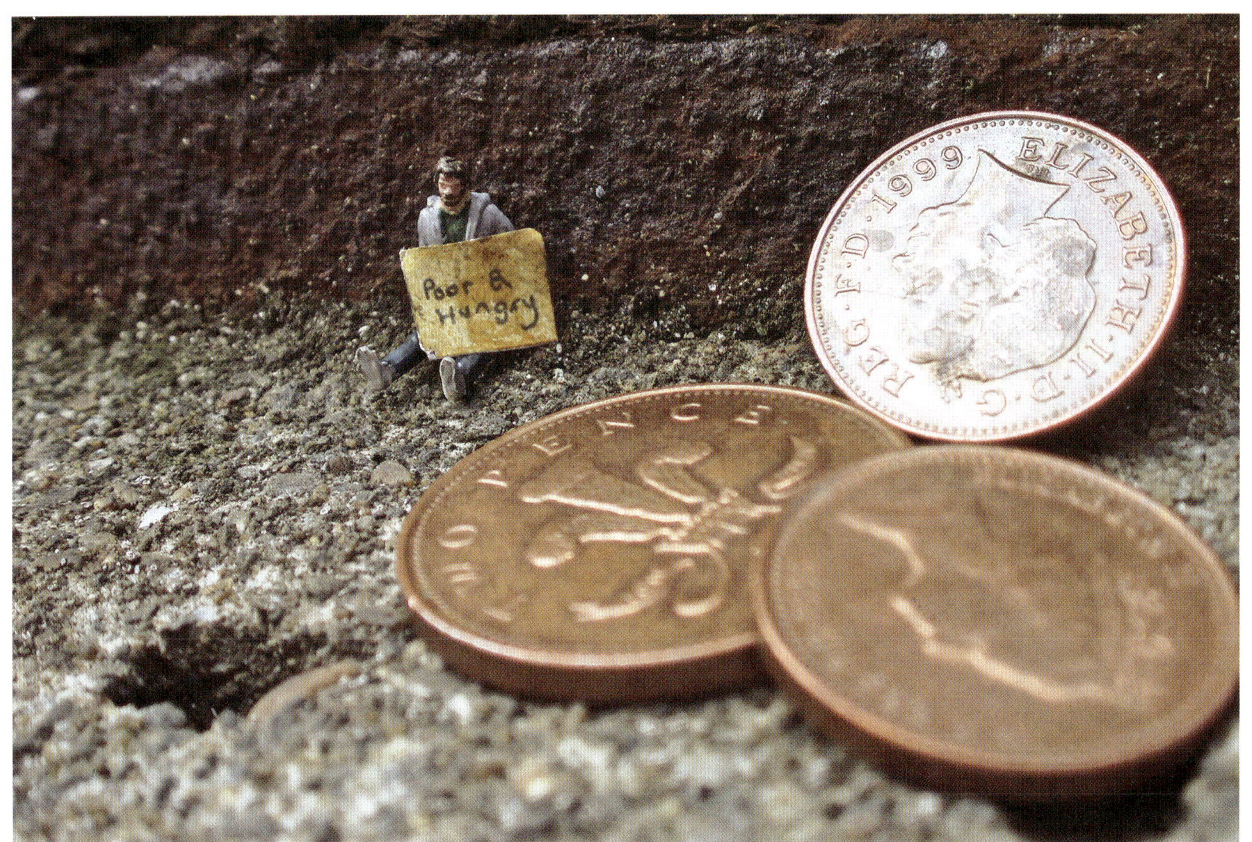

‘Spare some change’

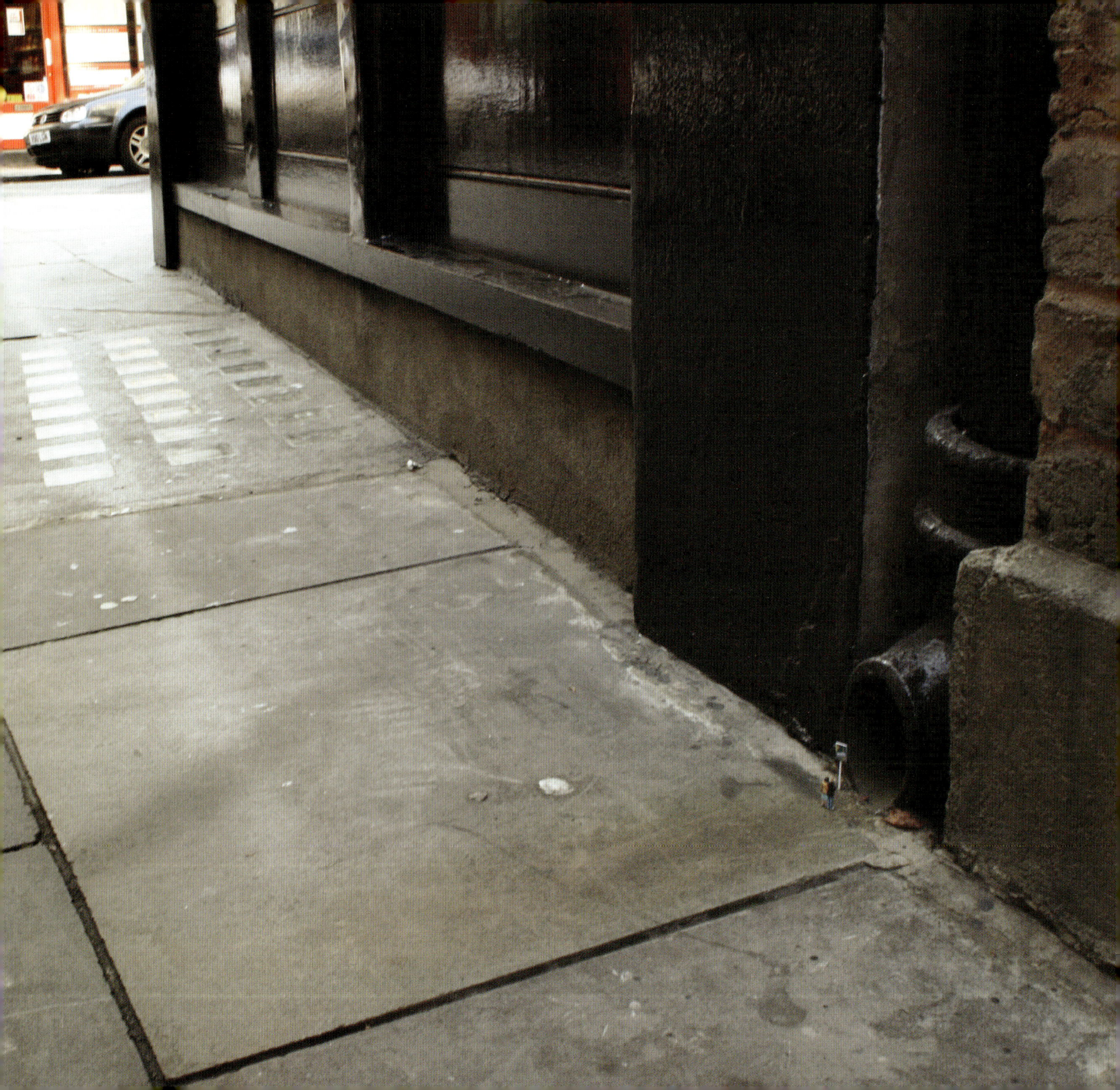

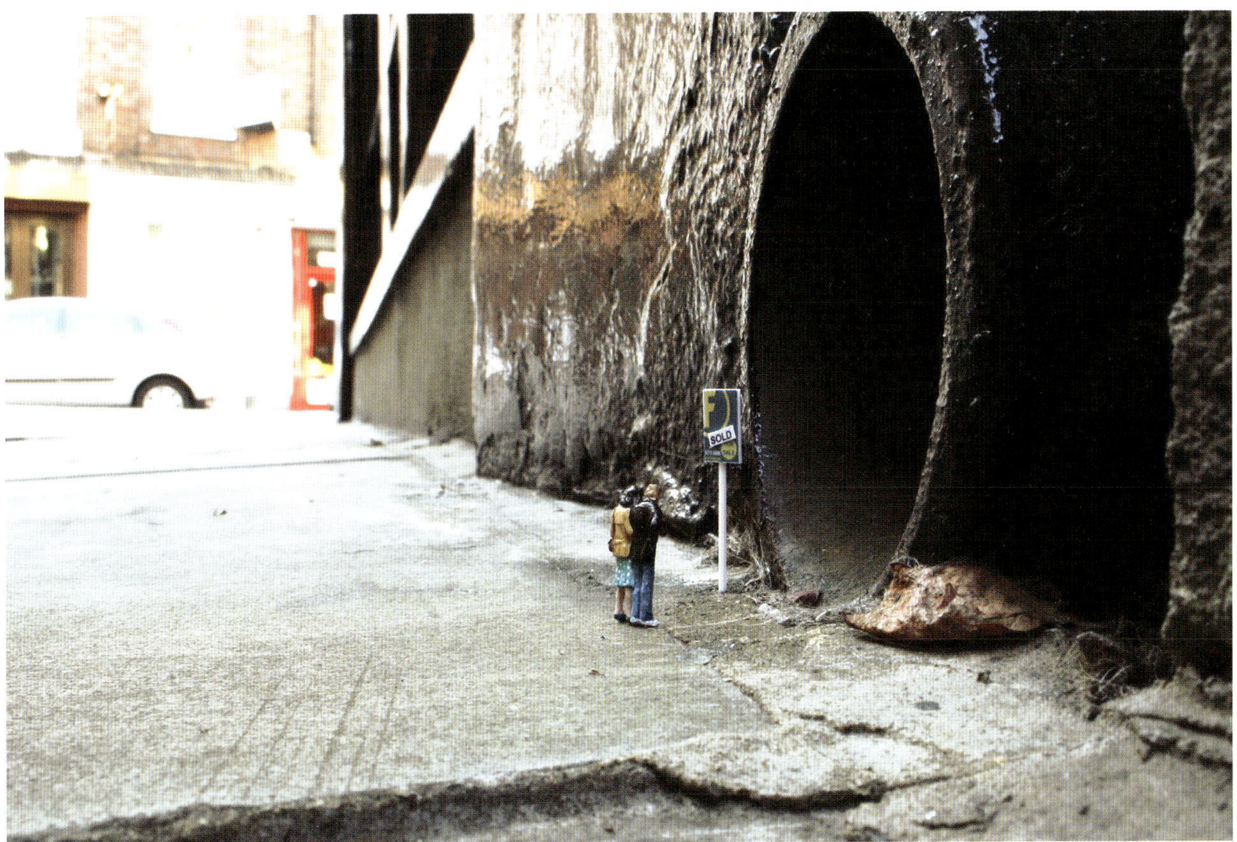

Our First Home

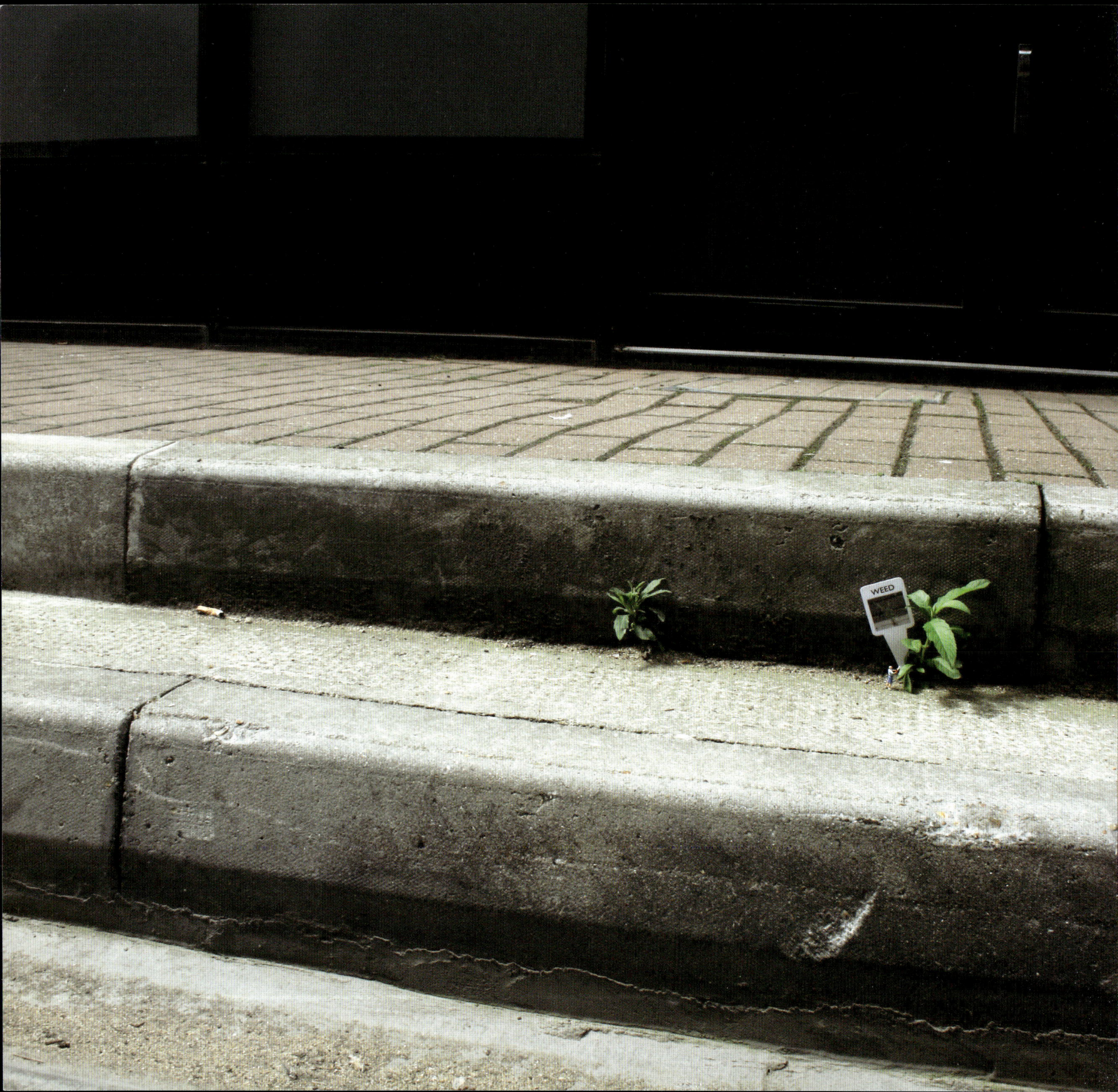
WEED

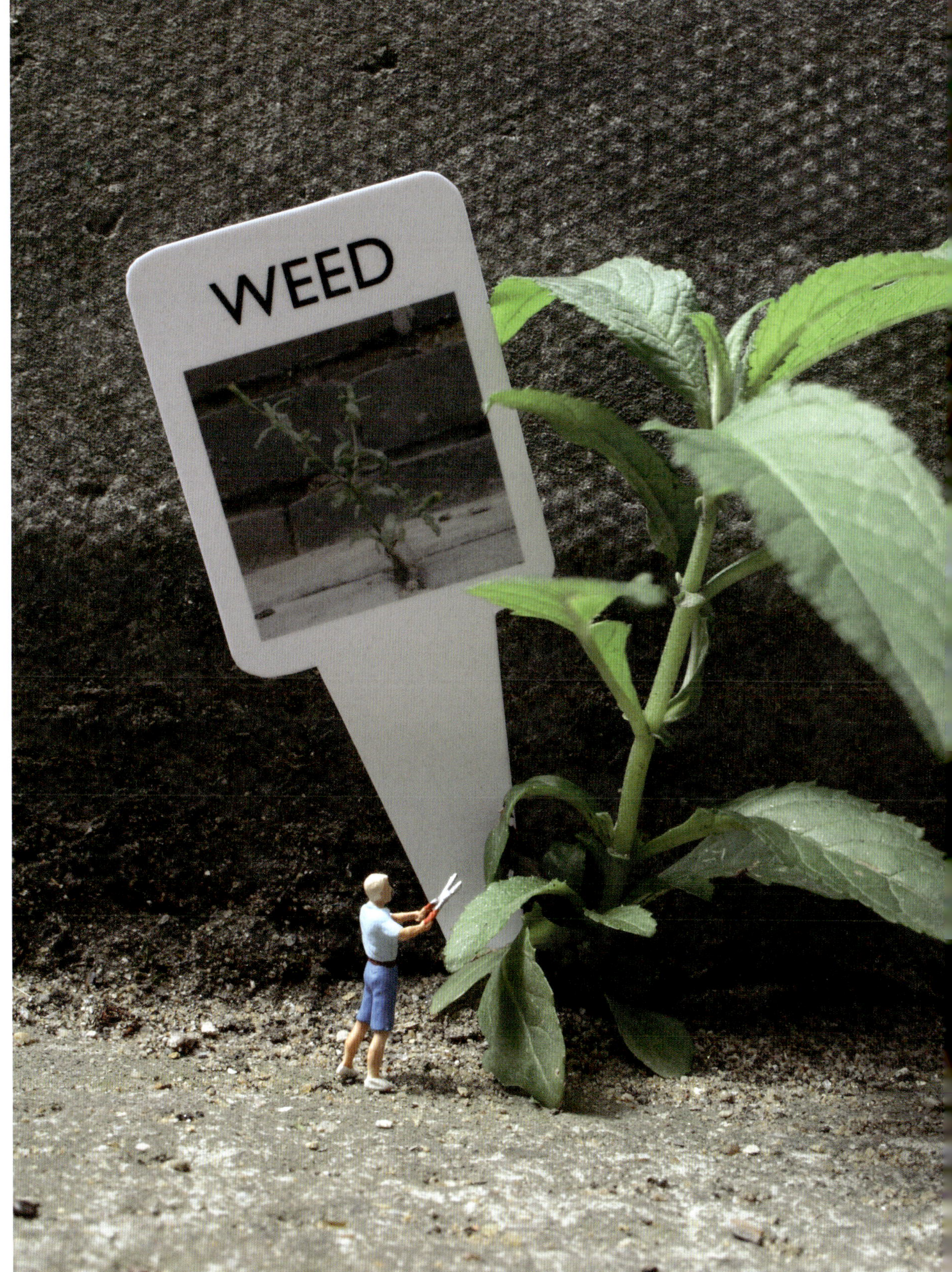

Britain in Bloom

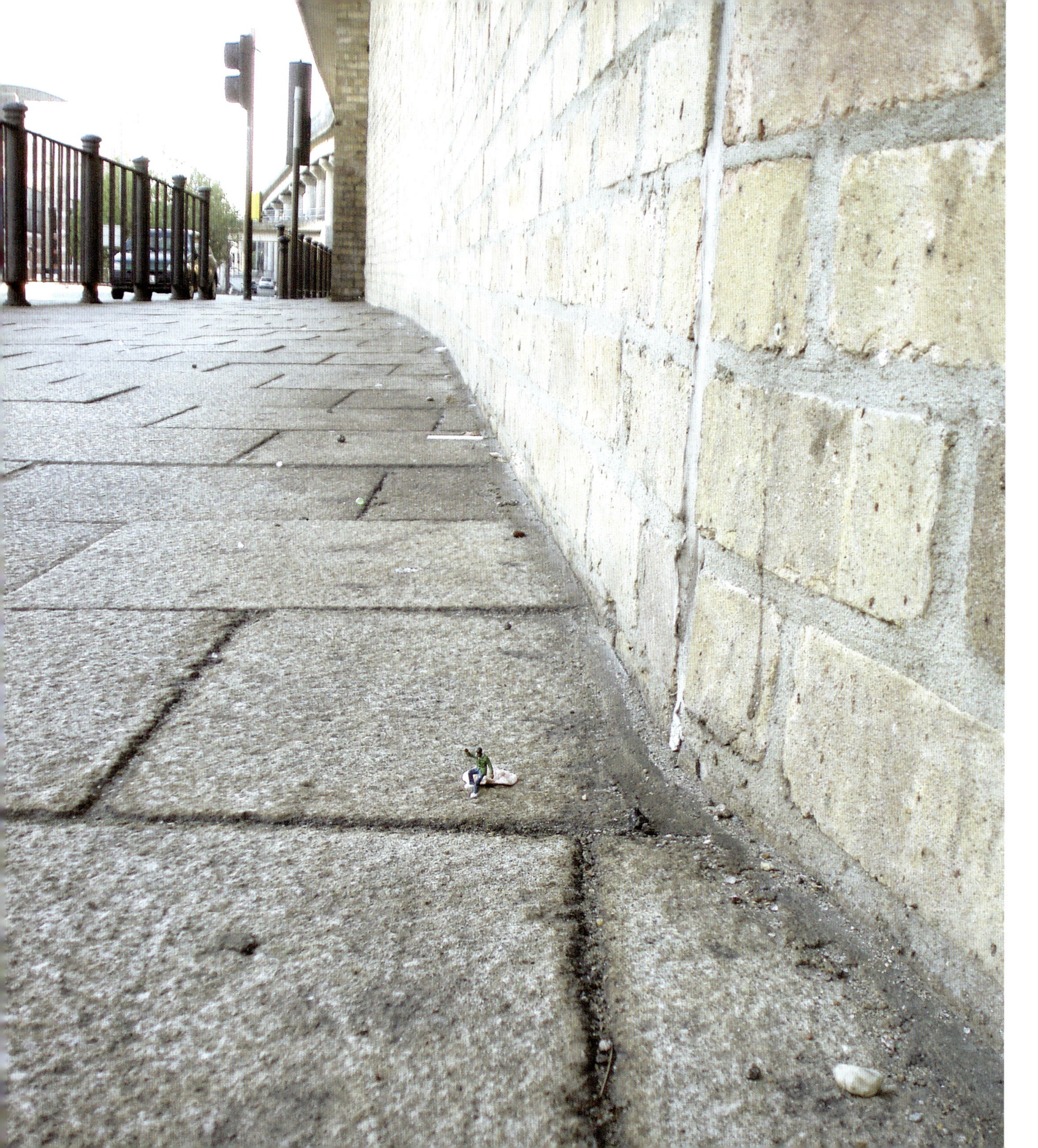

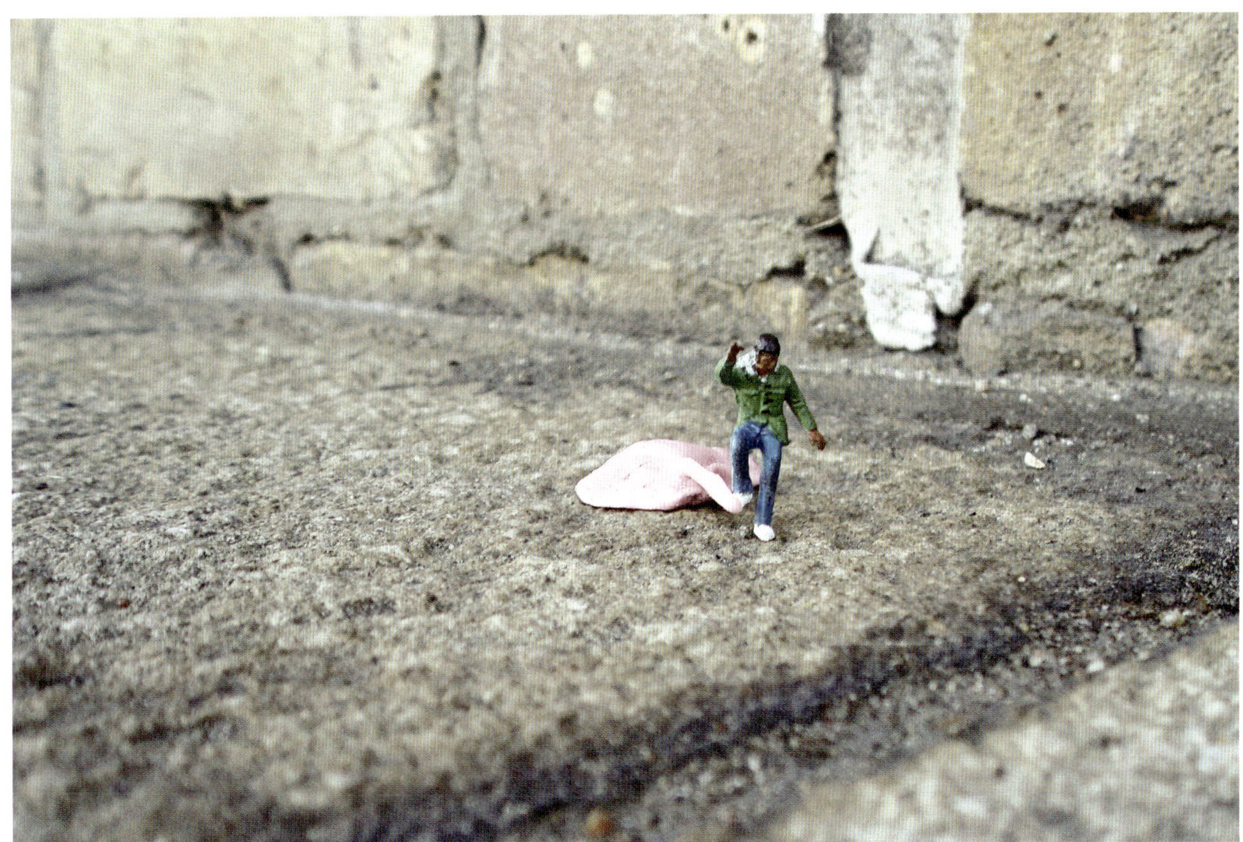

Gum

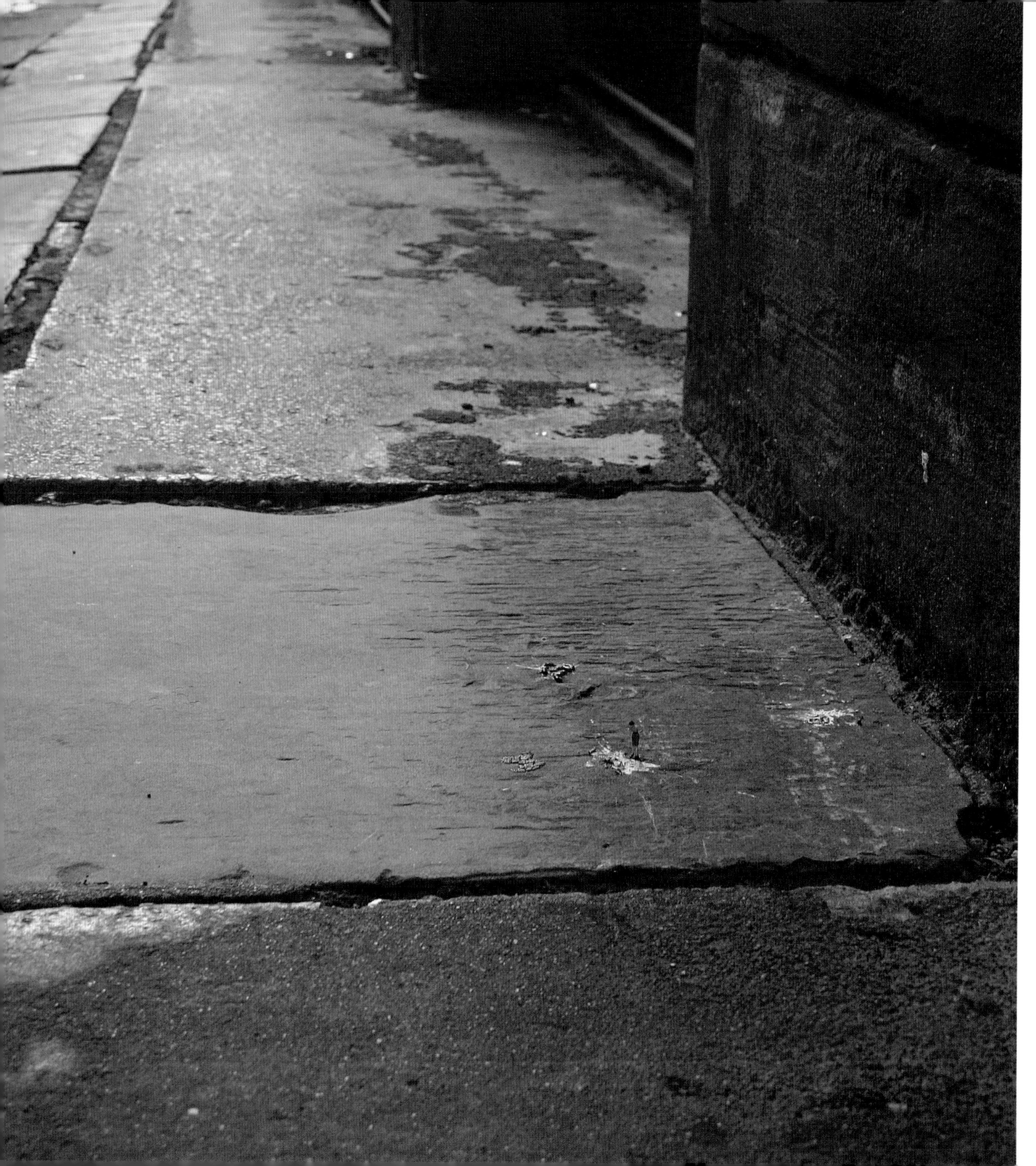

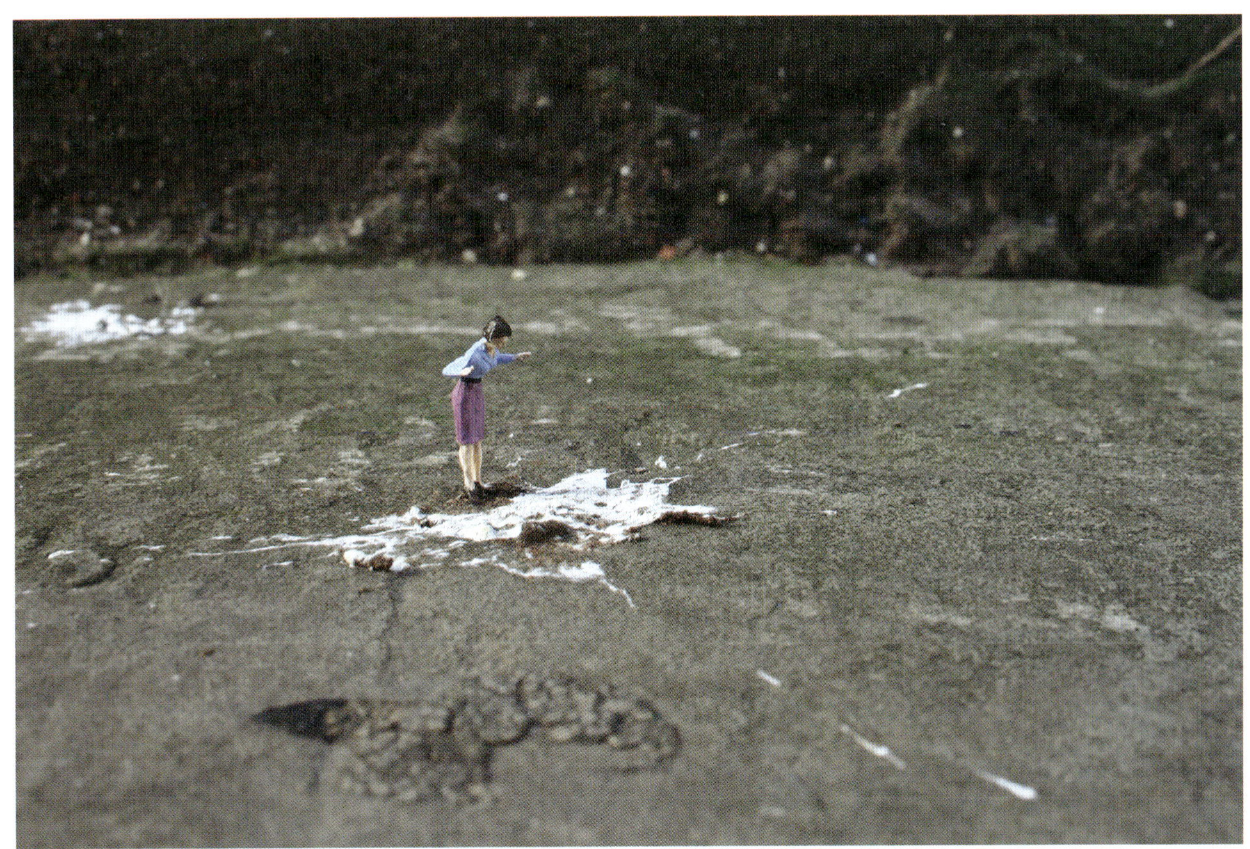

One False Move

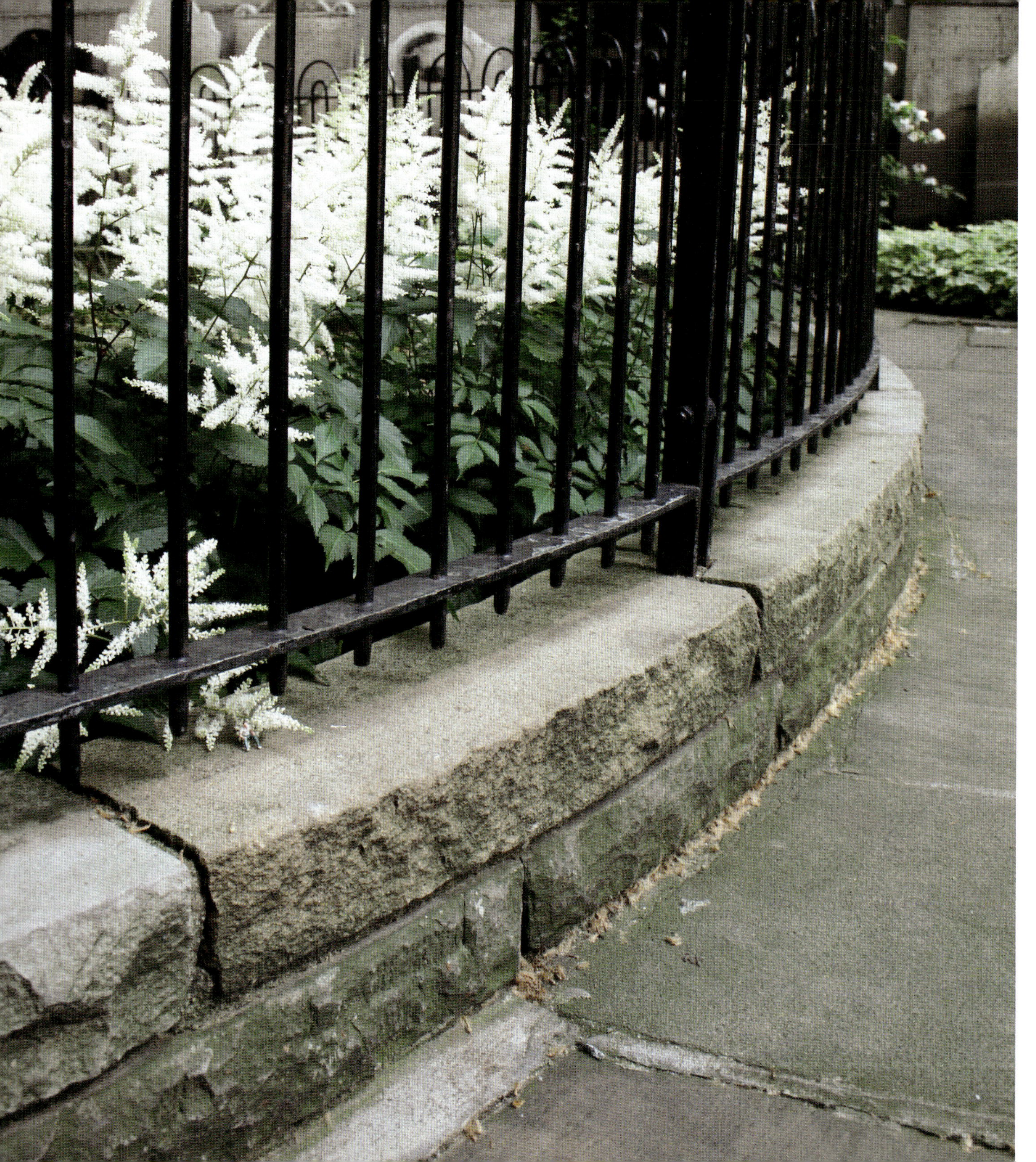

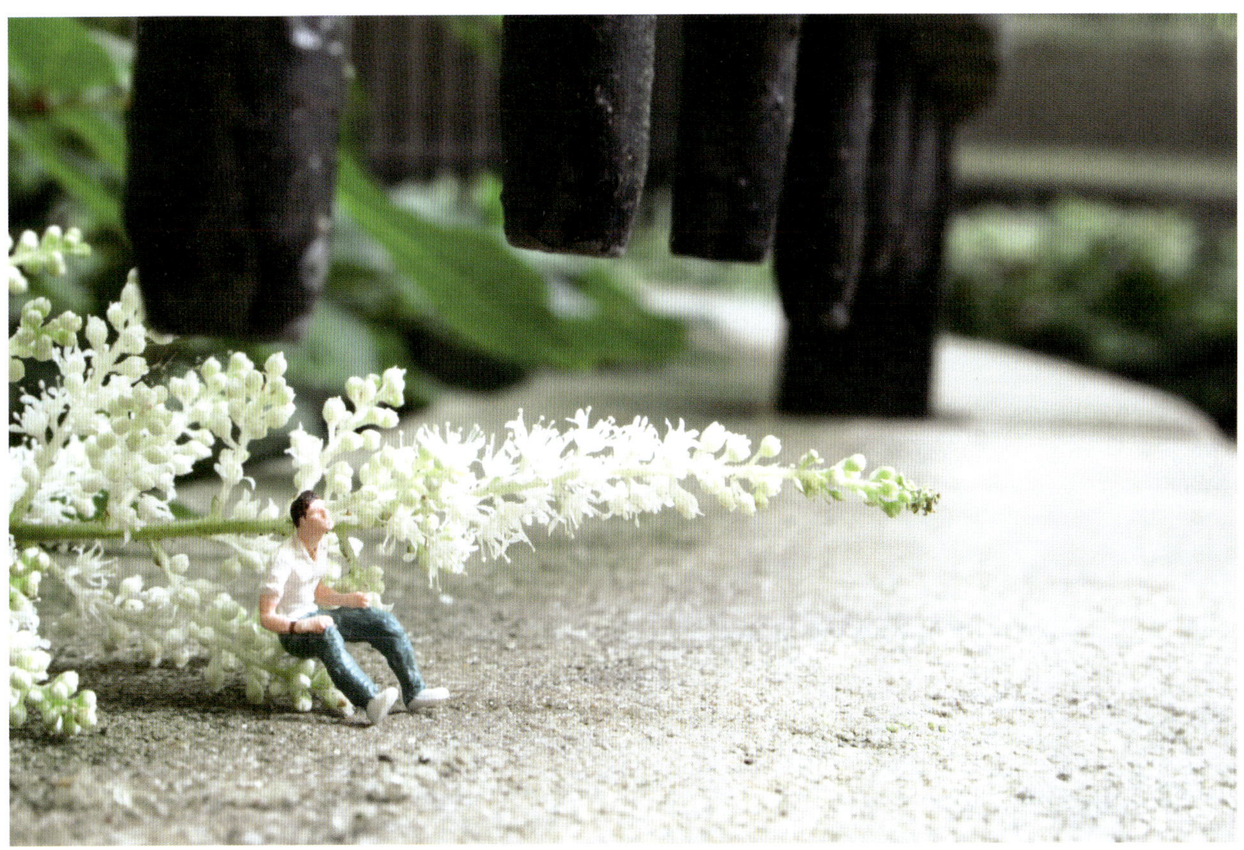

30 minutes

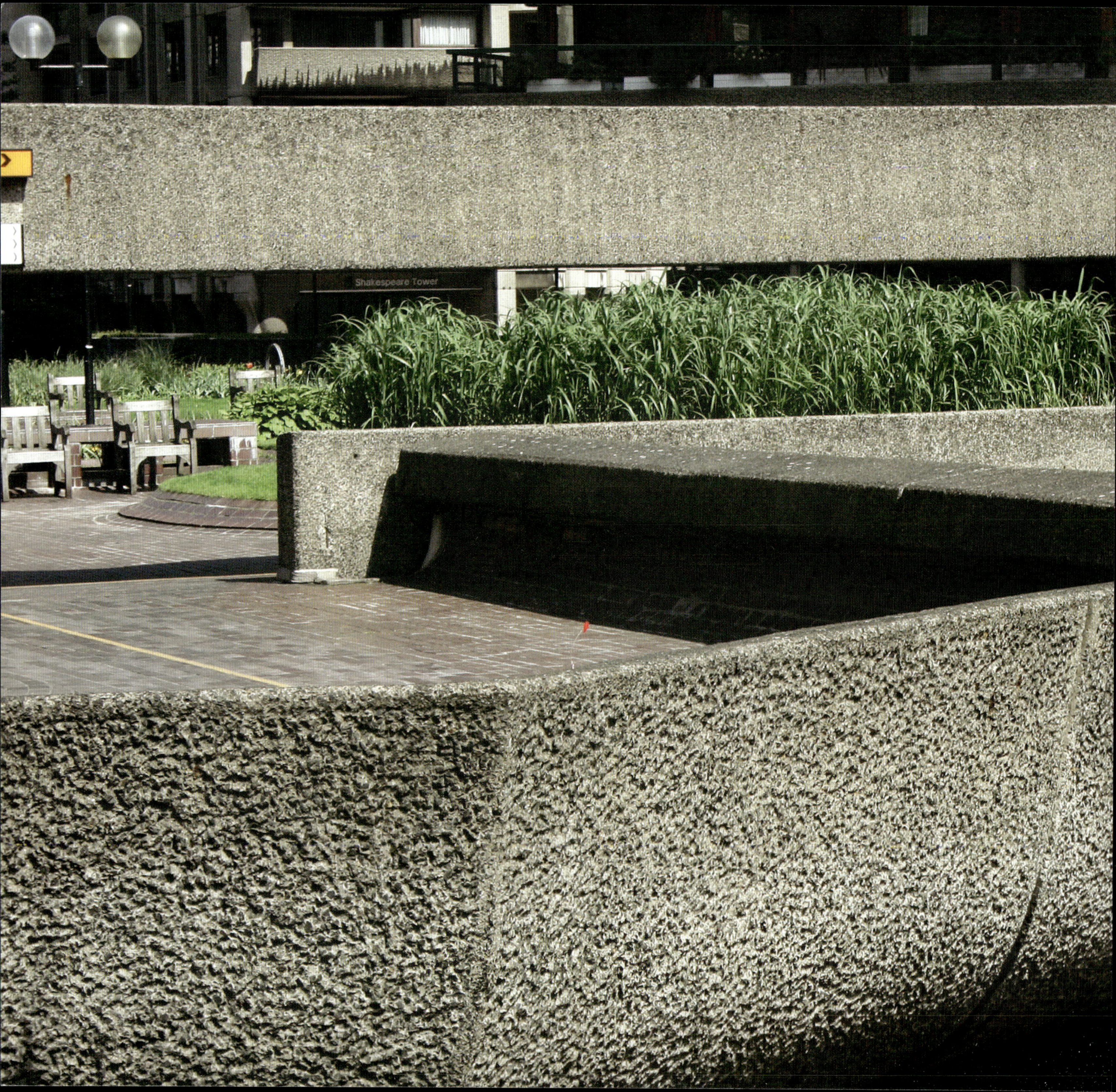
Shakespeare Tower

High as a Kite

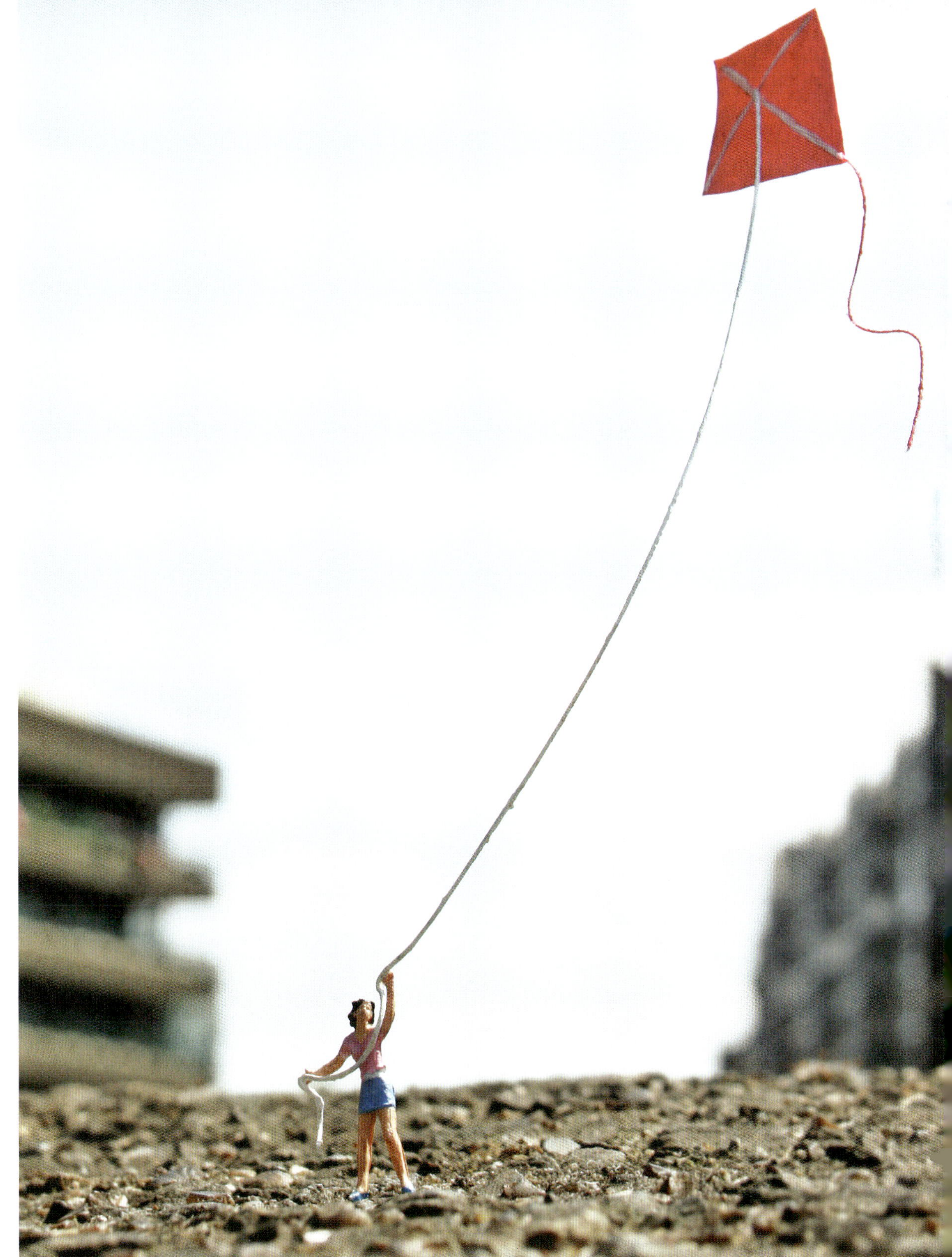

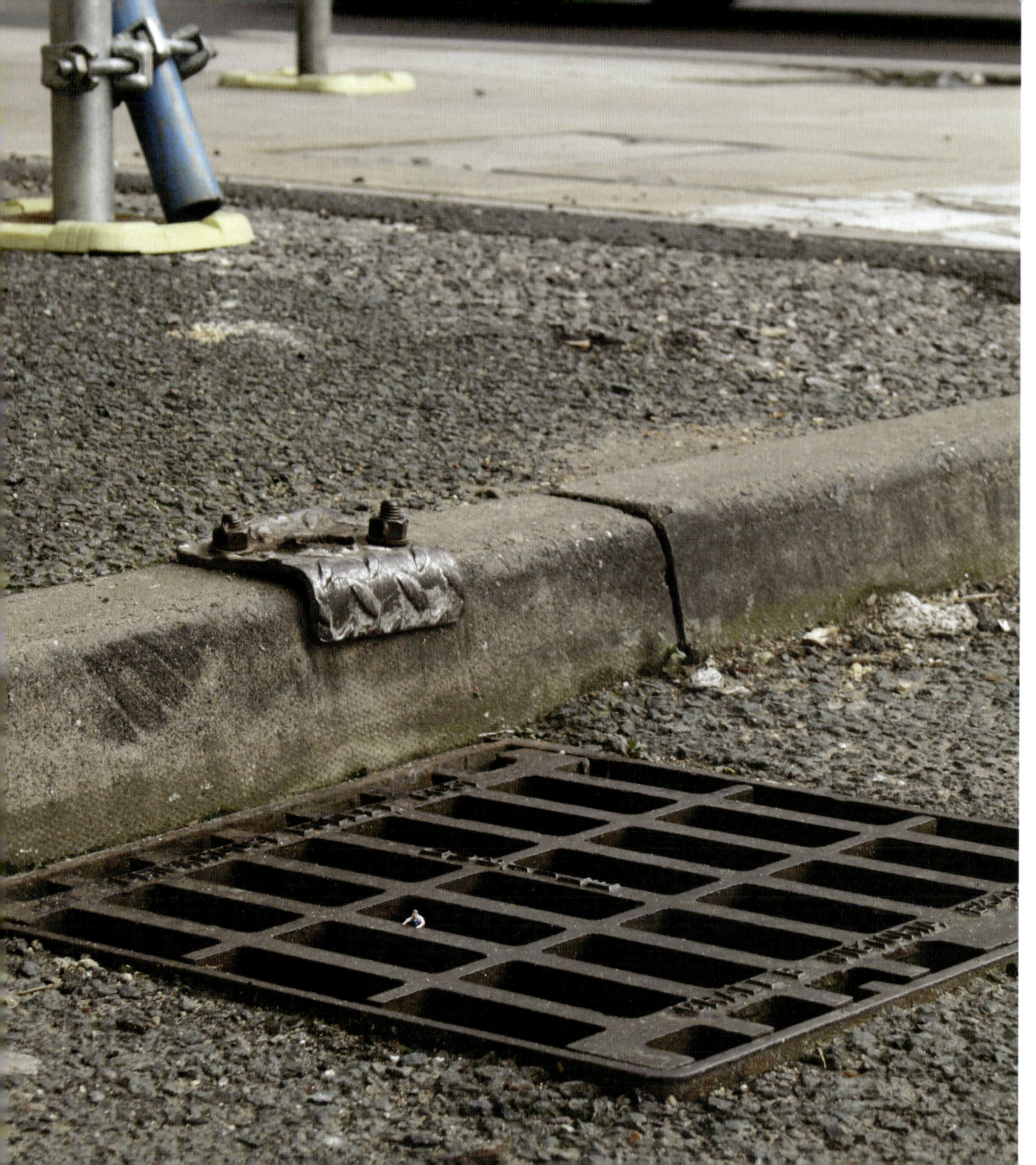

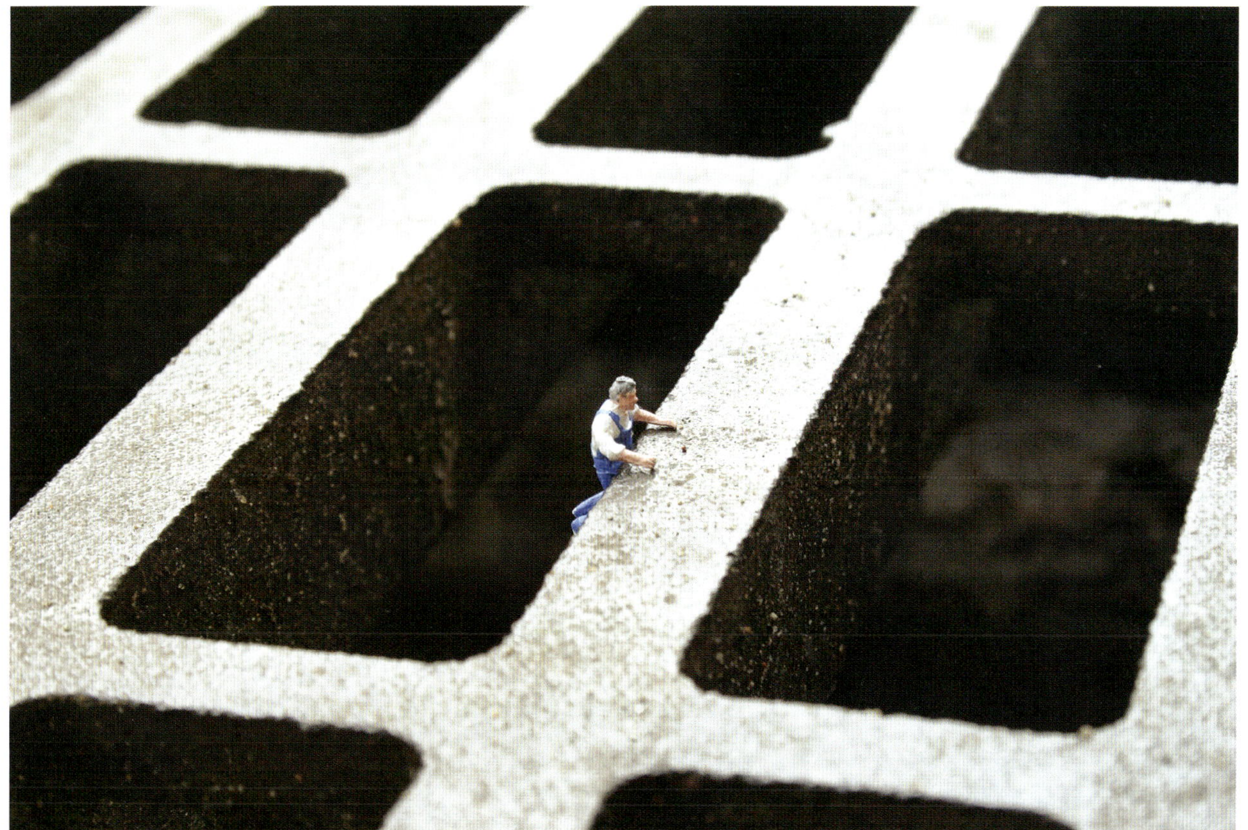

Drain Guy

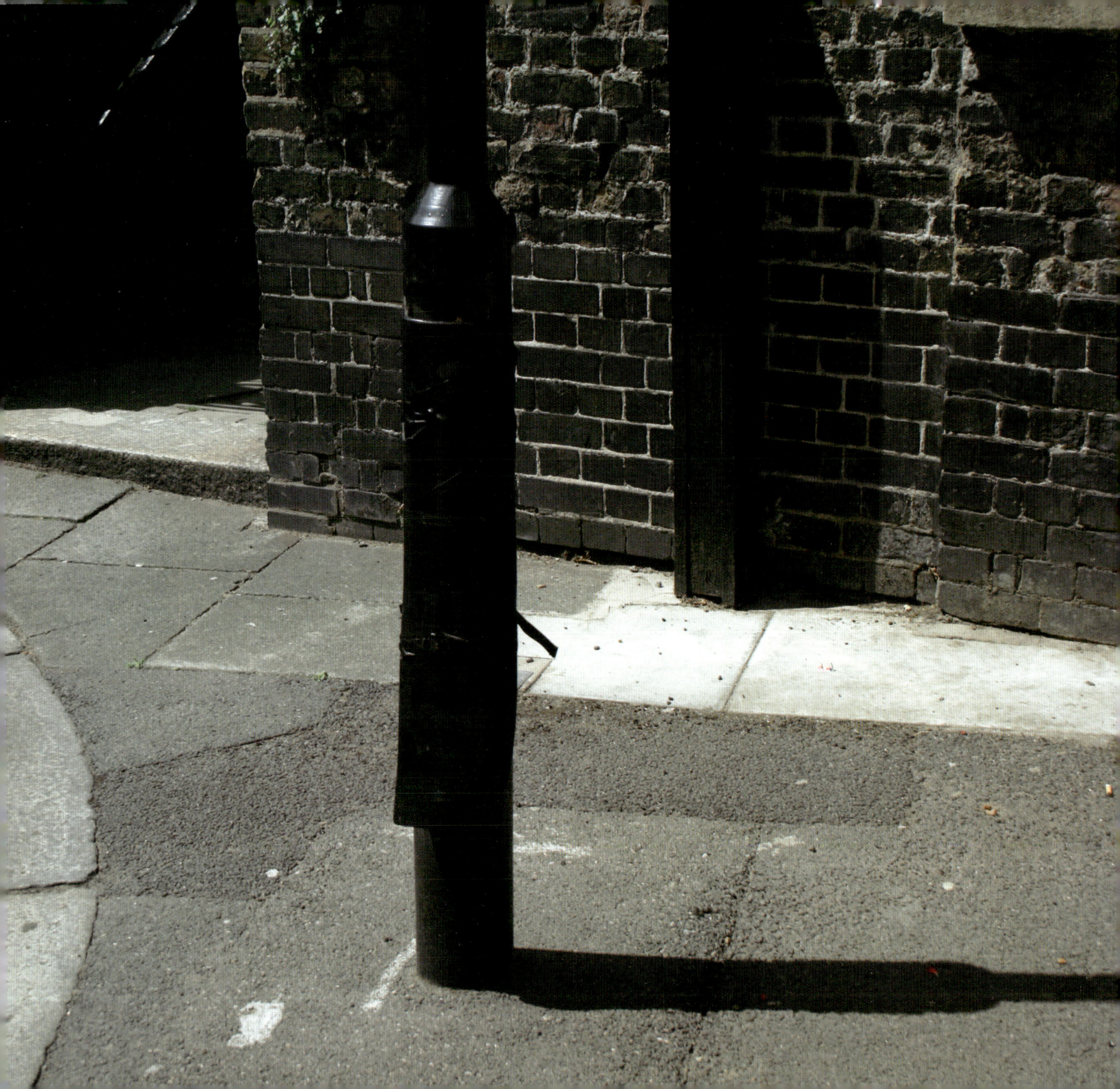

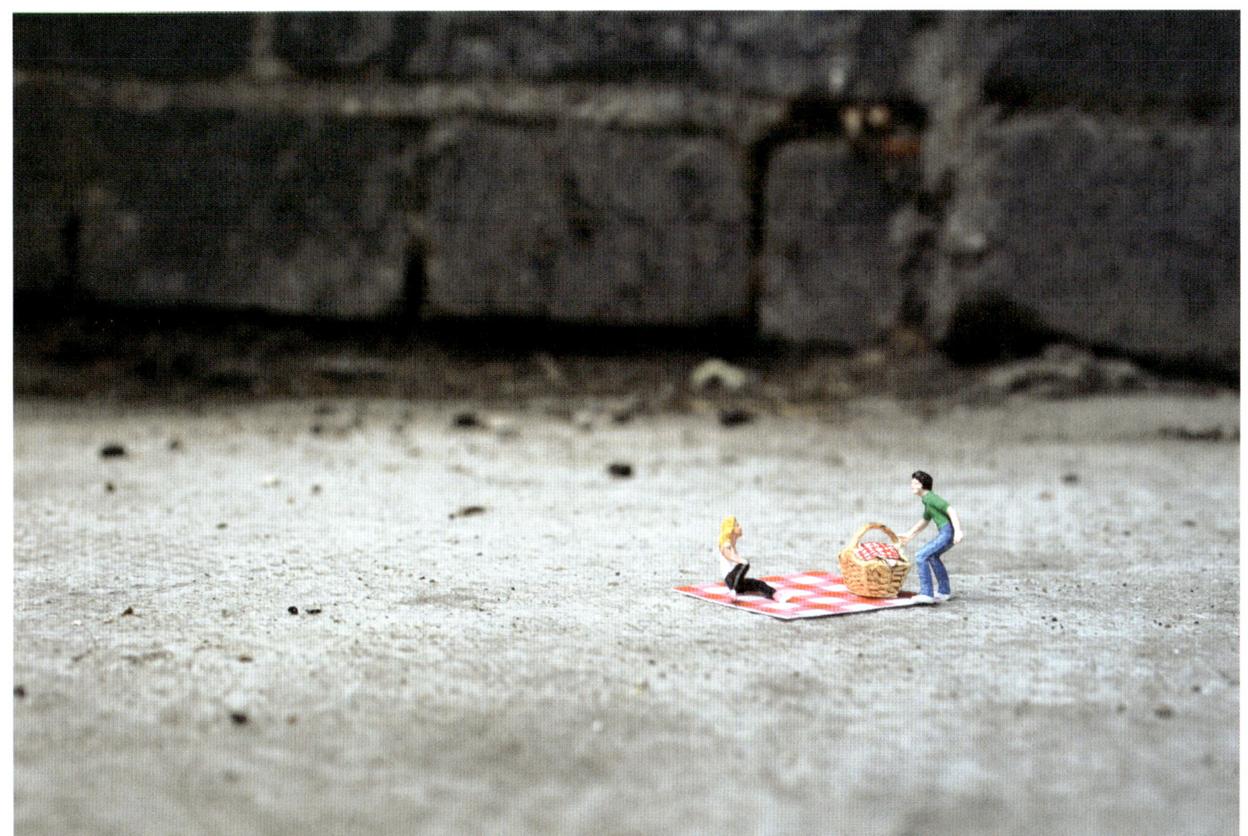

Last Chance to Impress

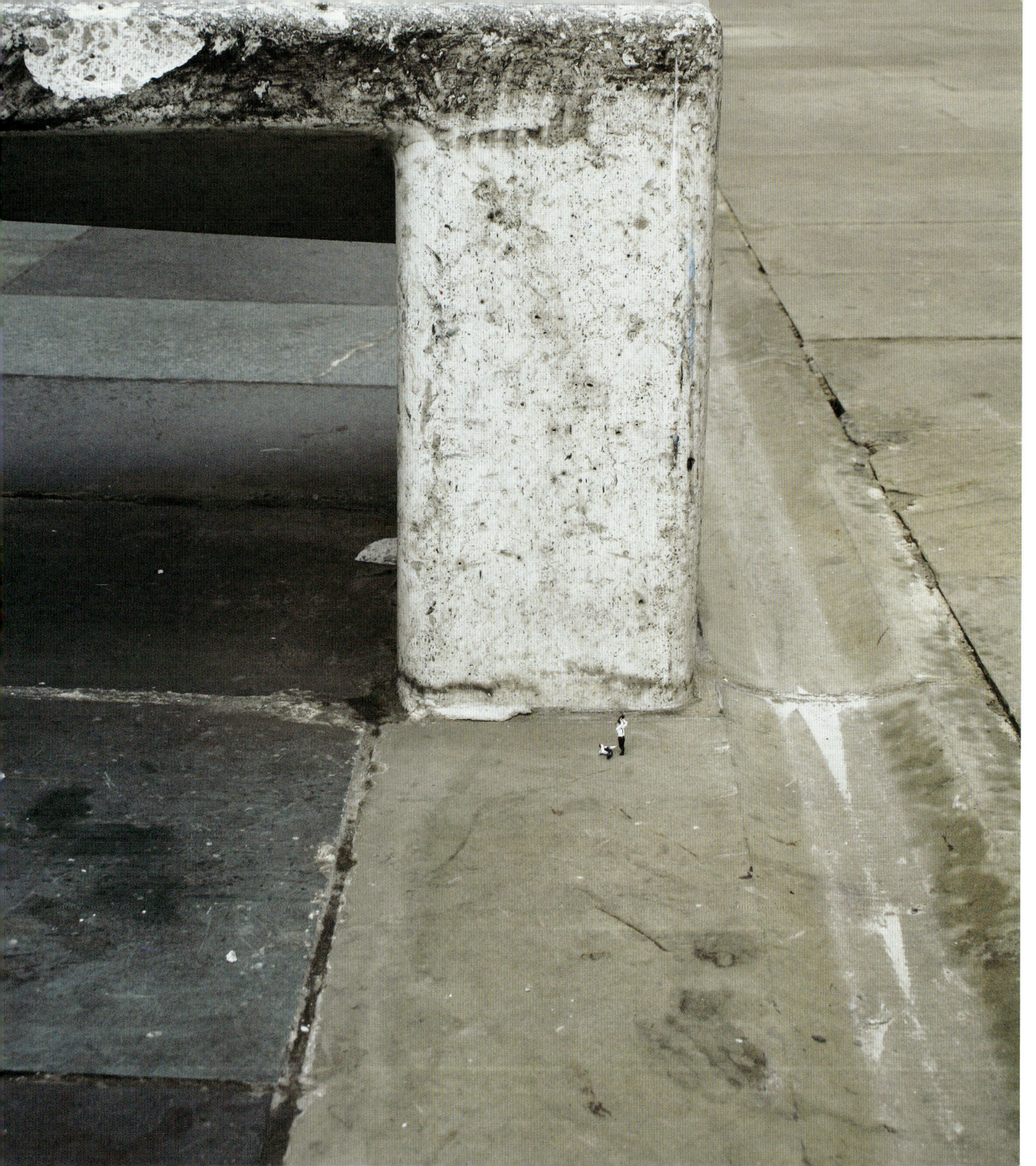

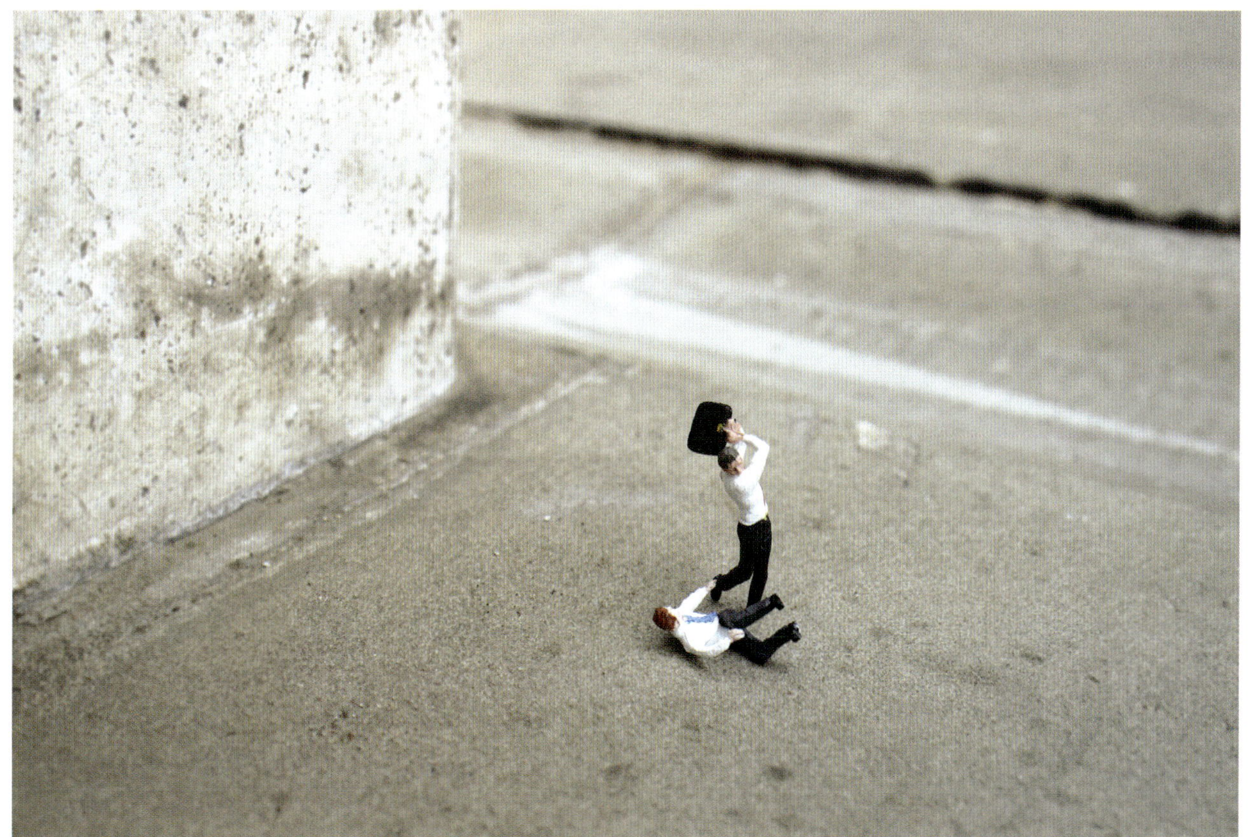

Office Politics

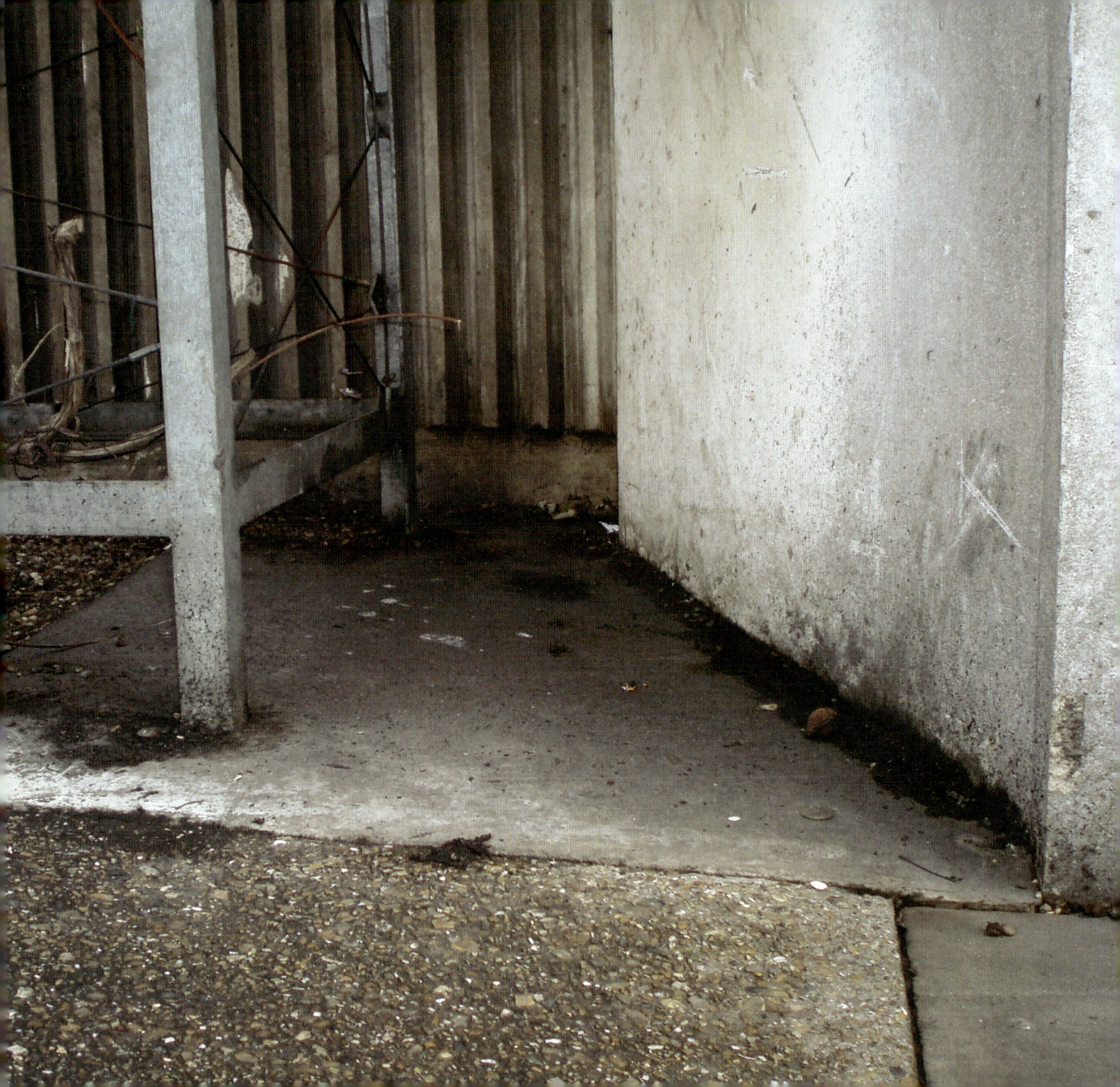

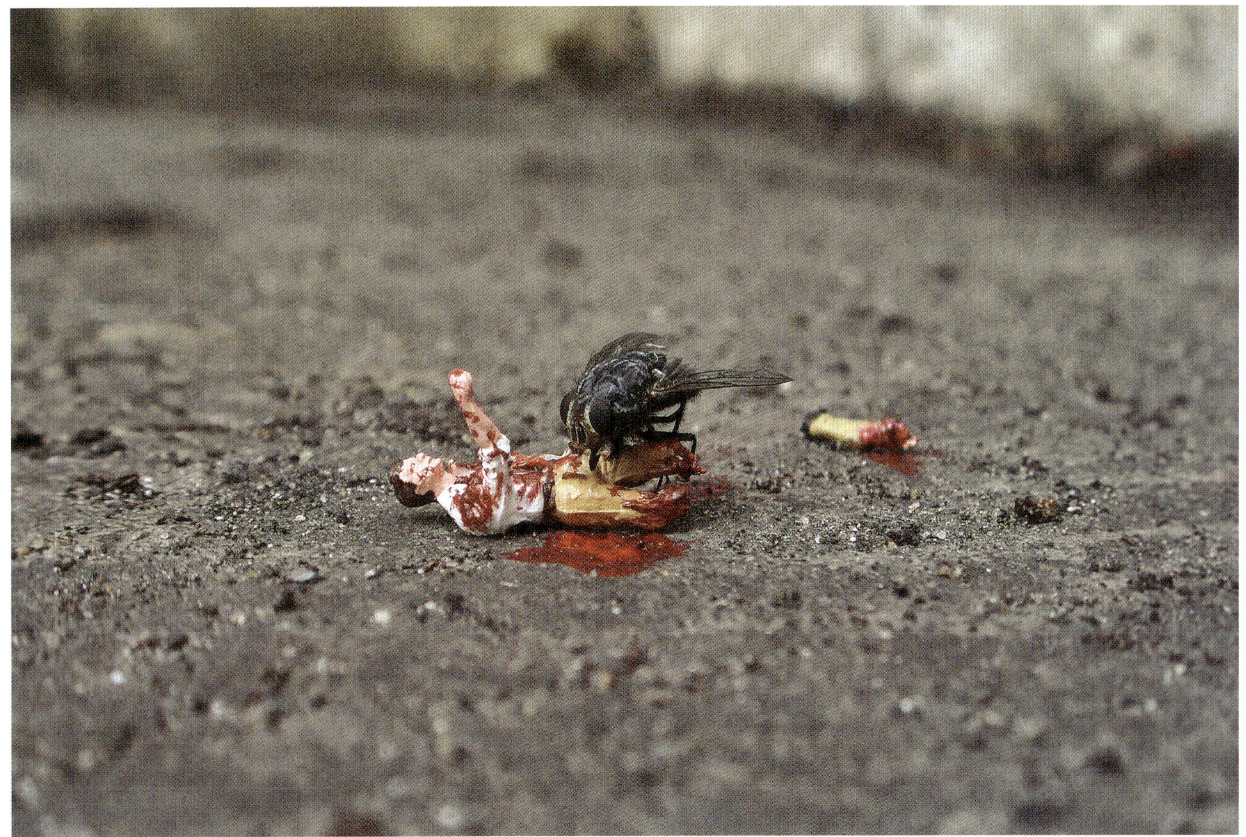

The Feast

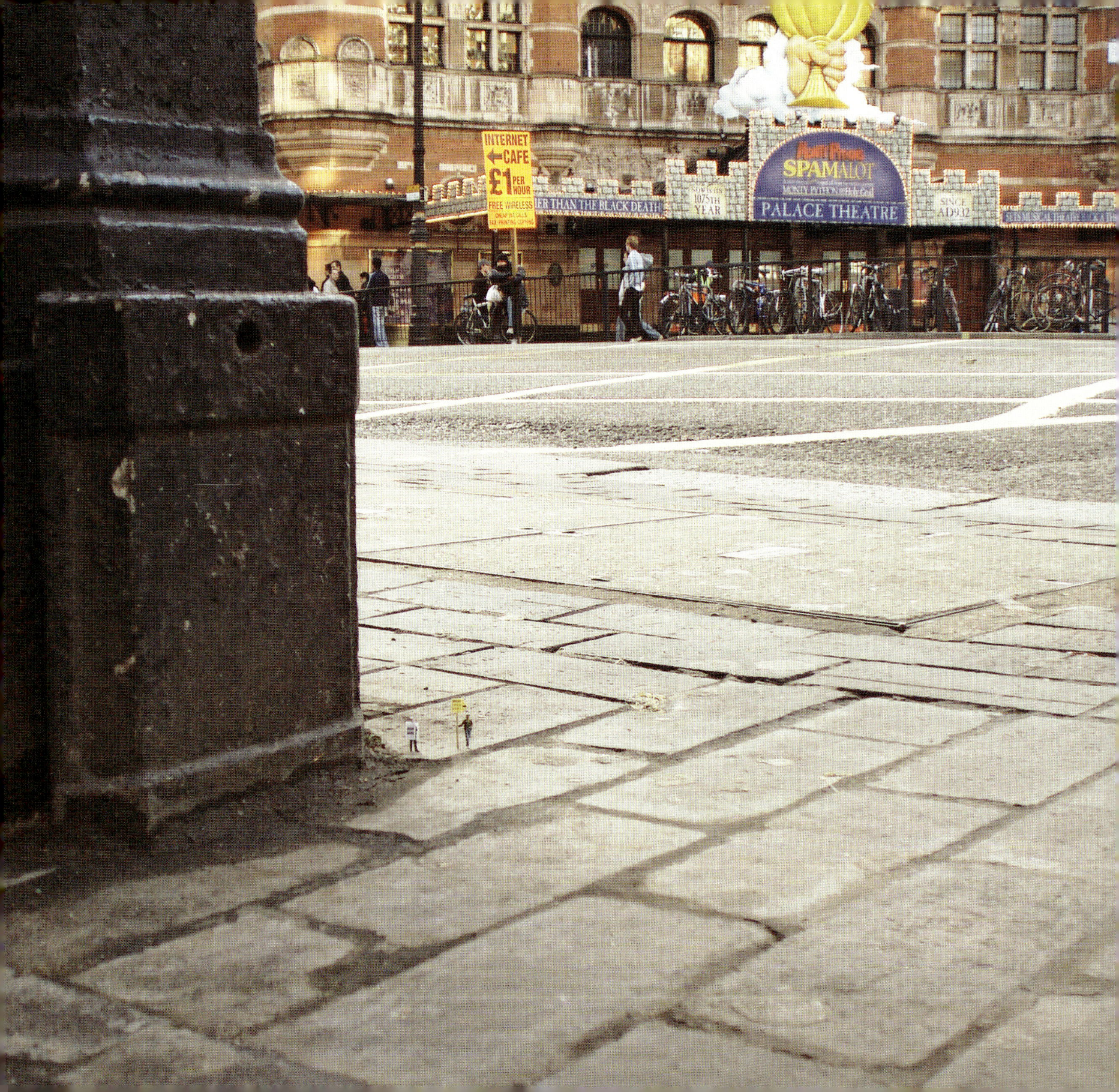
INTERNET
CAFE
£1 PER HOUR
FREE WIRELESS
SPAMALOT
MONTY PYTHON
NOW IN ITS
1075TH
YEAR
PALACE THEATRE
SINCE
AD932

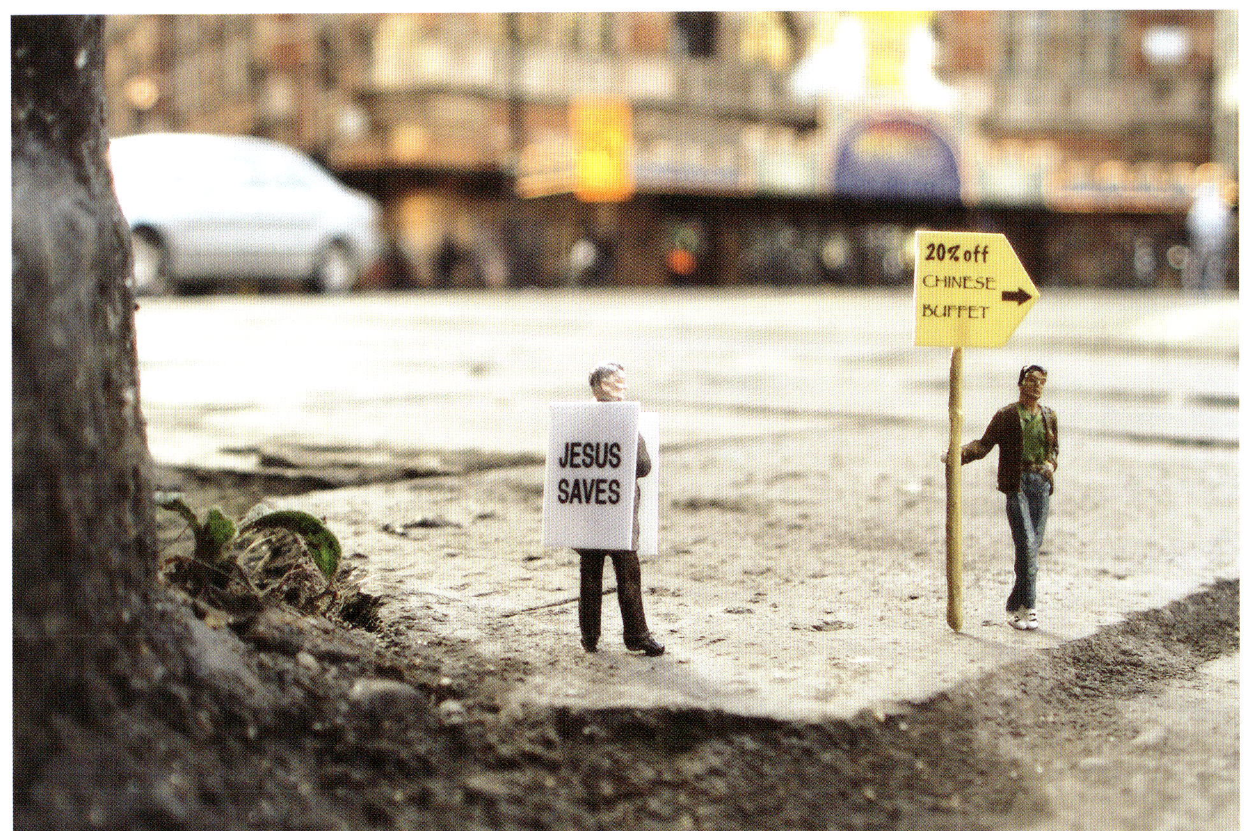

Jesus Saves

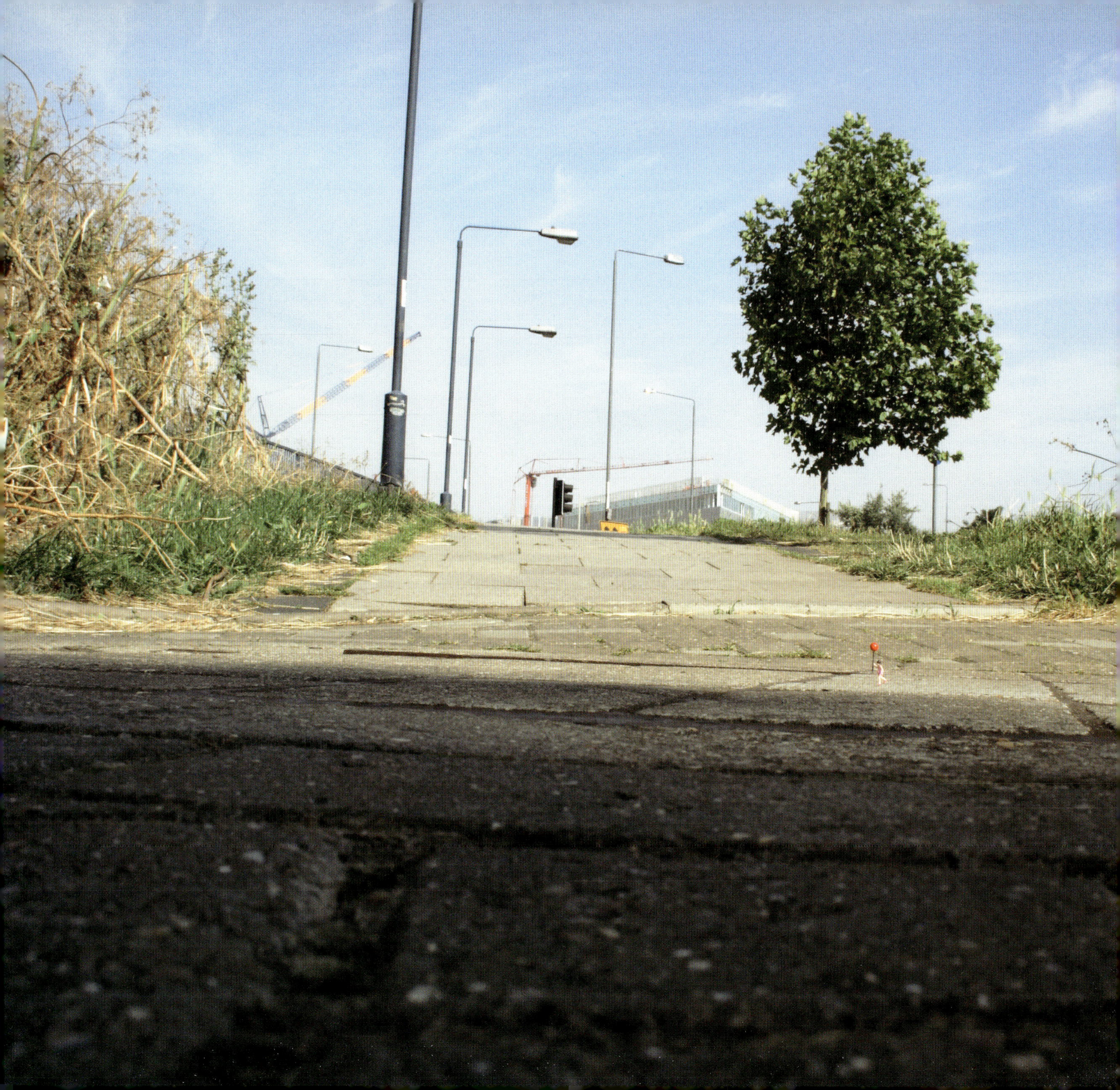

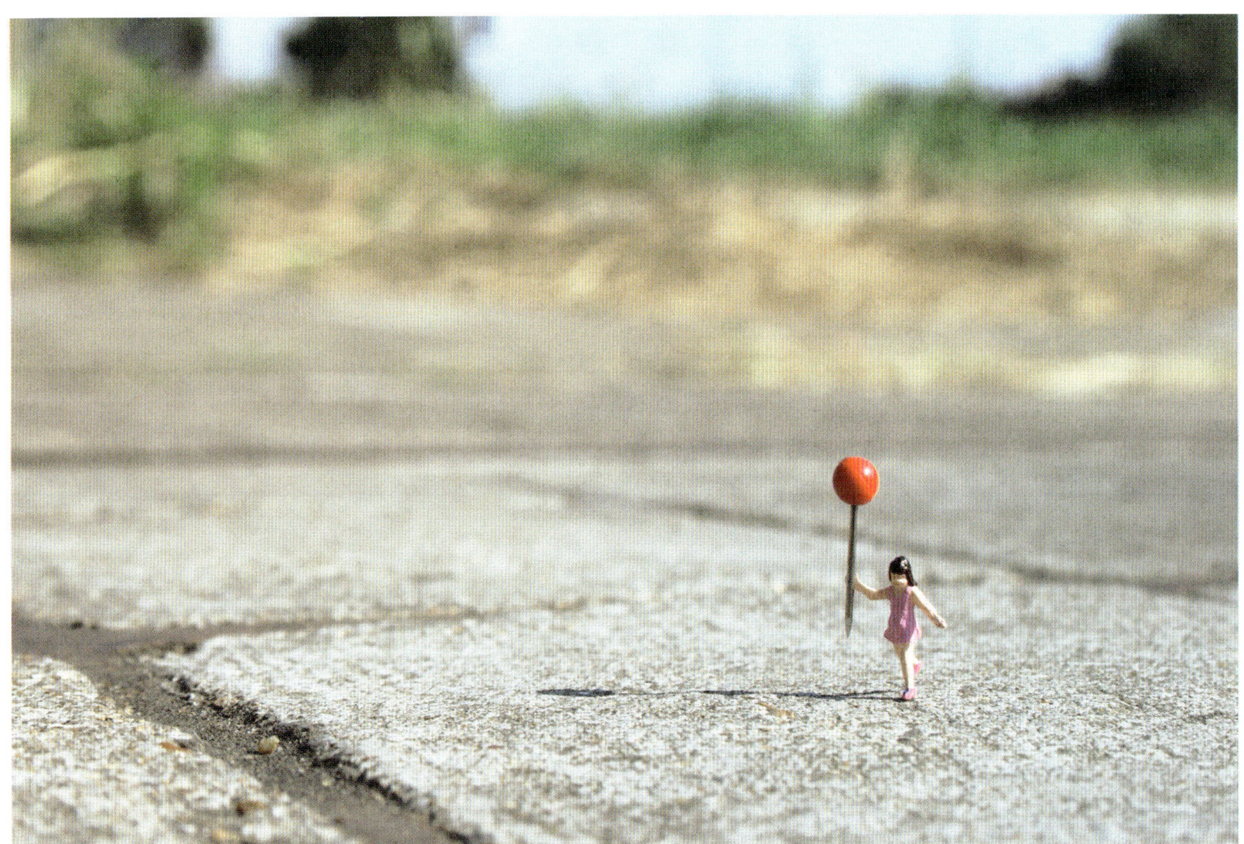

Concealed Weapon

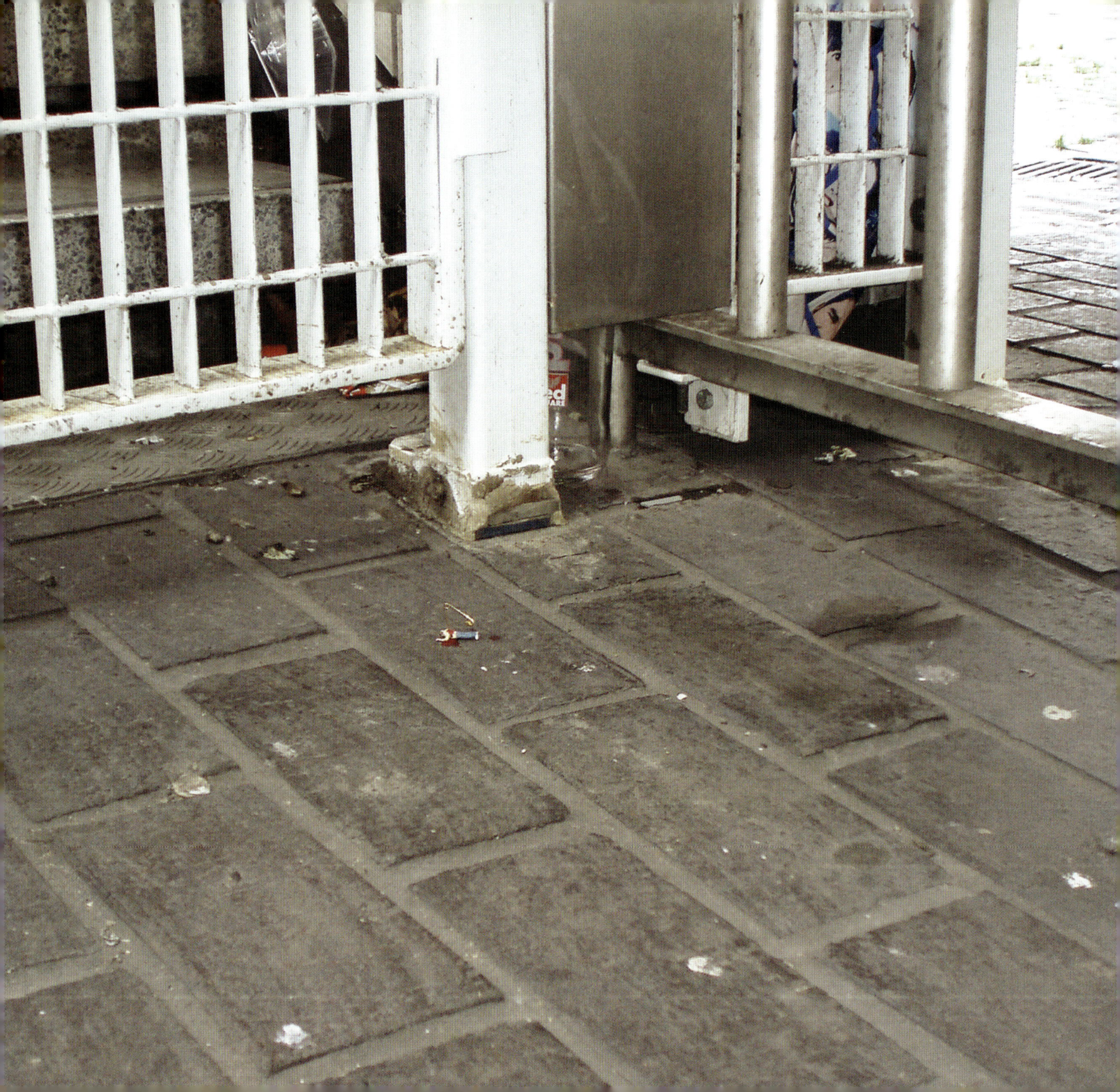

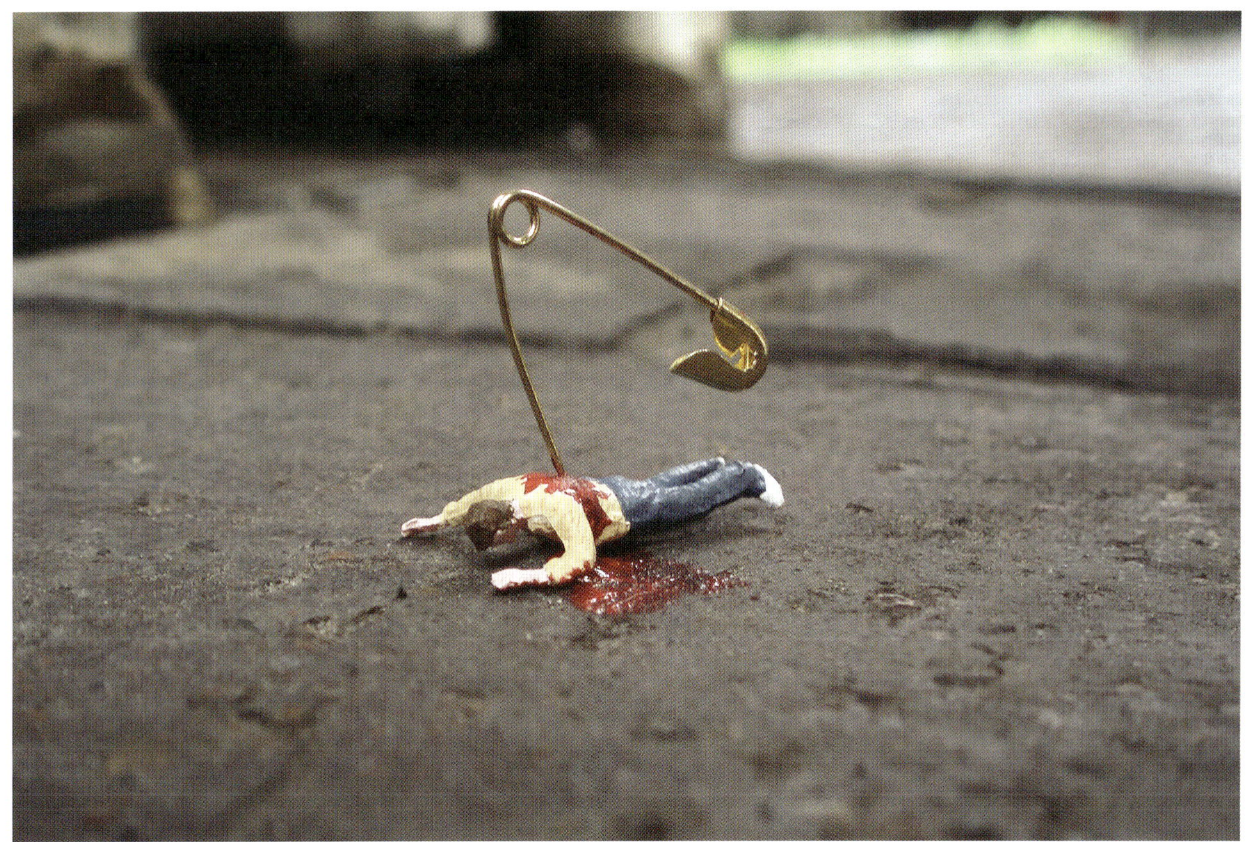

Pinned Down

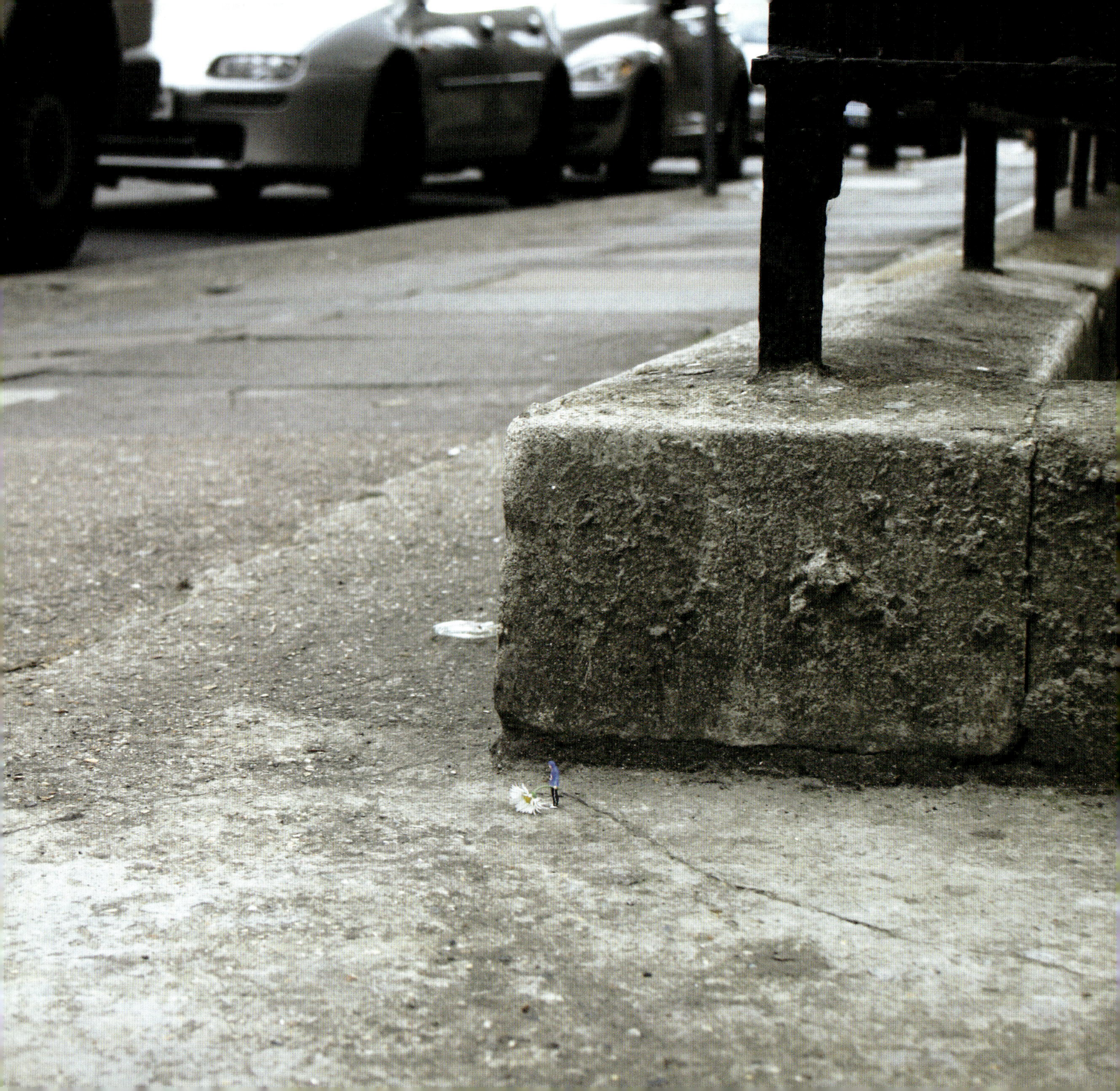

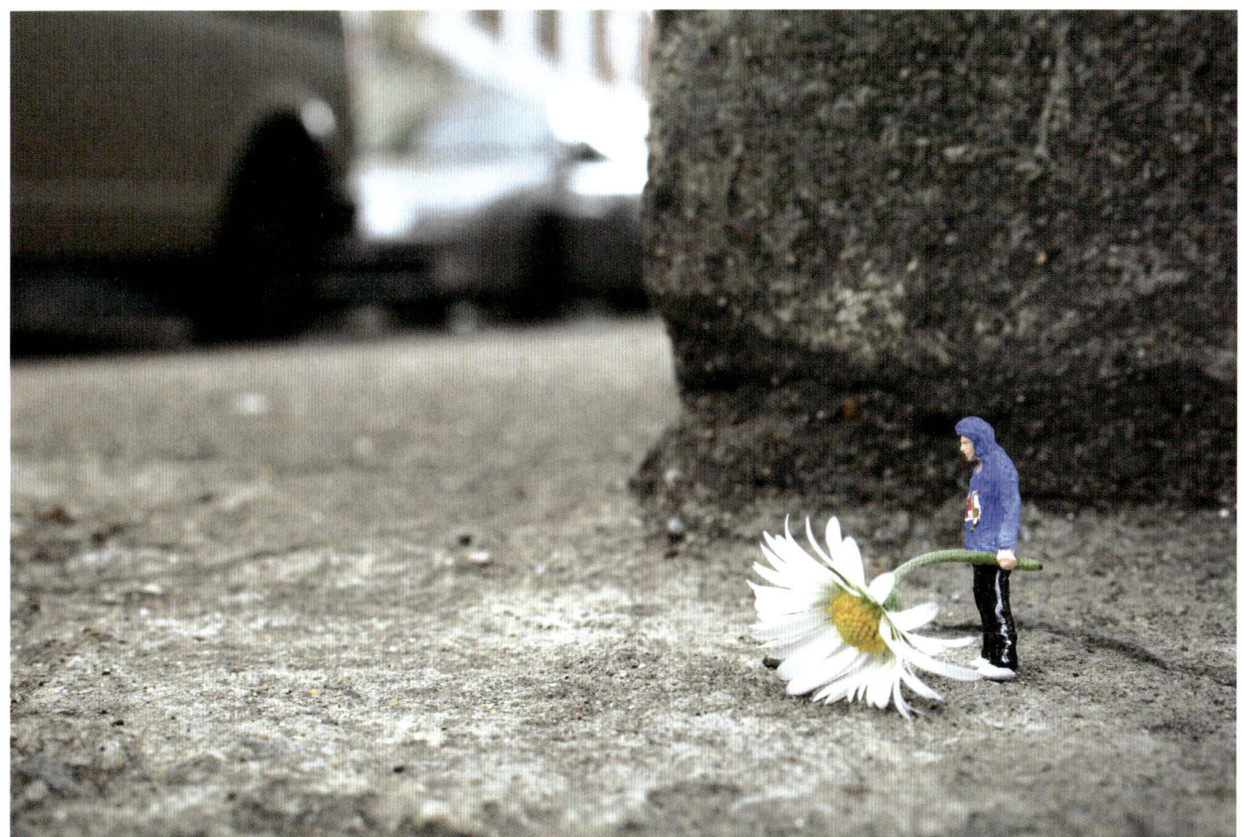

Ground Zero

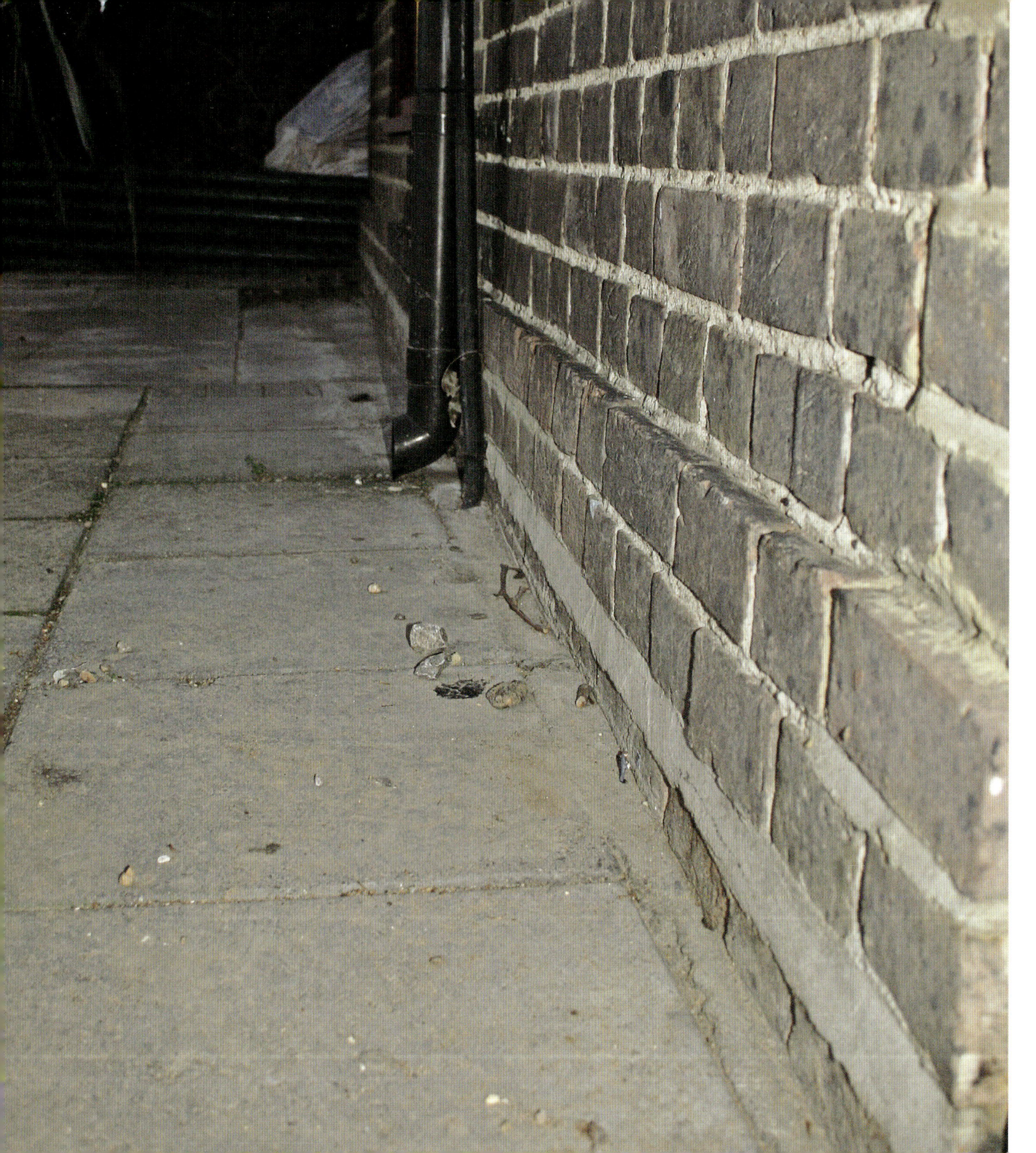

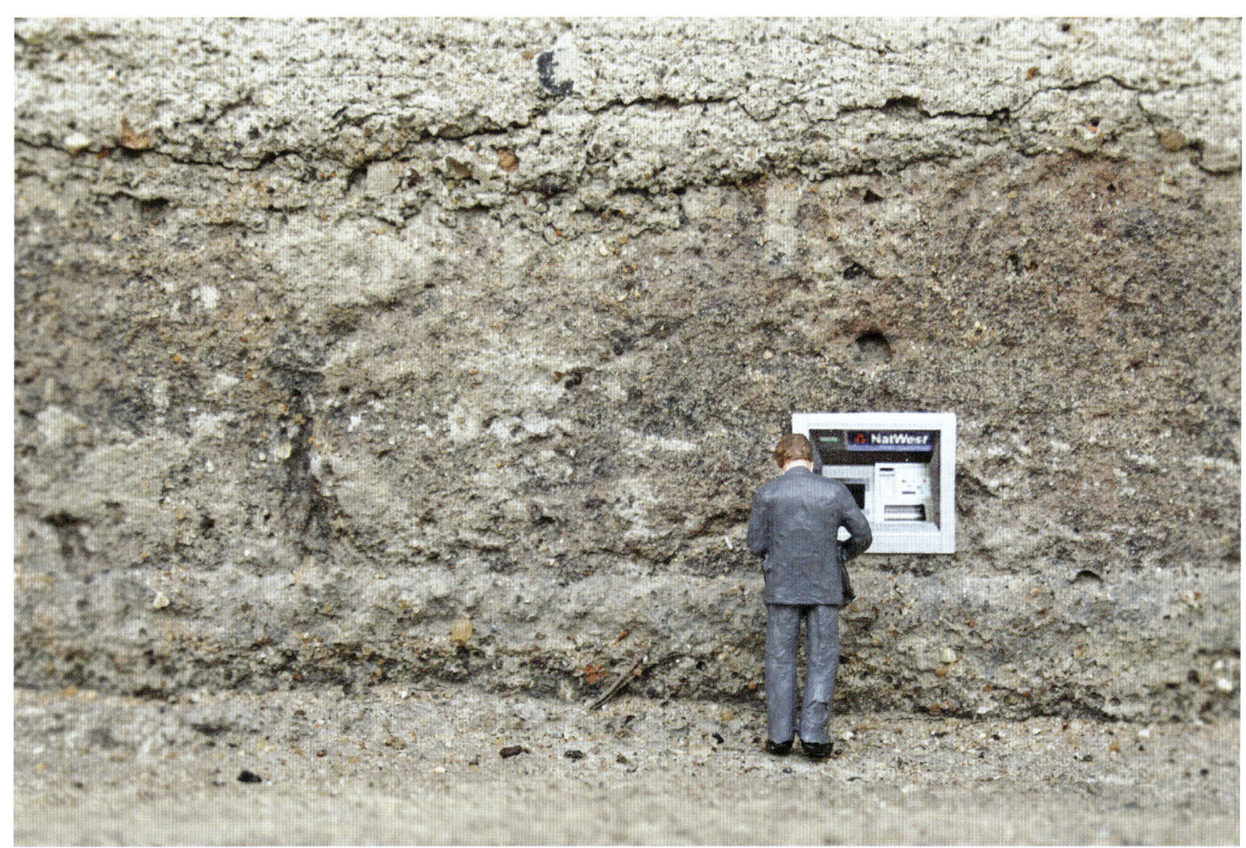

Cash Machine

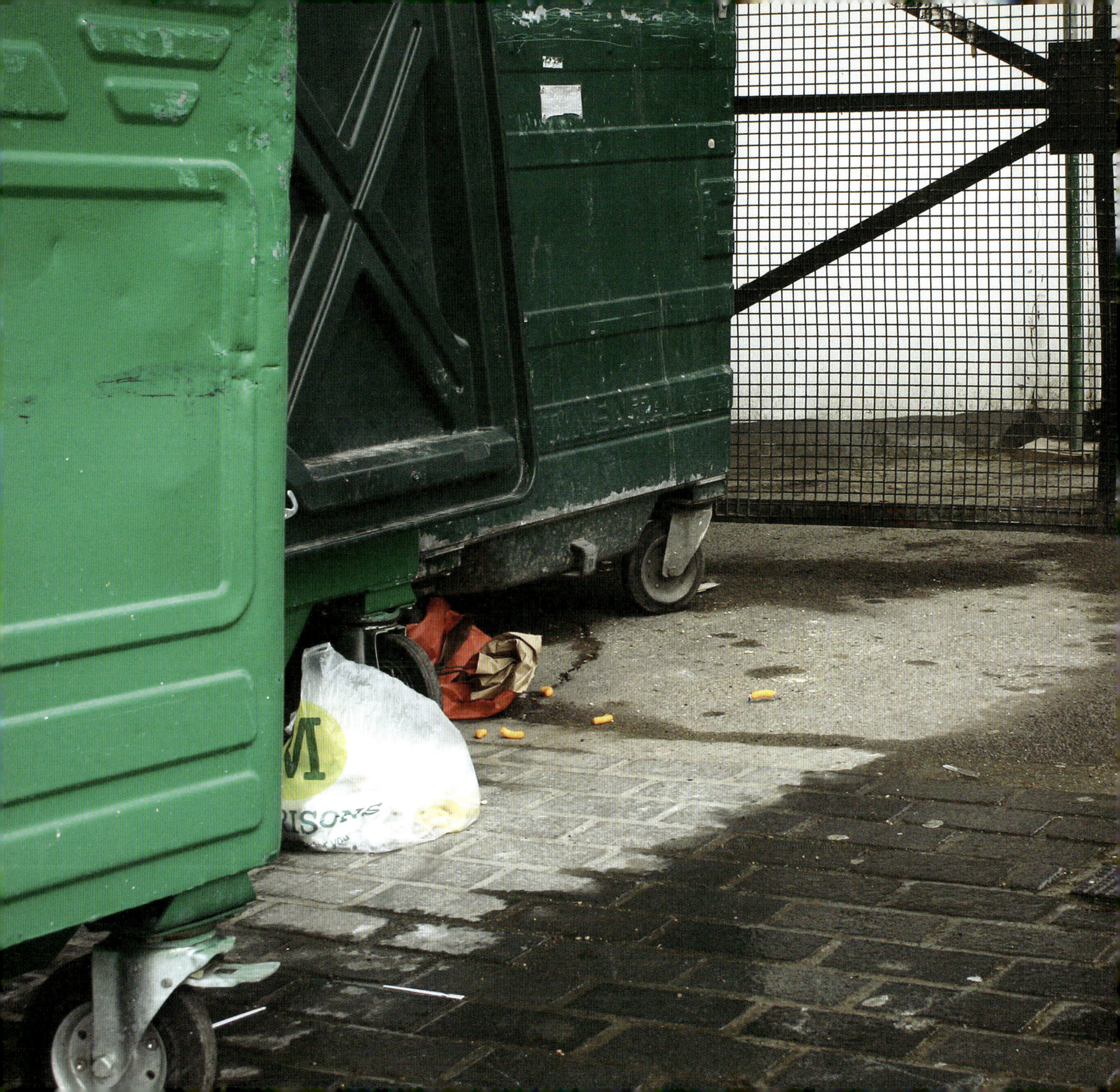
RISONS

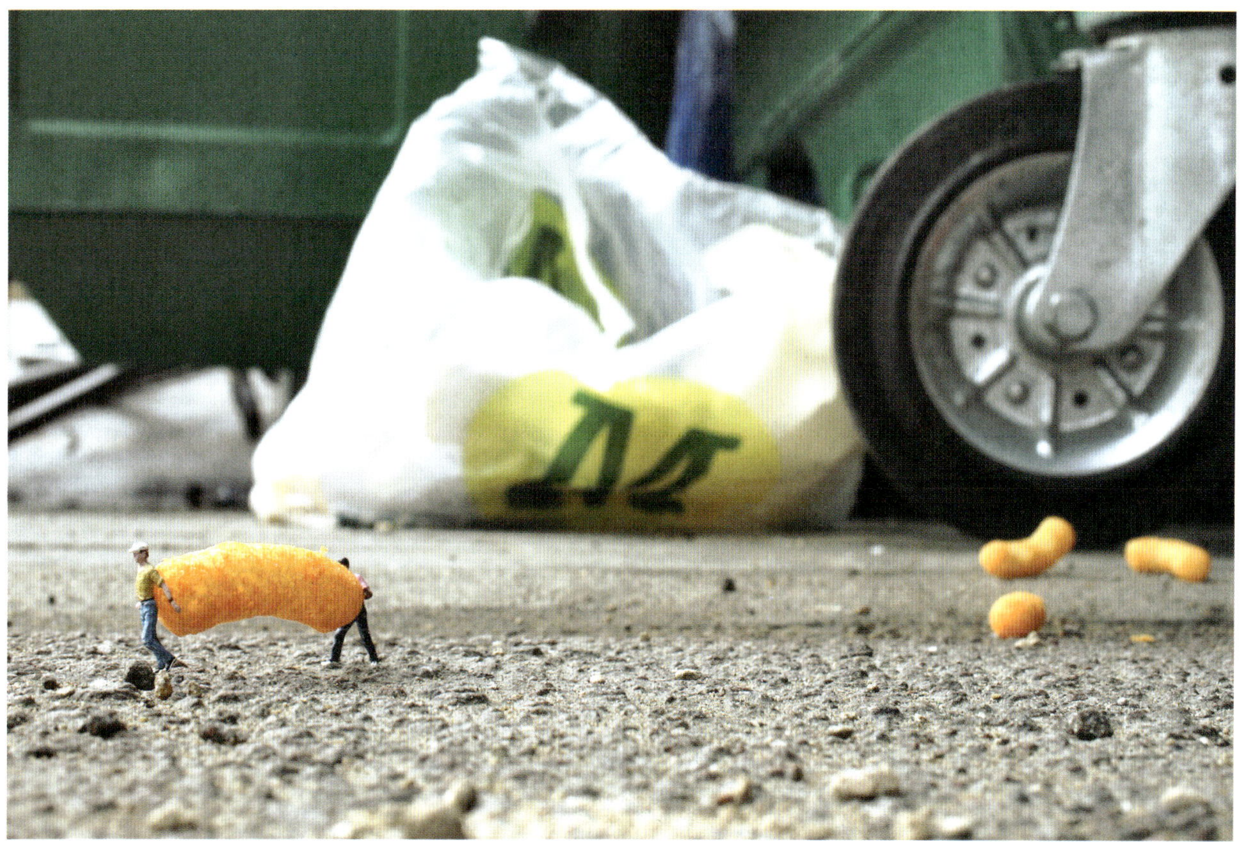

Scavengers

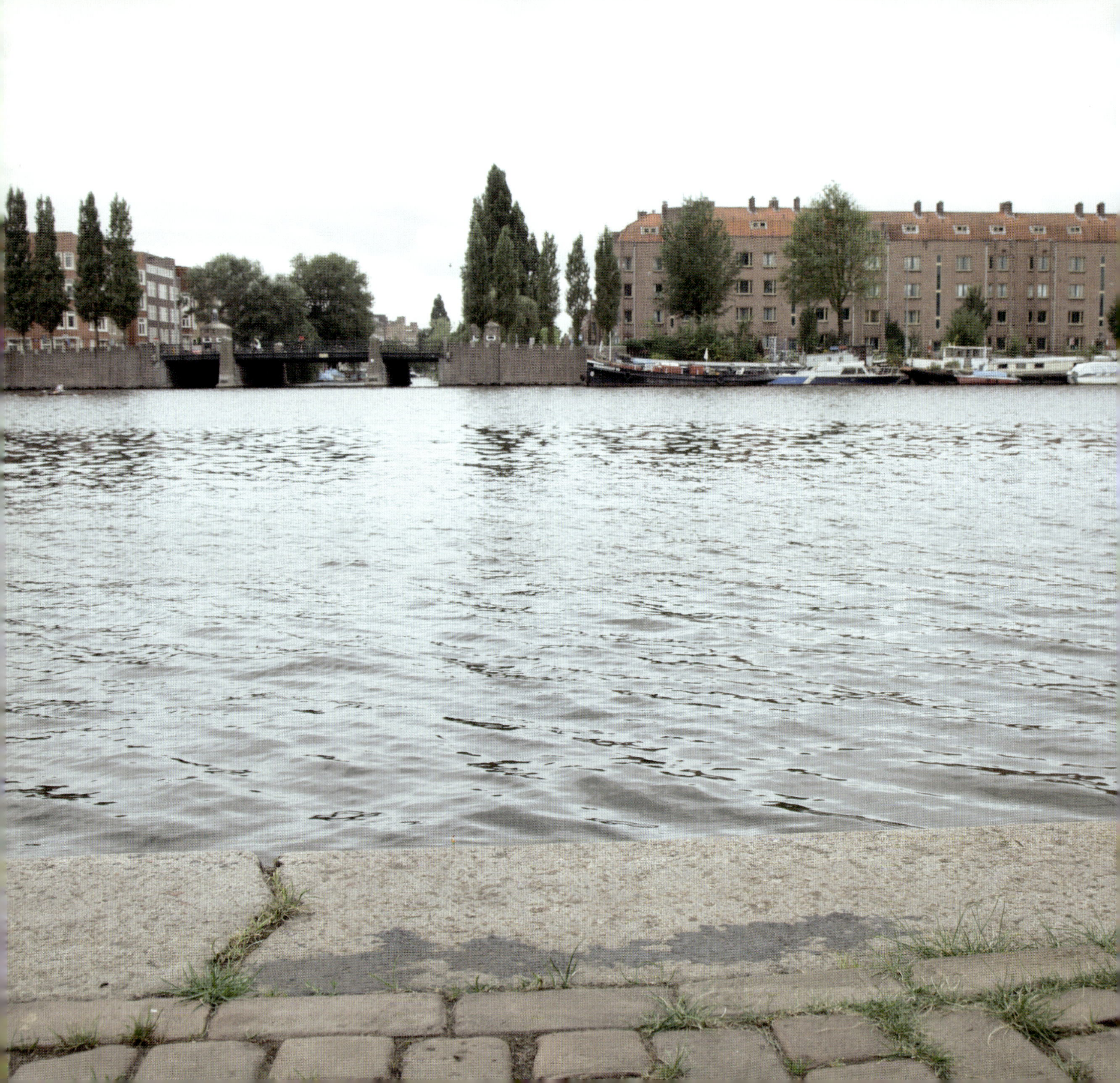

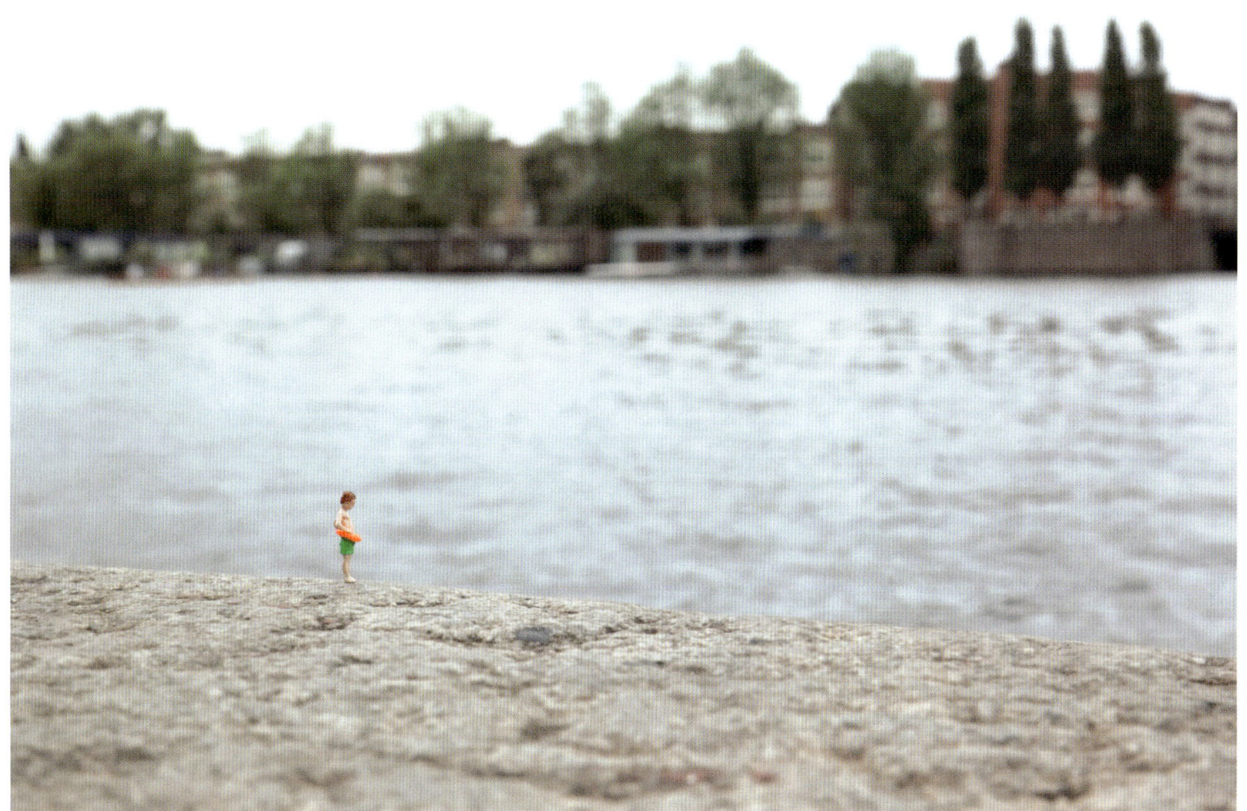

Flotsam

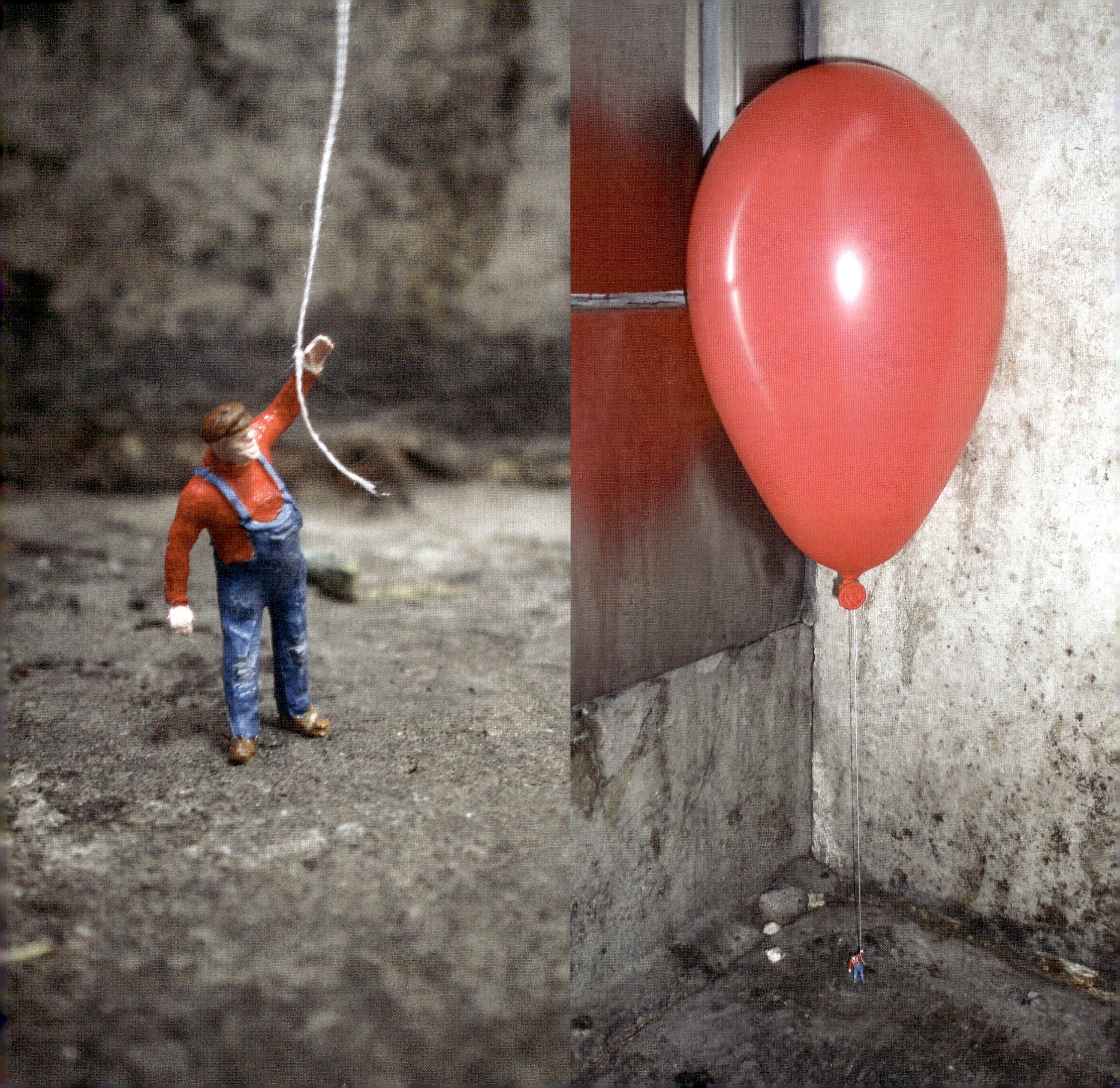

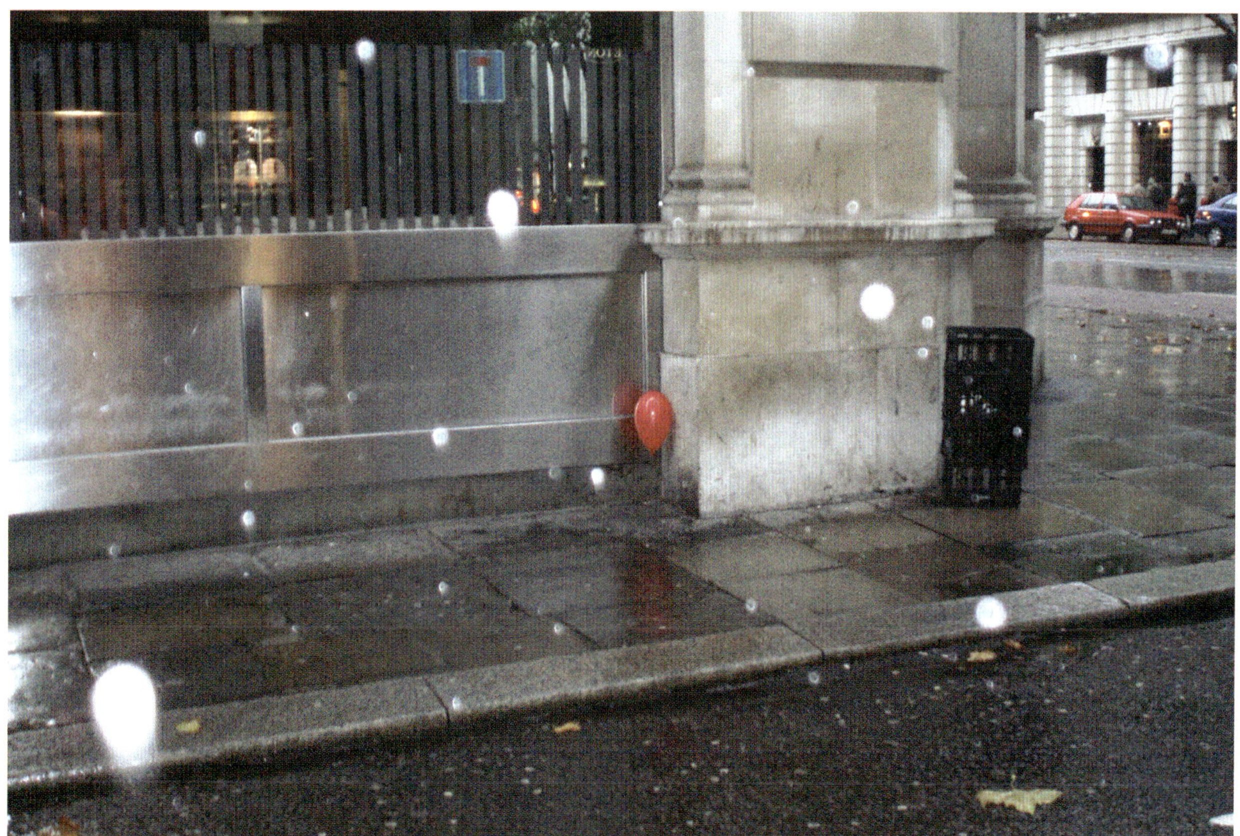

Balloon Man

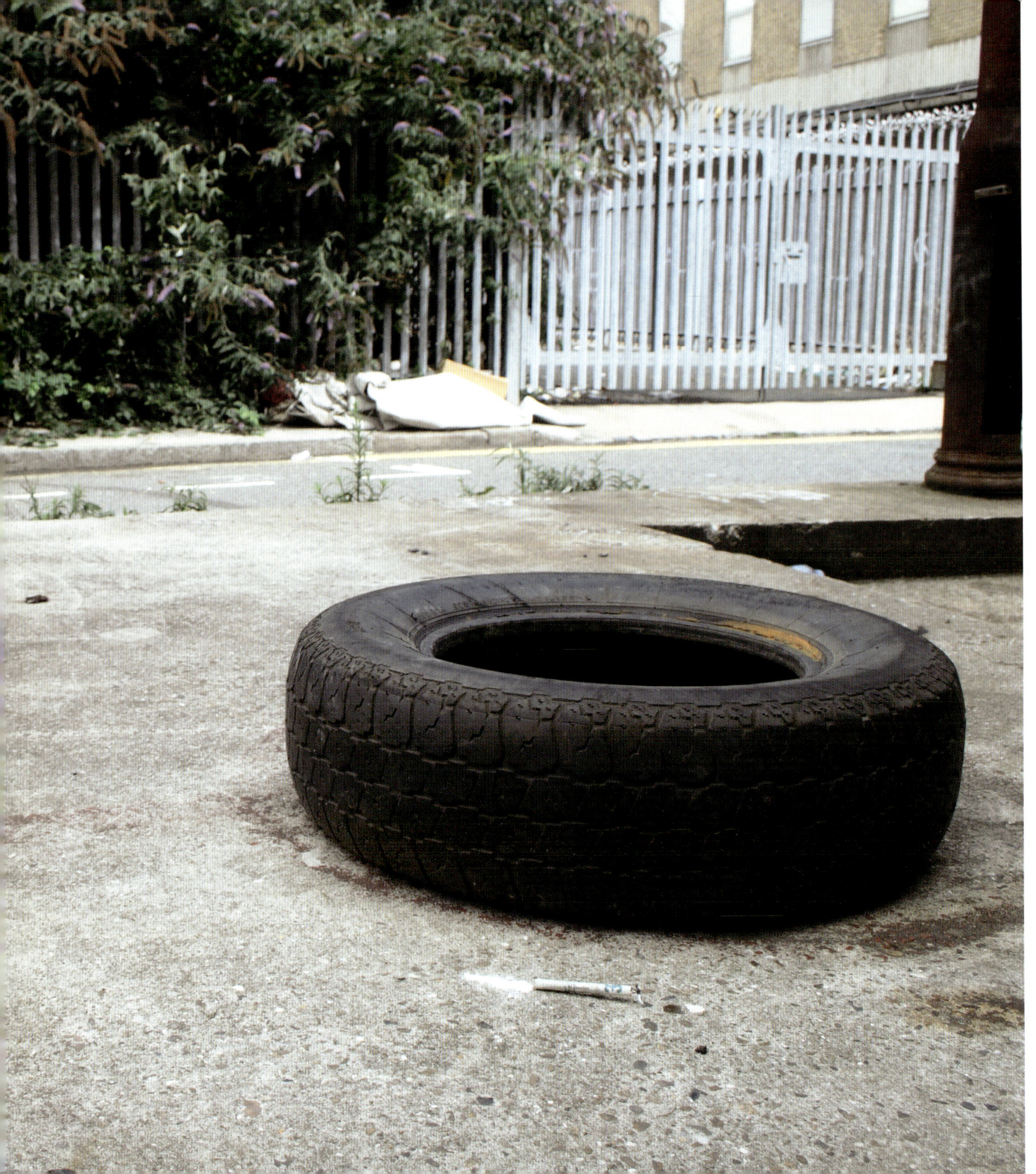

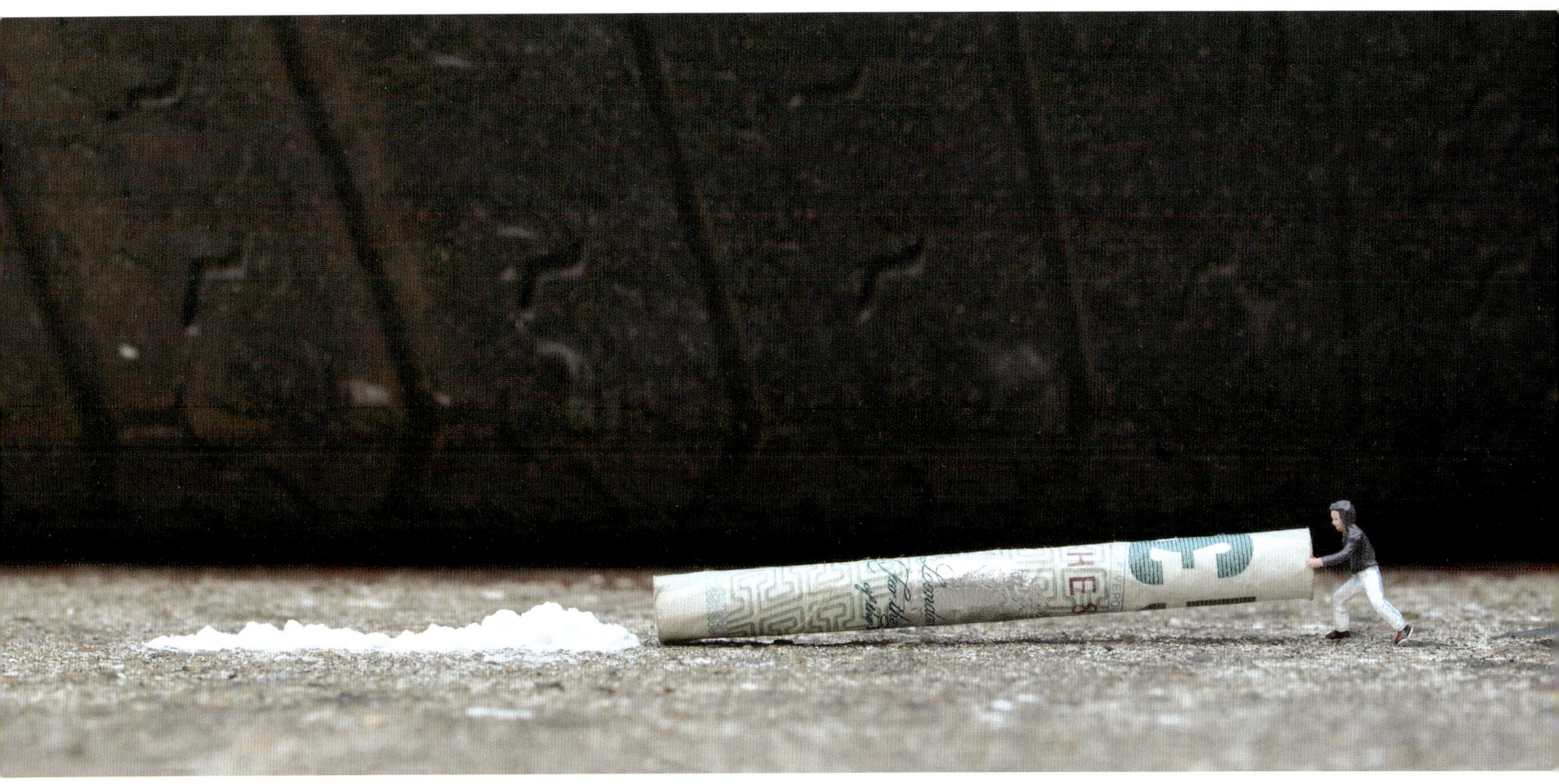

Pocket Money

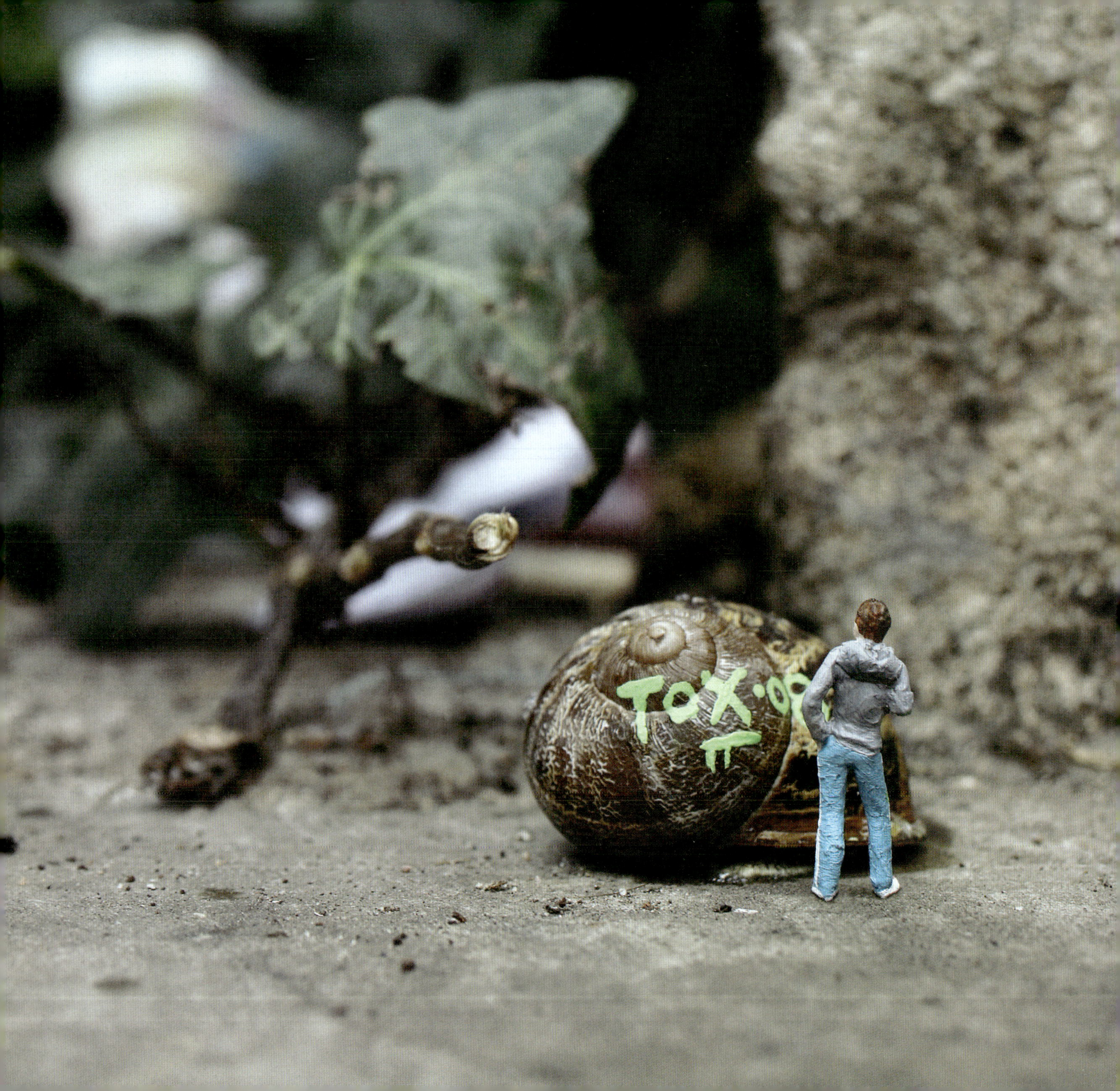
TOX

Tagging

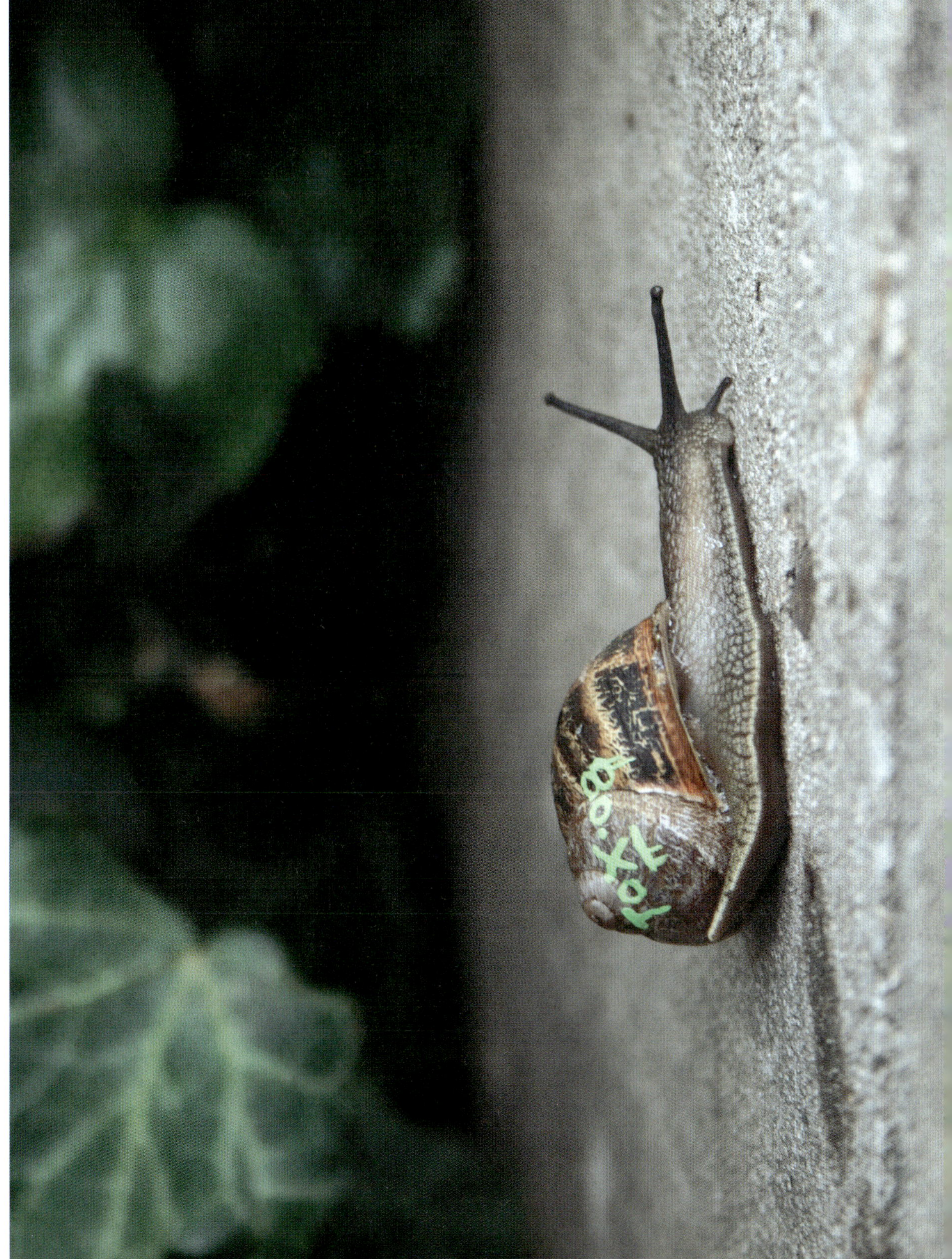

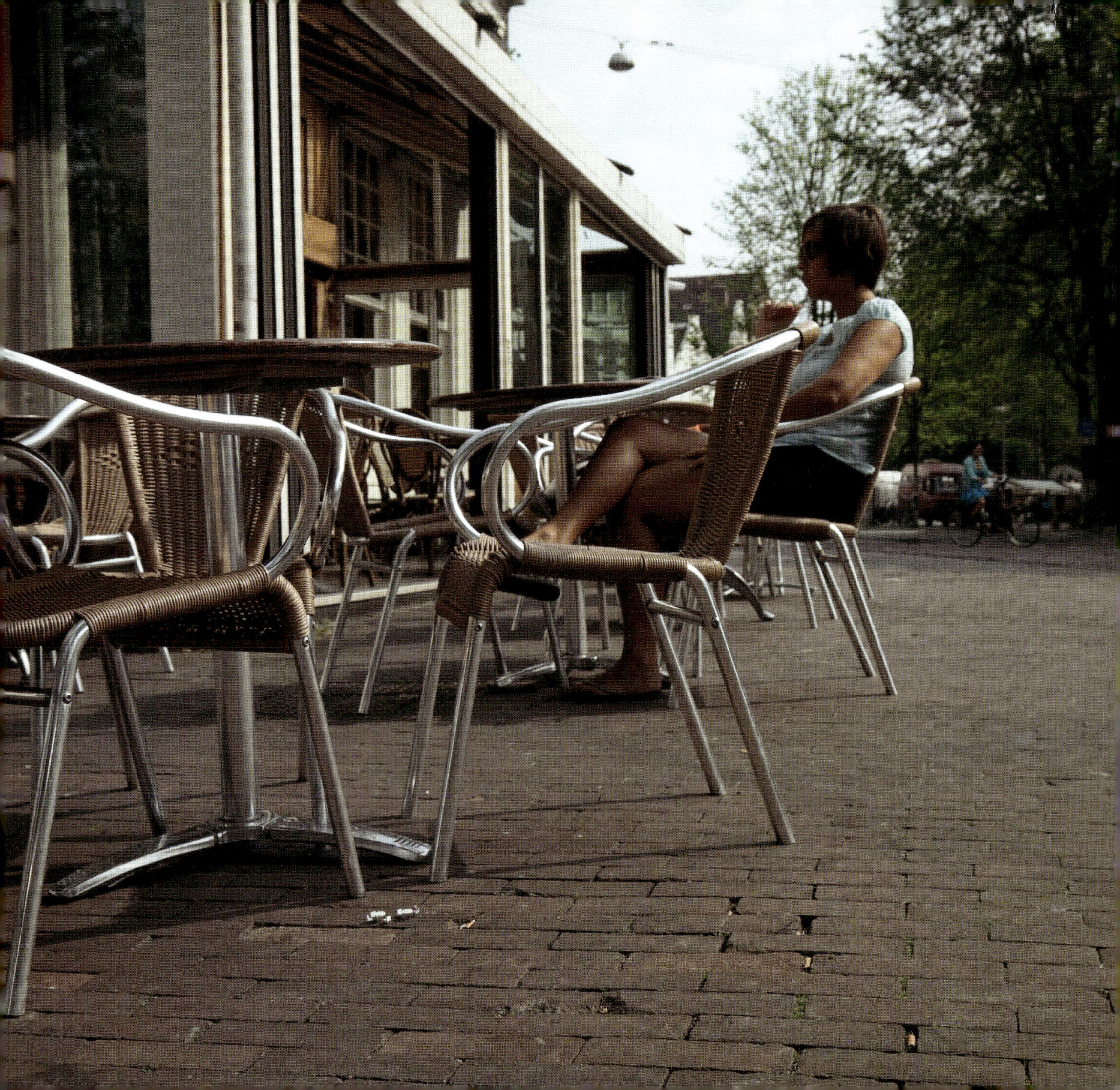

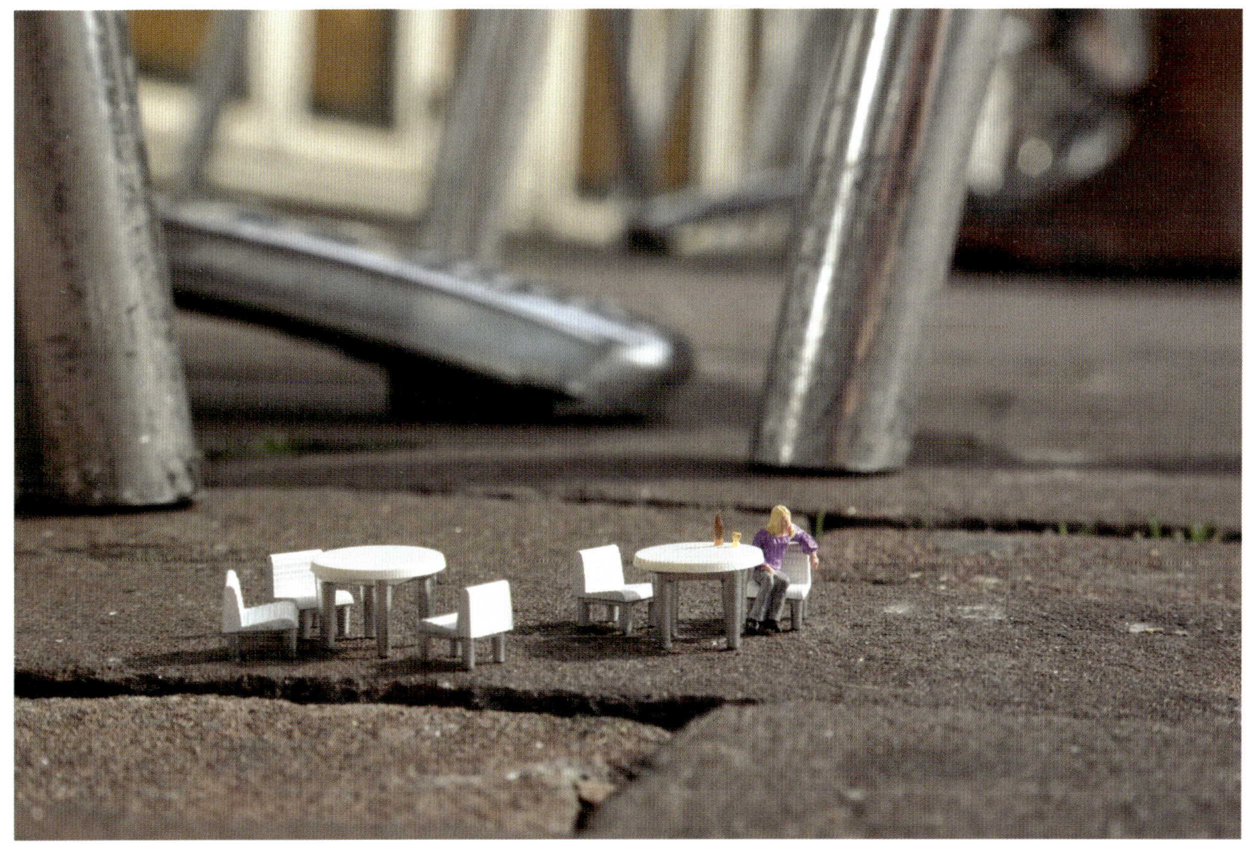

Spare Chair

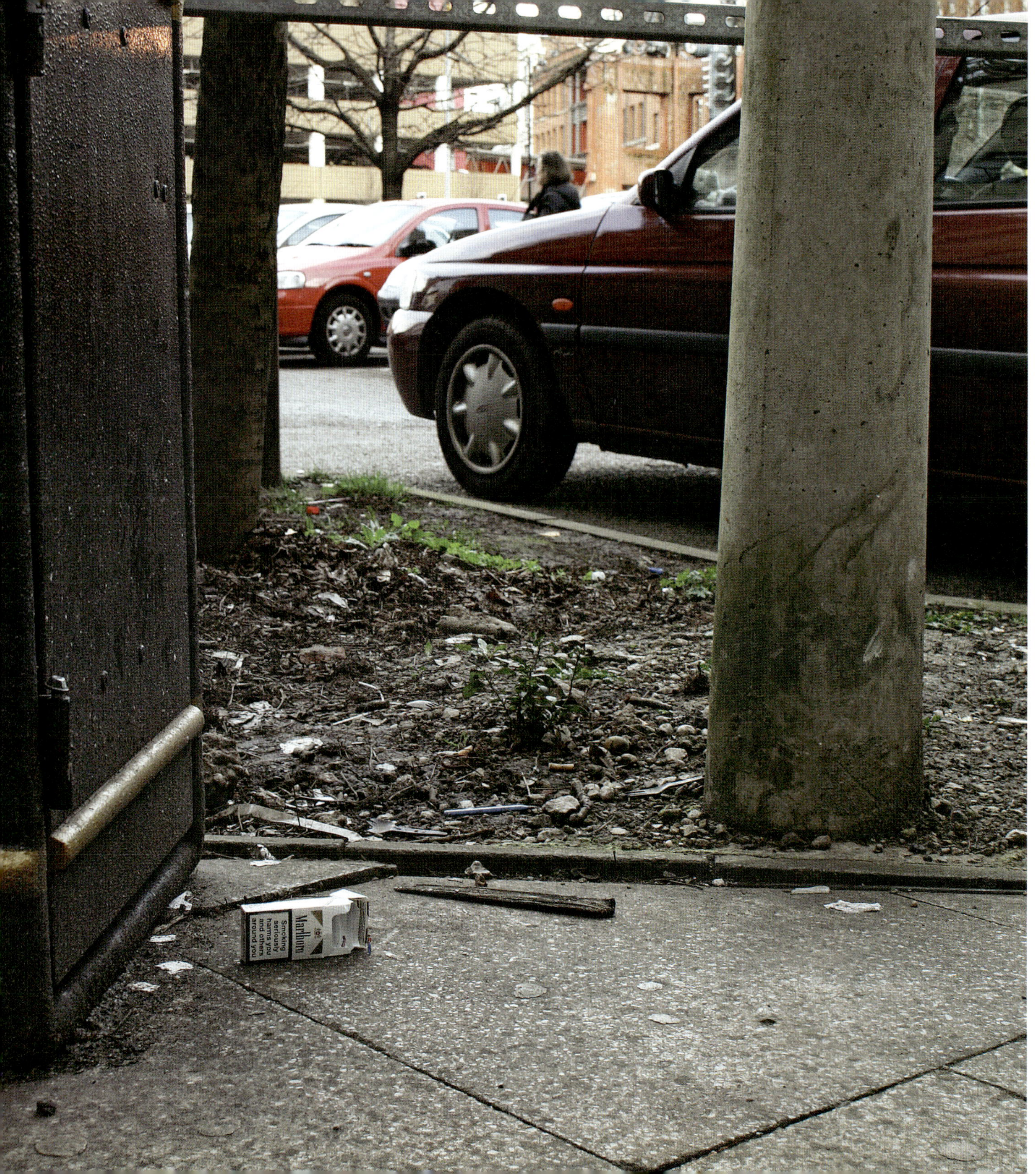
Marlboro
Smoking seriously harms you and others around you

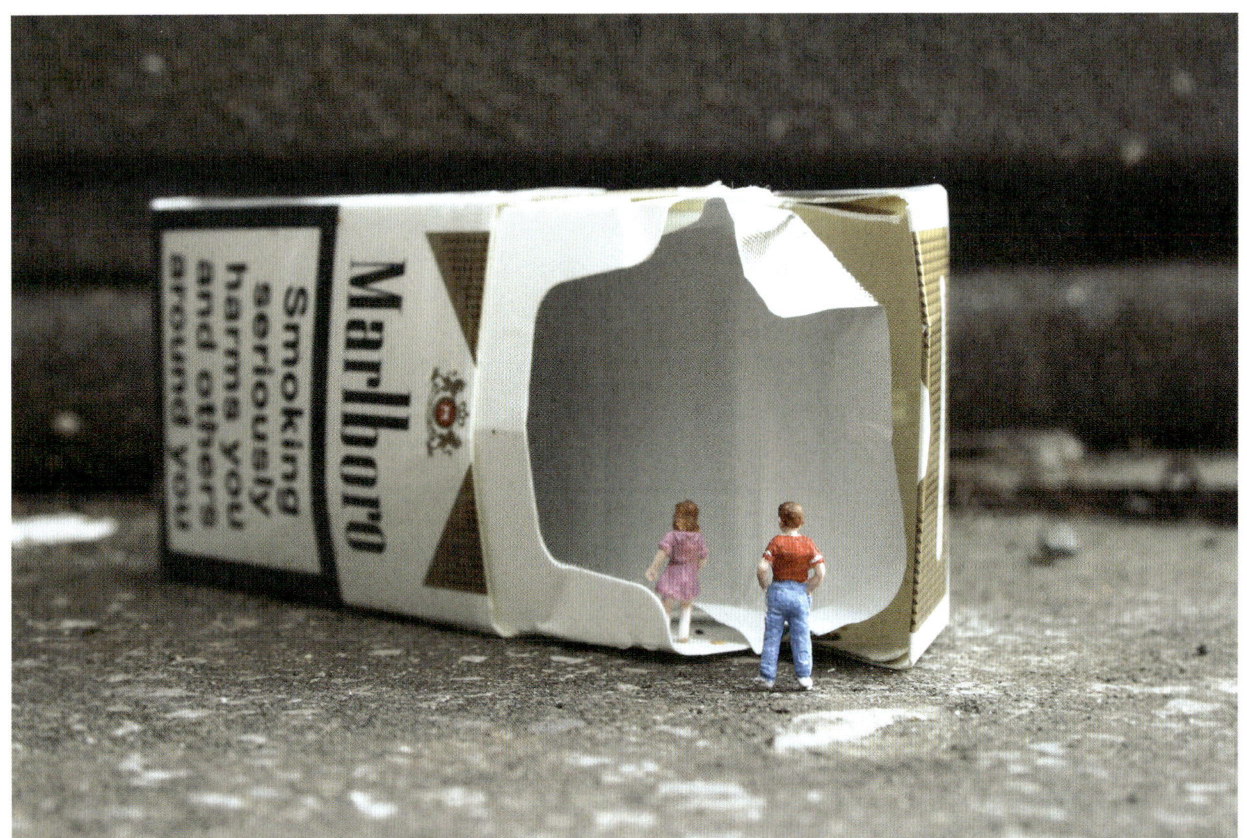
Marlboro
Smoking seriously harms you and others around you

The Den

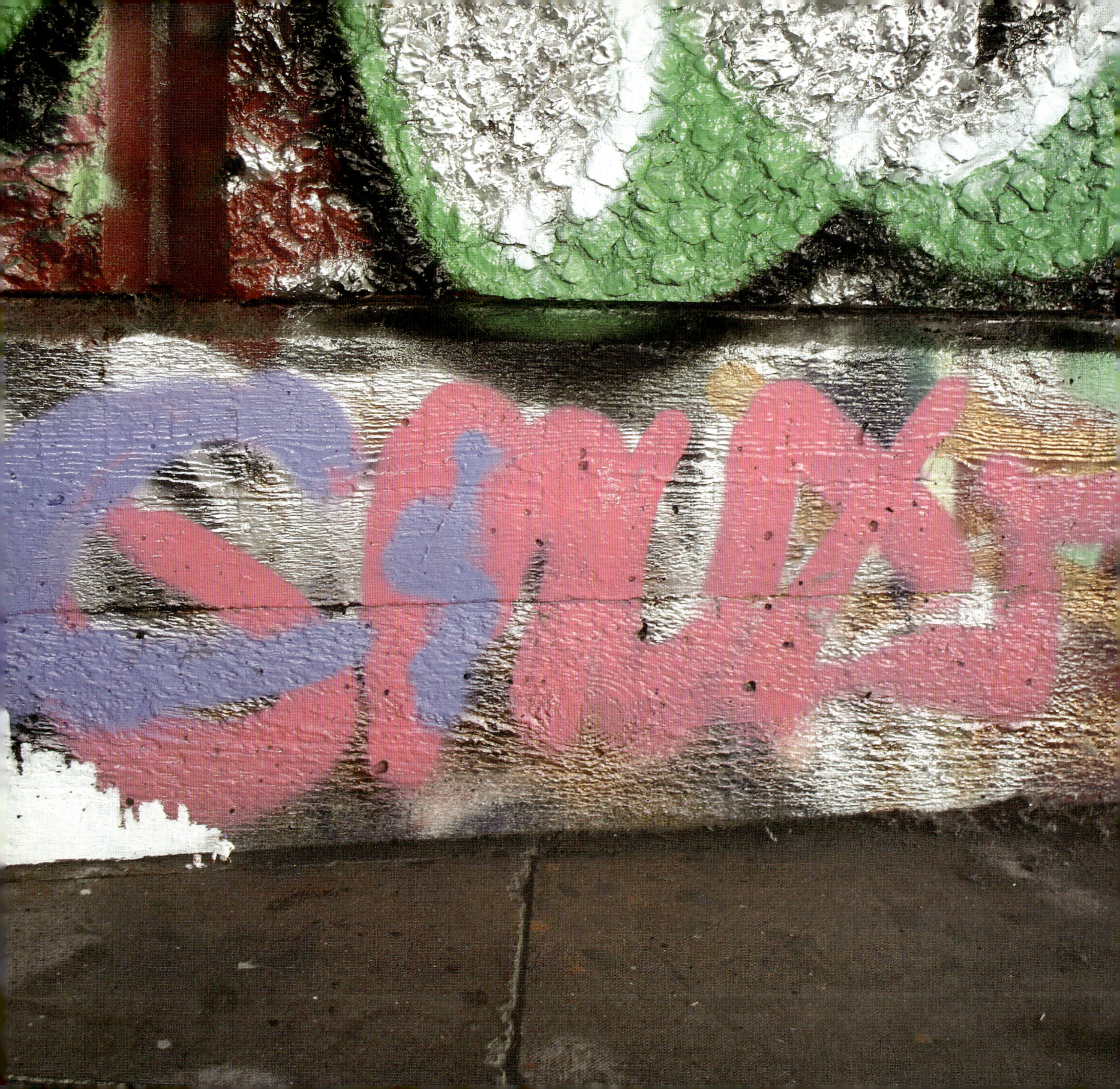

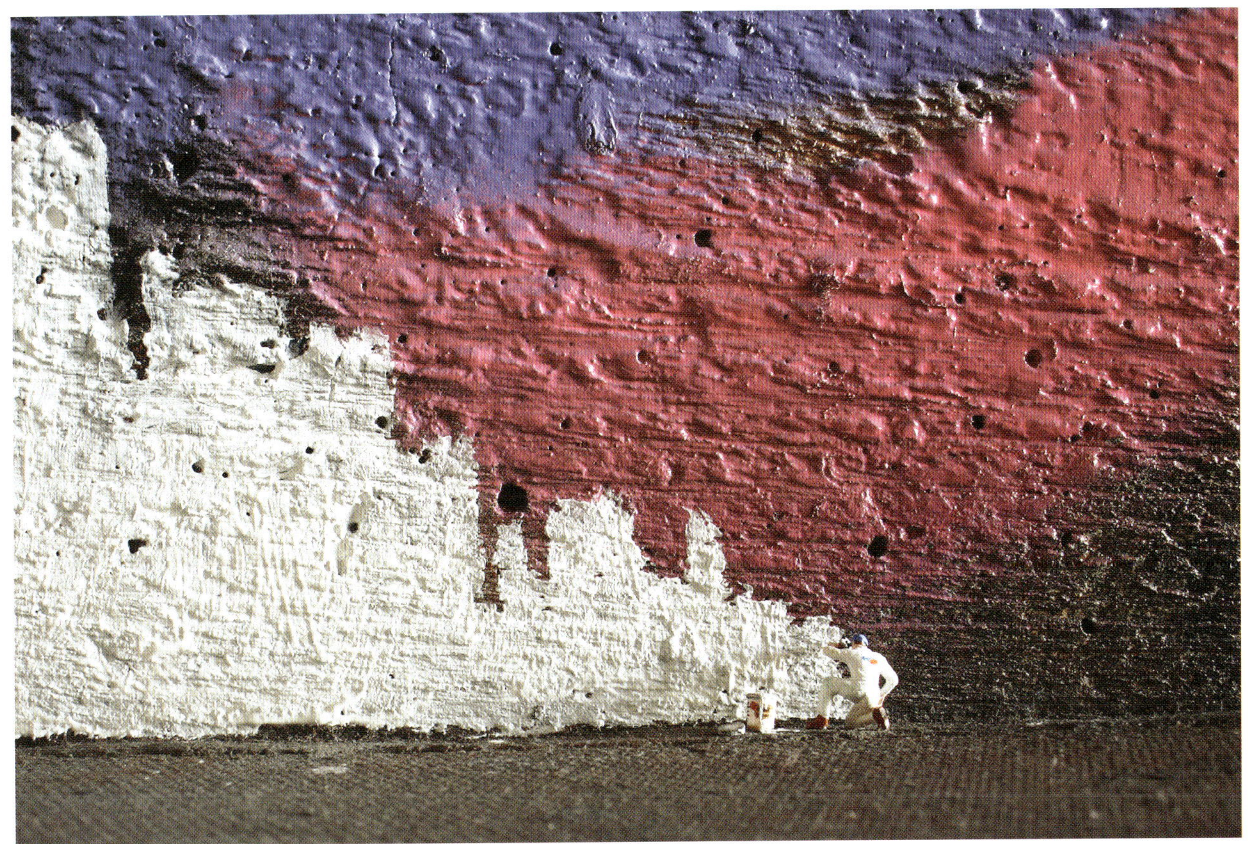
Buffing

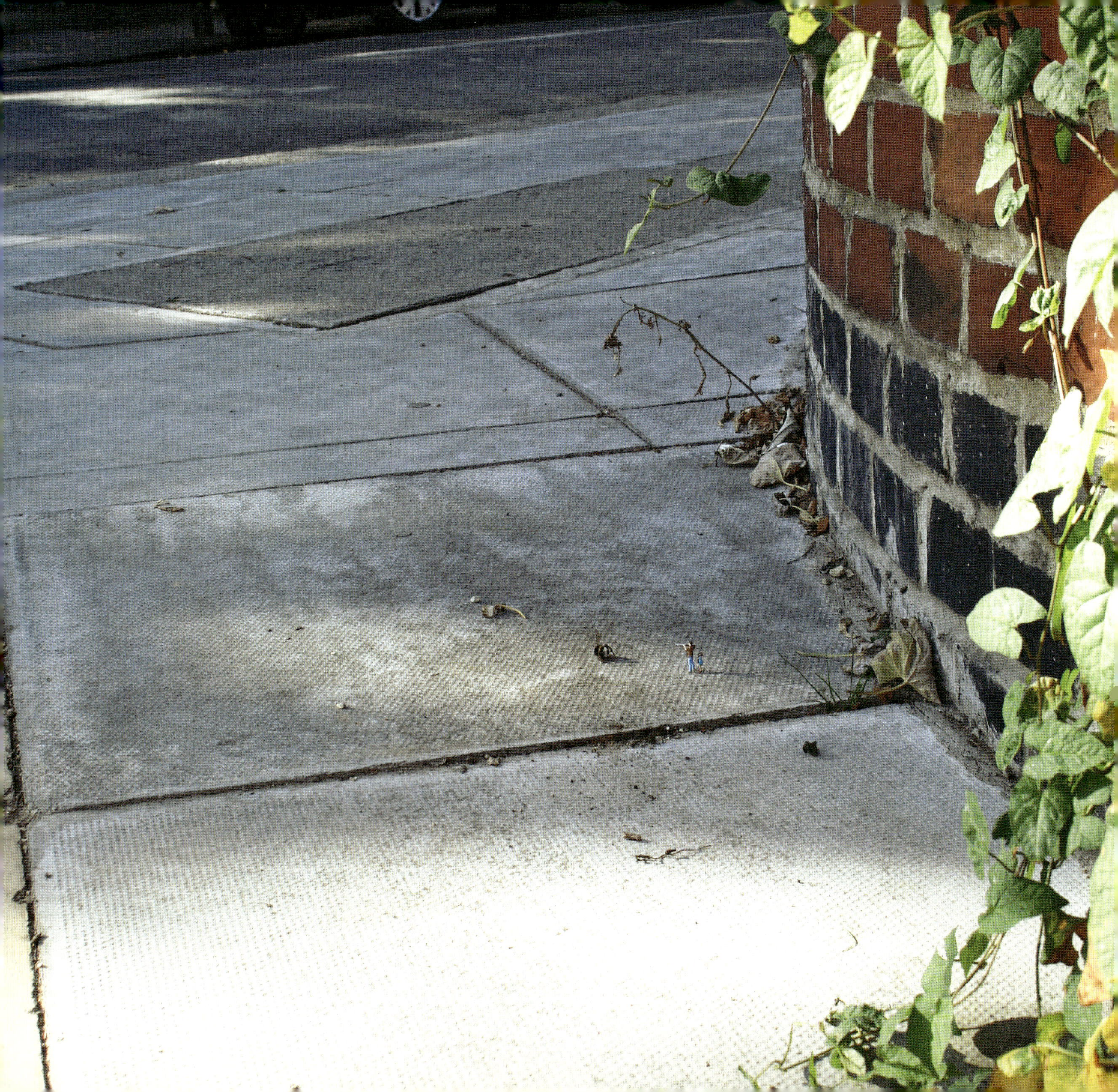

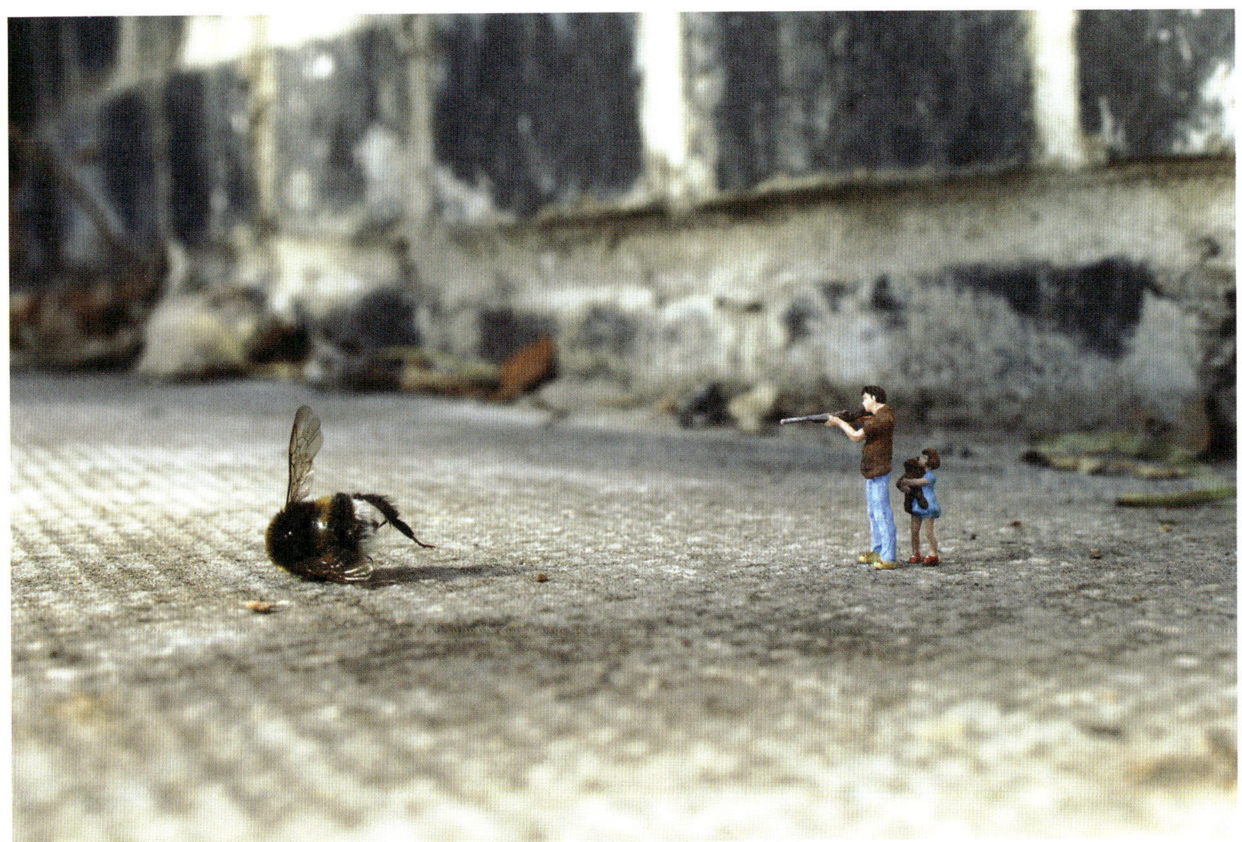

'They're not pets, Susan'

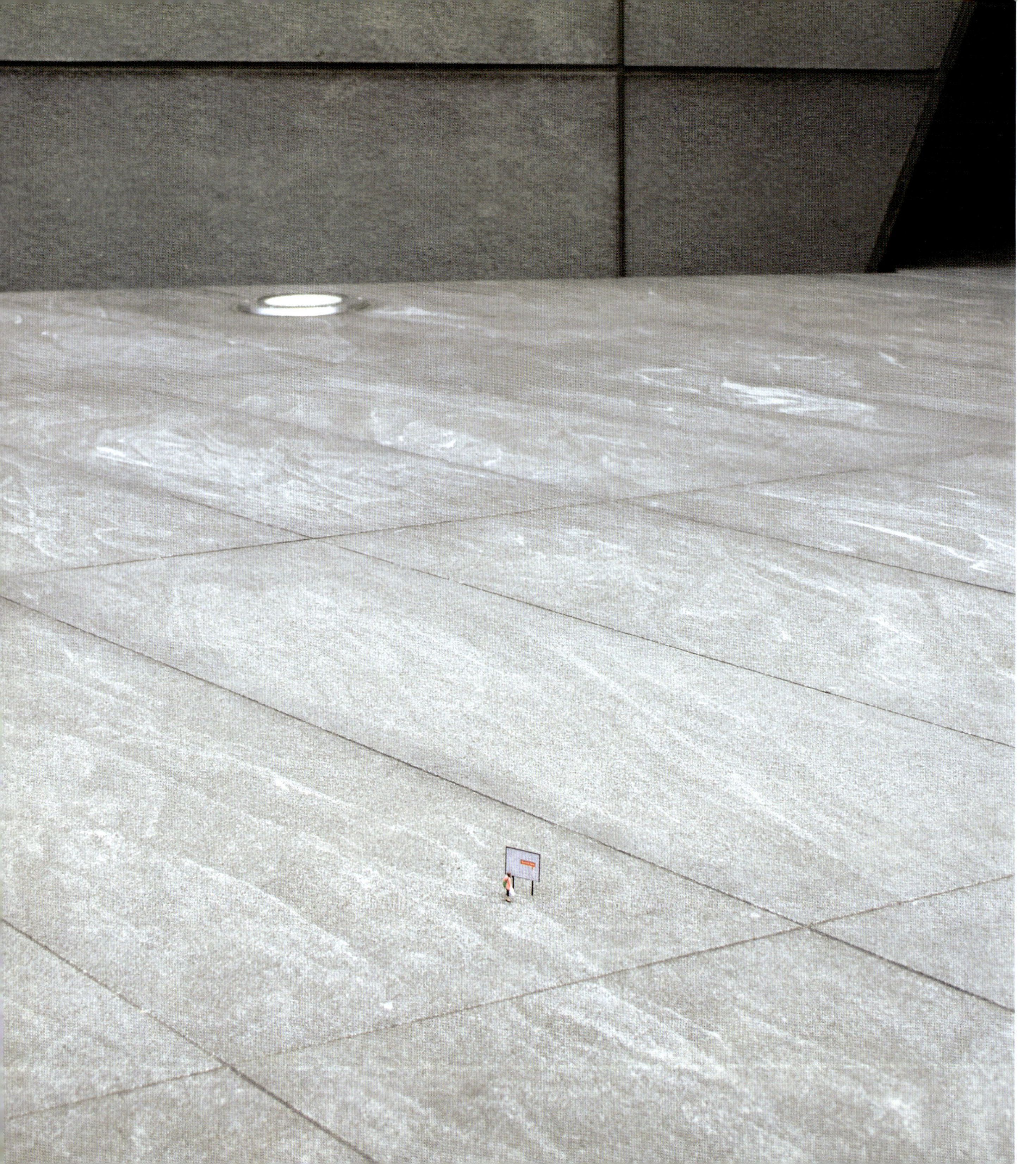

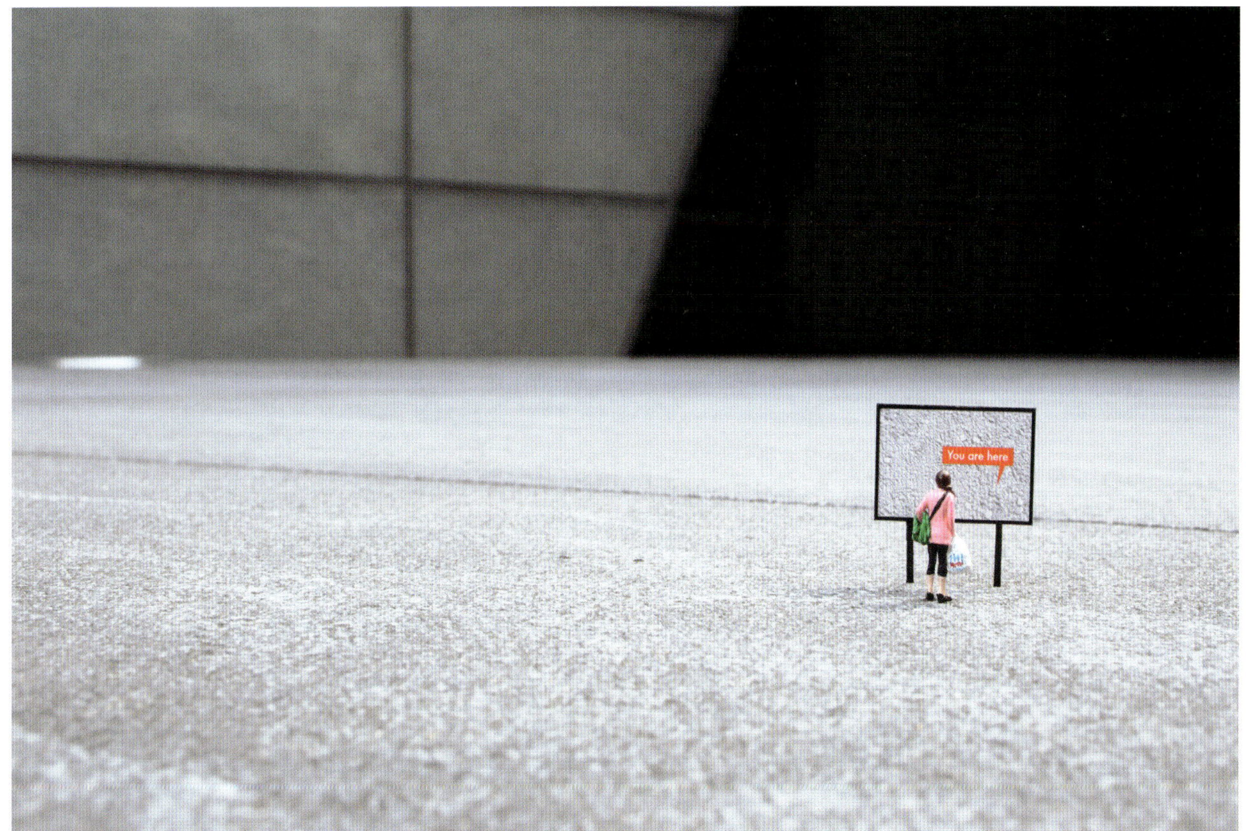

Tundra

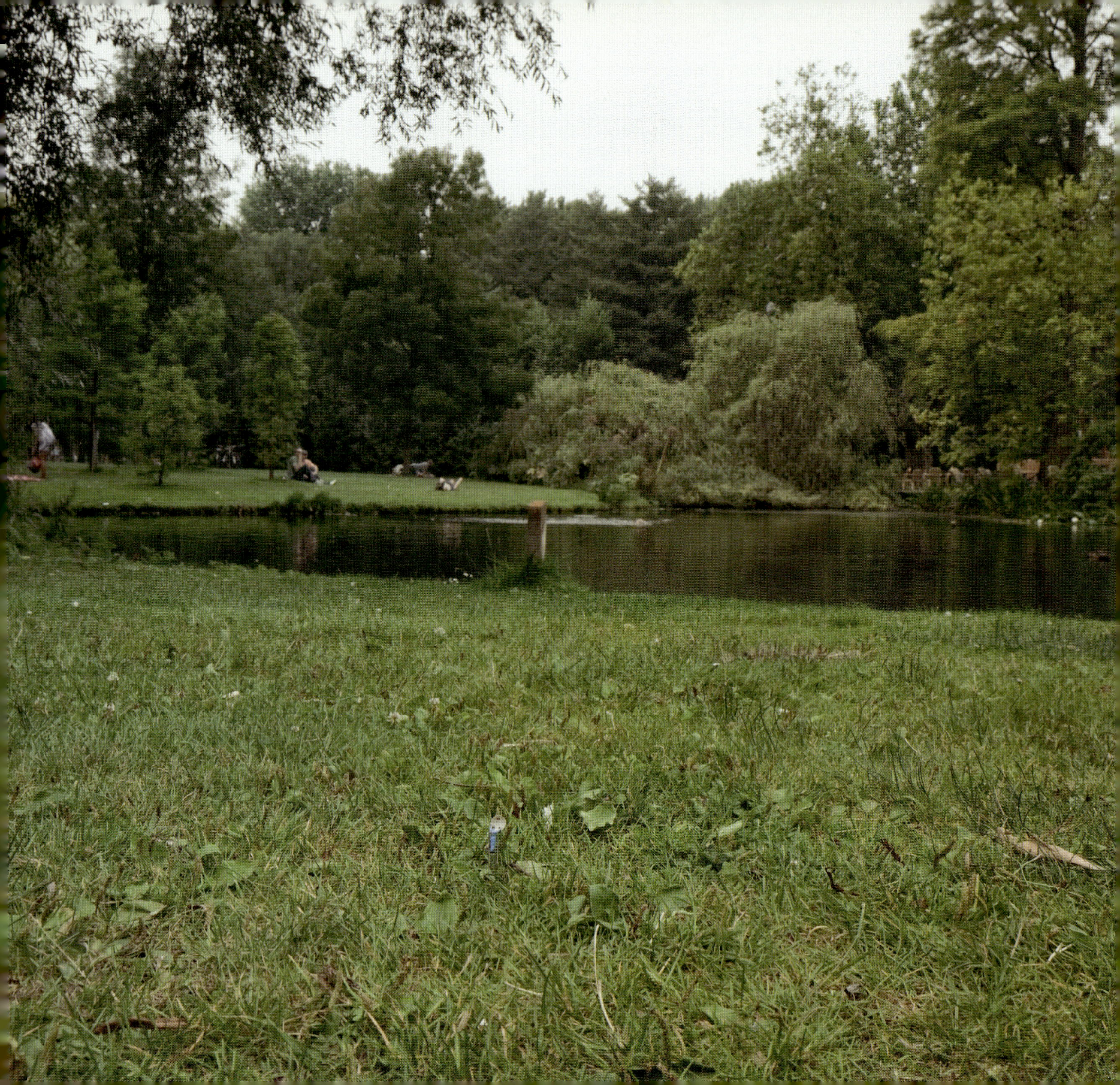

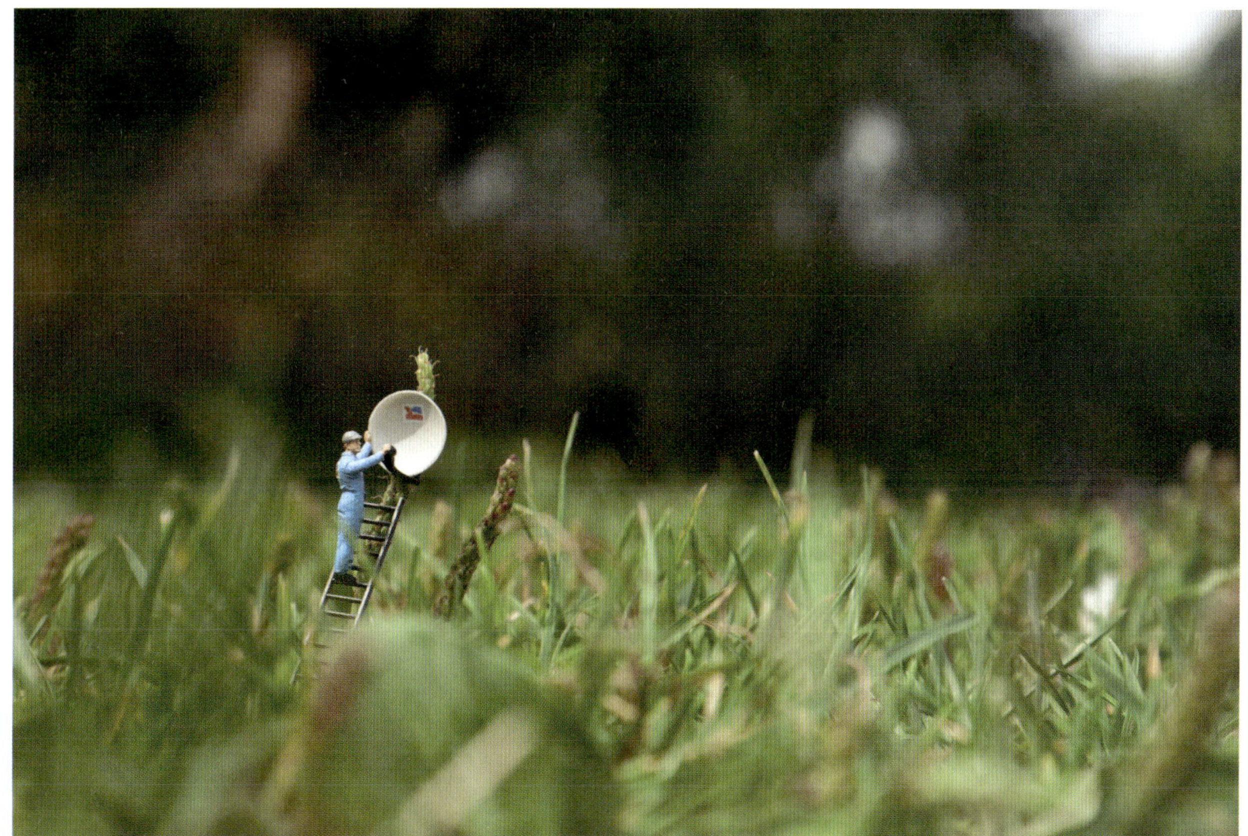

The Great Indoors

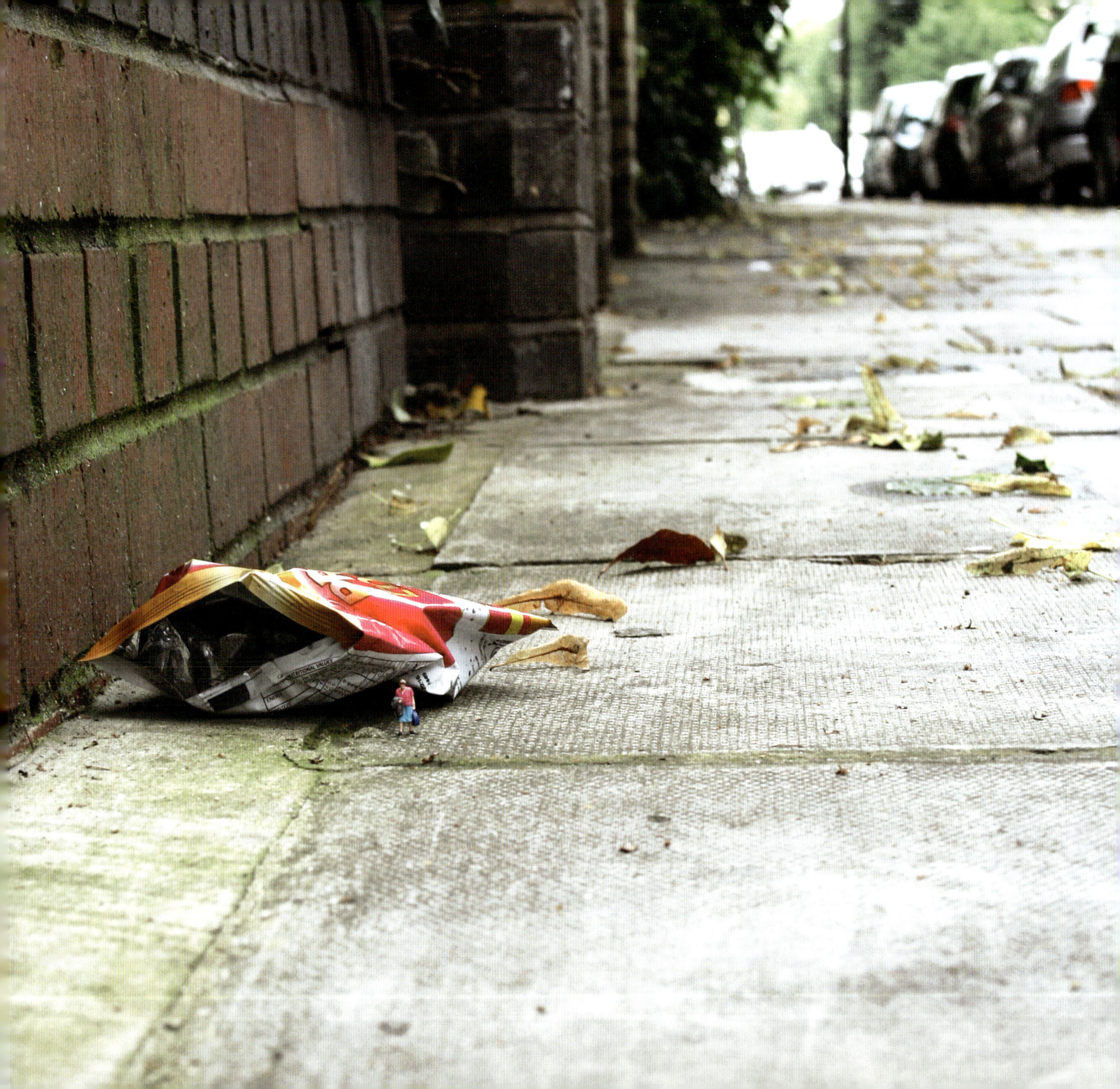

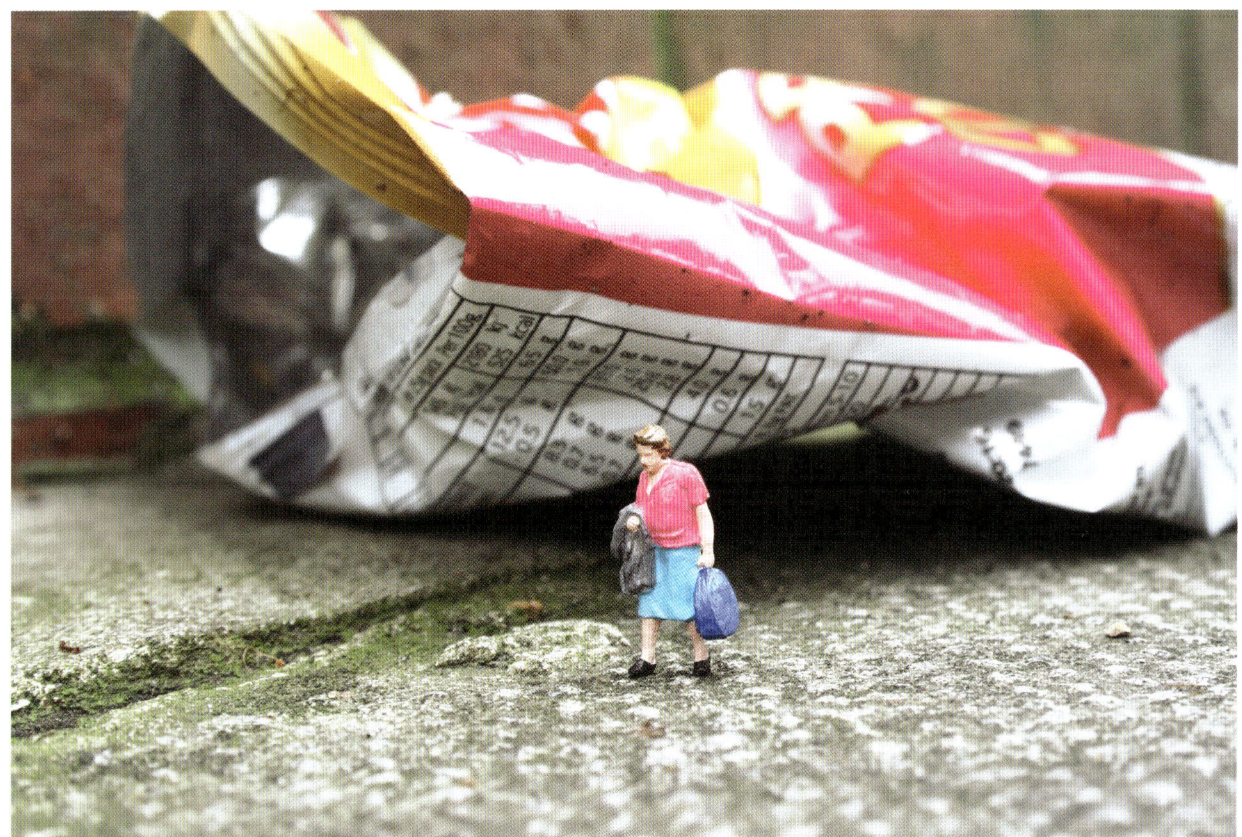

One Day He'll Notice Me

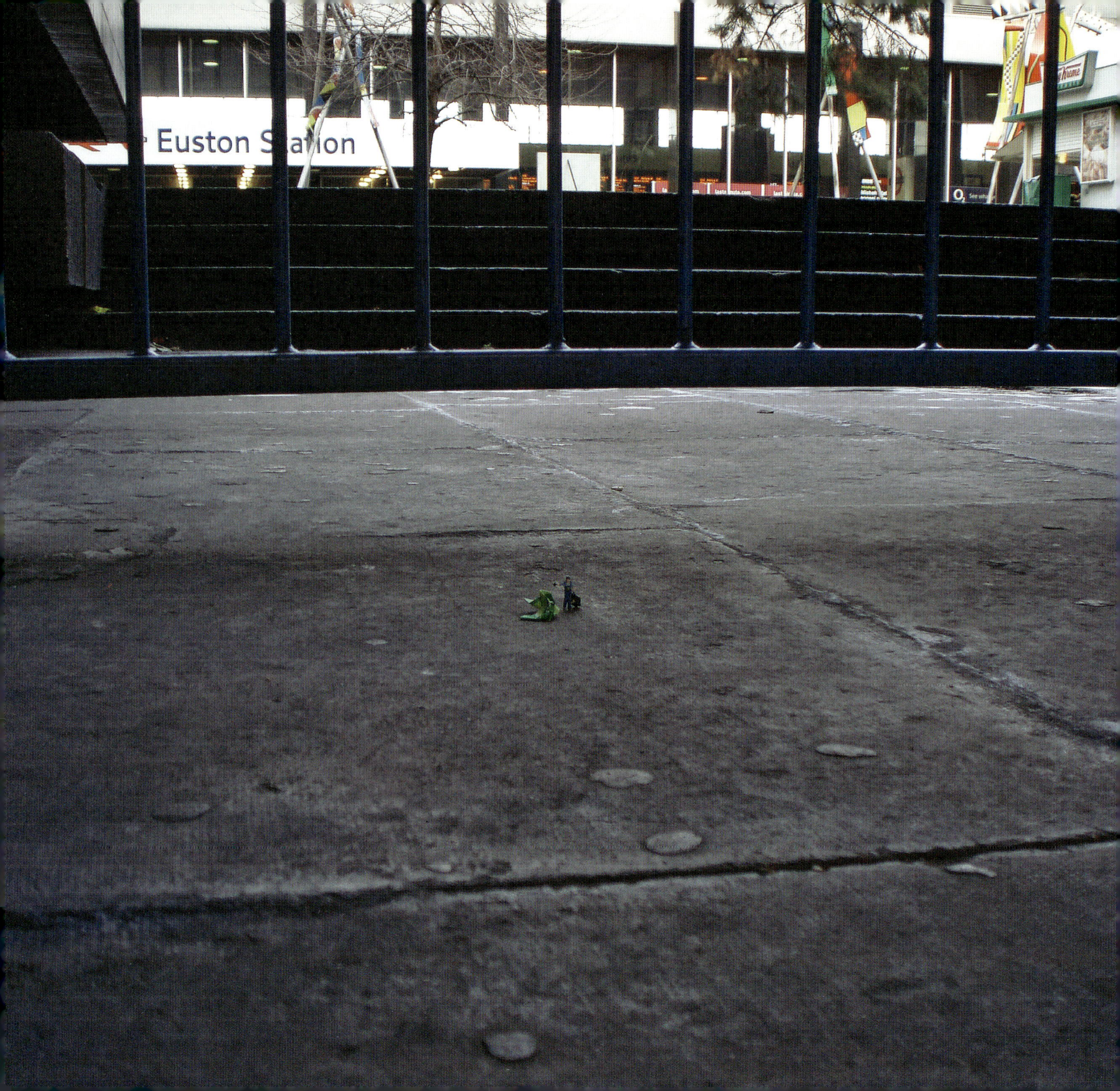
Euston

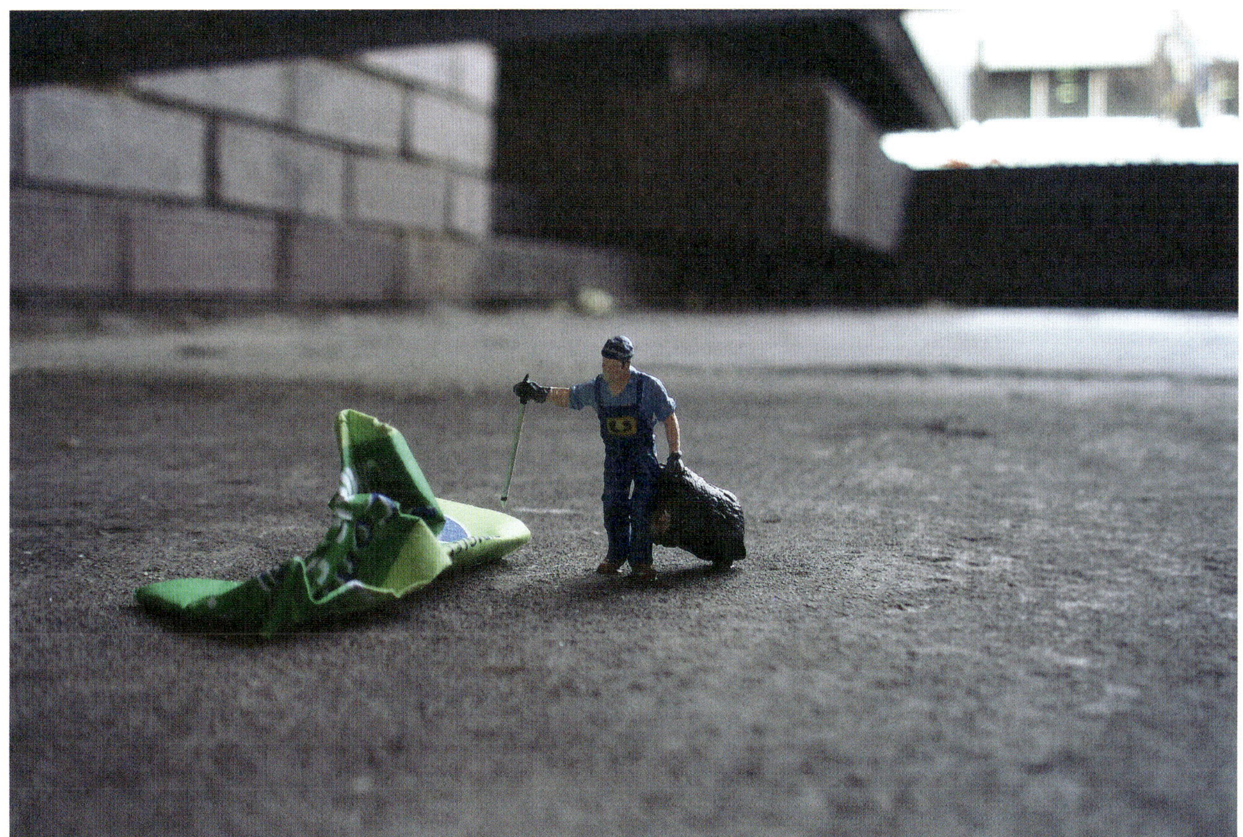

Rubbish

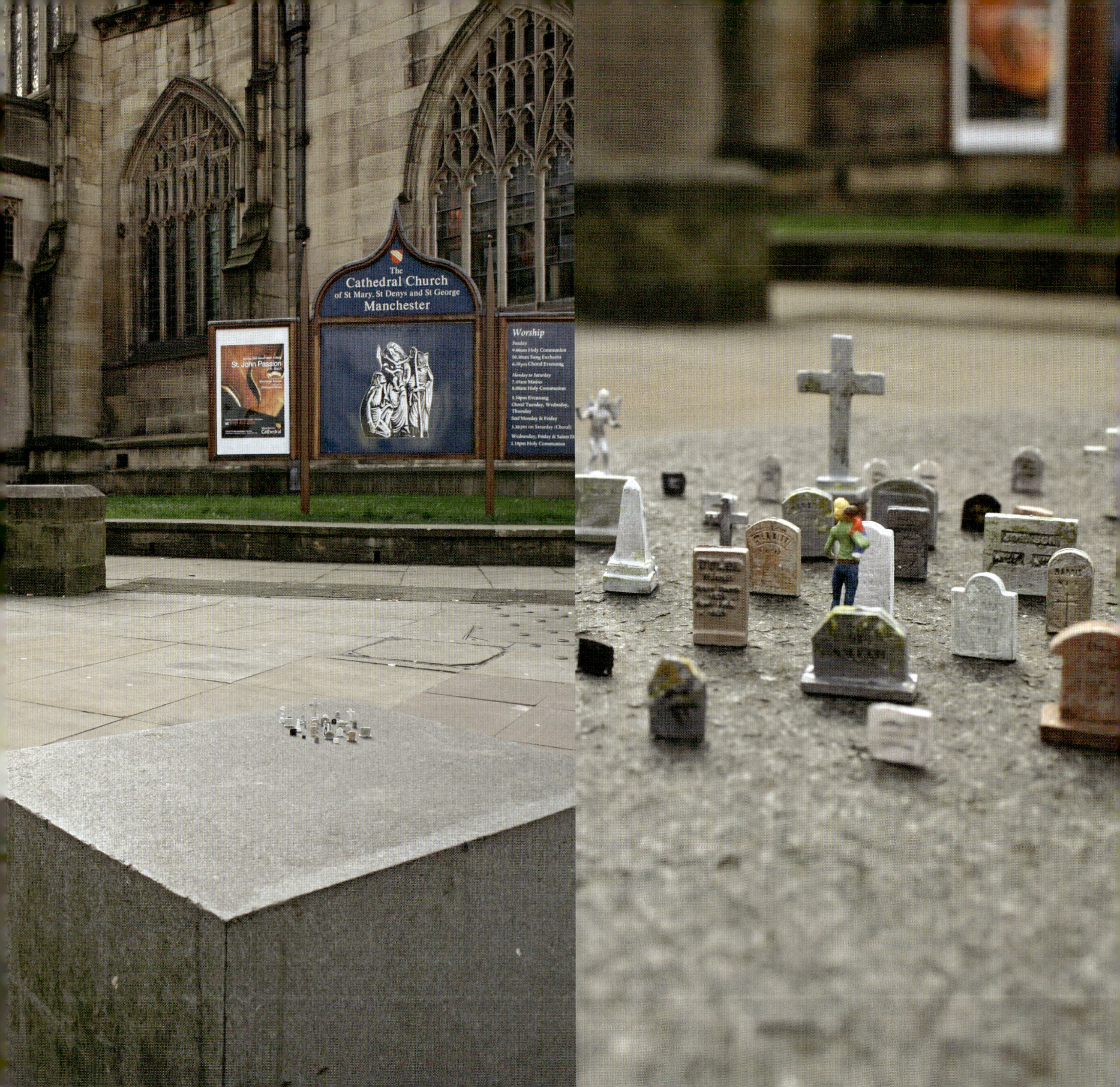
The
Cathedral Church
of St Mary, St Denys and St George
Manchester
St. John Passion
Worship
Sunday
9.00am Holy Communion
10.30am Sung Eucharist
6.30pm Choral Evensong
Monday to Saturday
7.45am Matins
8.00am Holy Communion
Choral Tuesday, Wednesday, Thursday
Said Monday & Friday
1.10pm Holy Communion
JOHNSON

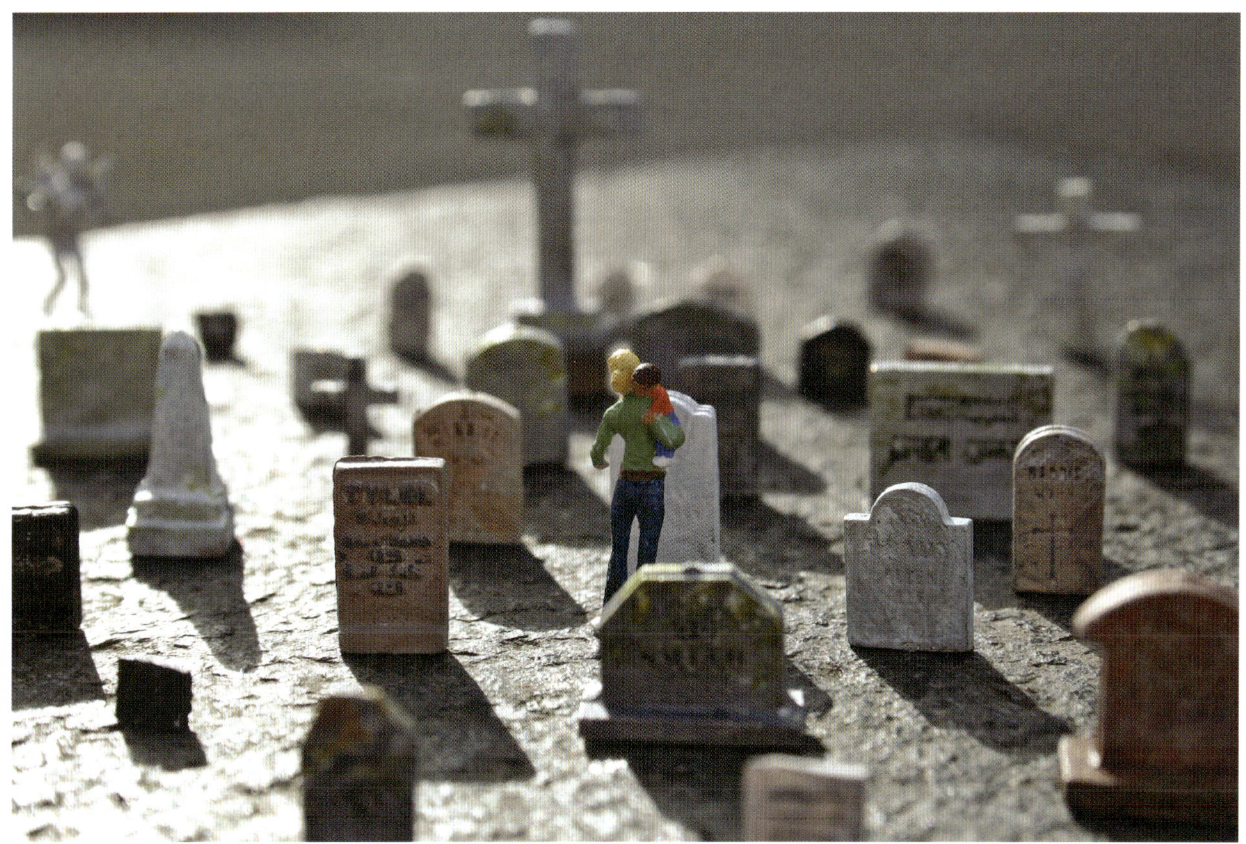

Twelve Months Later

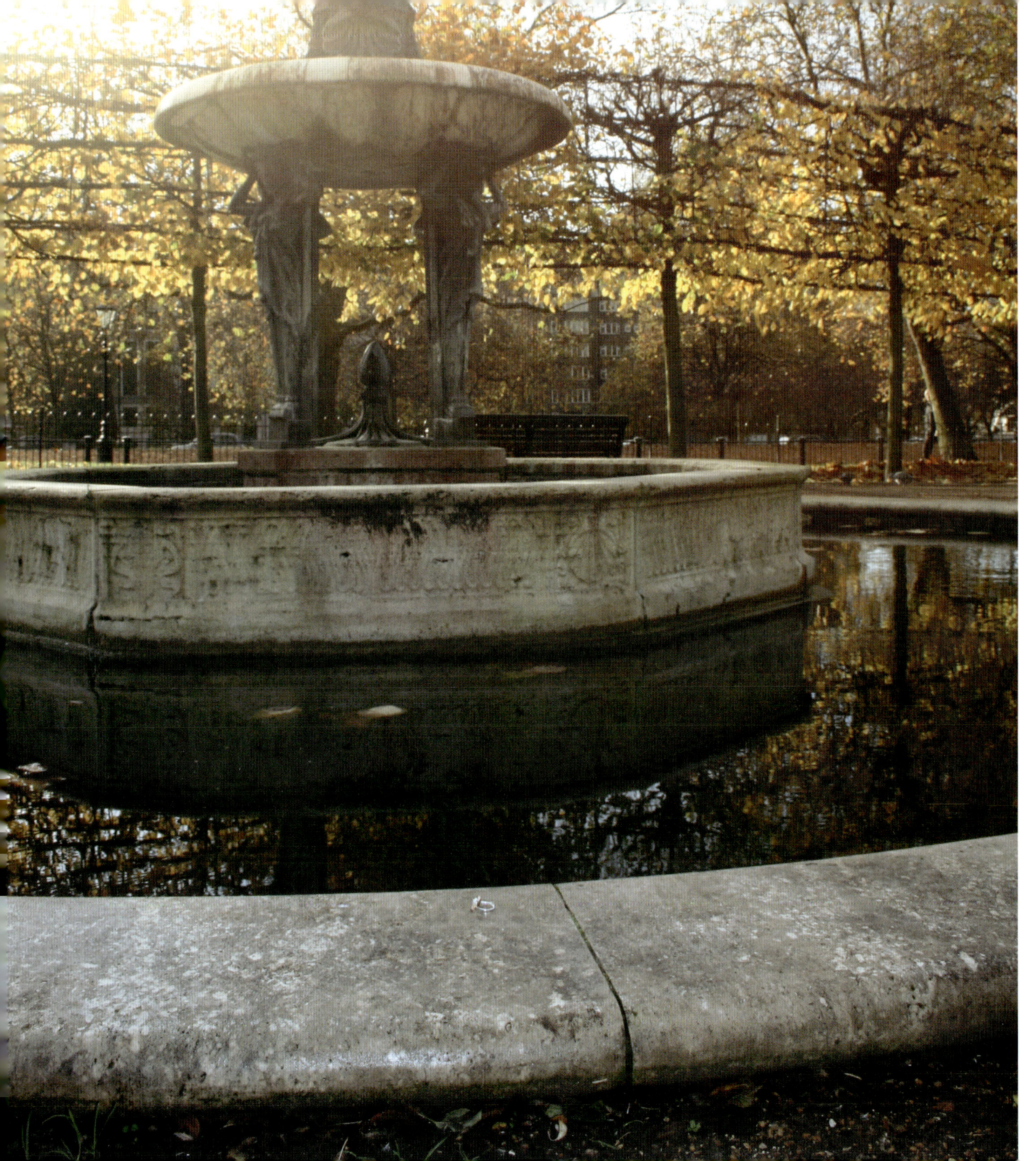

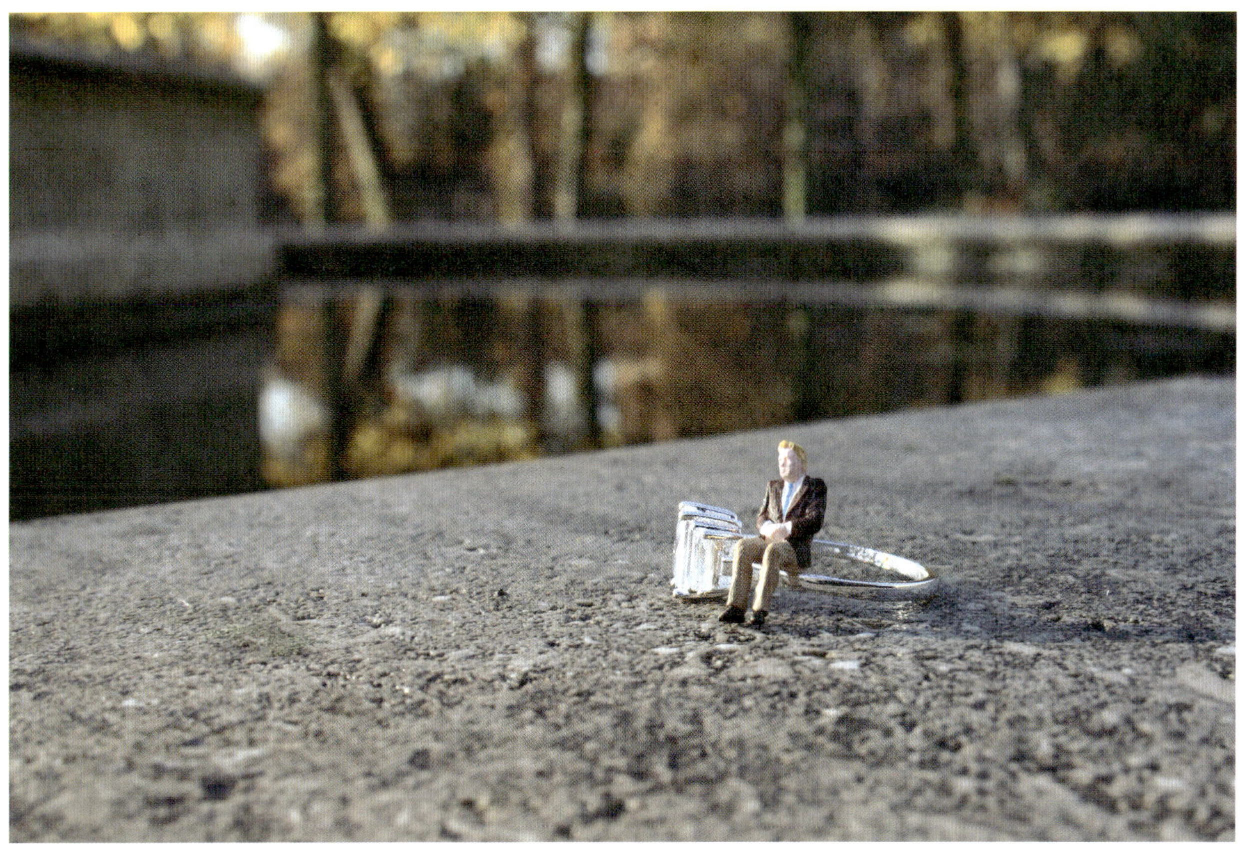

Plan B

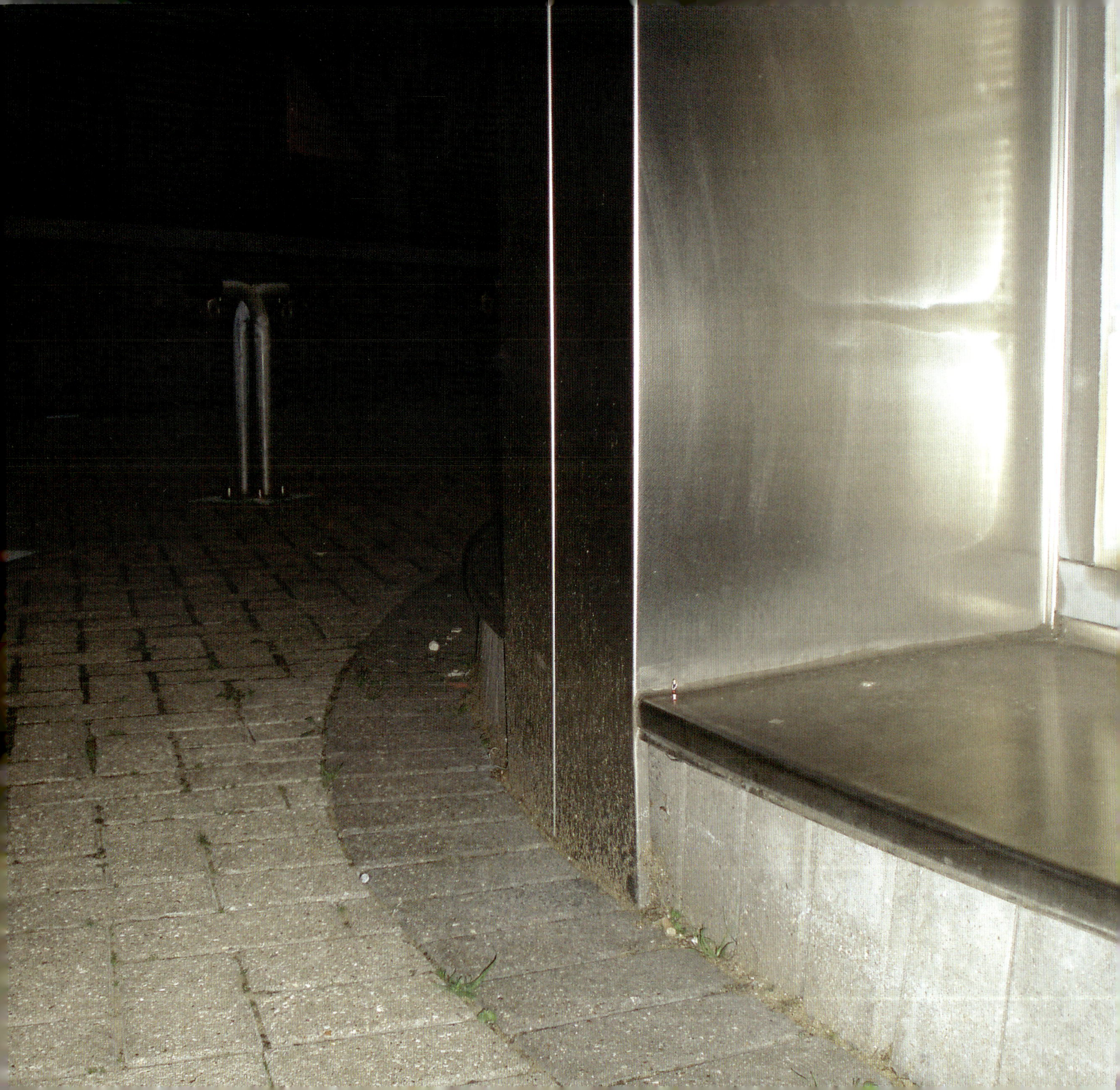

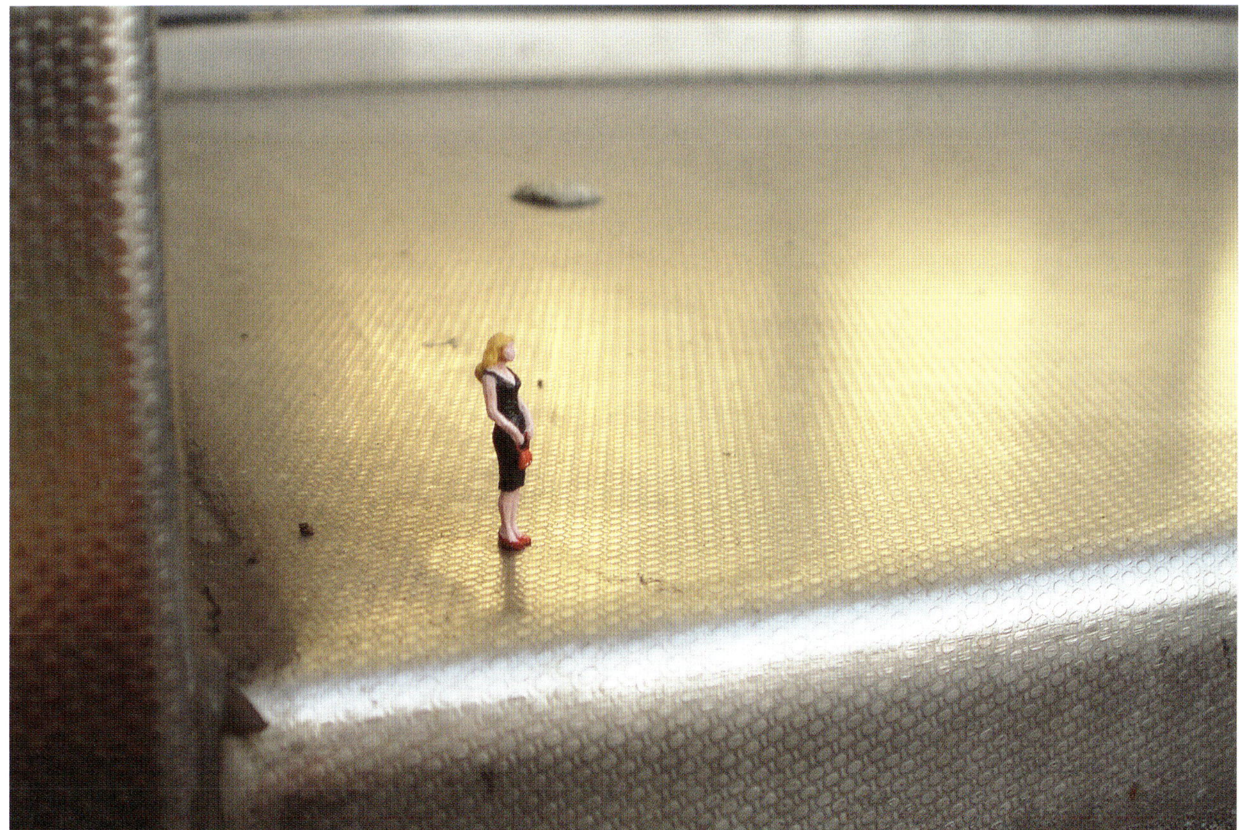

Stood Up Again

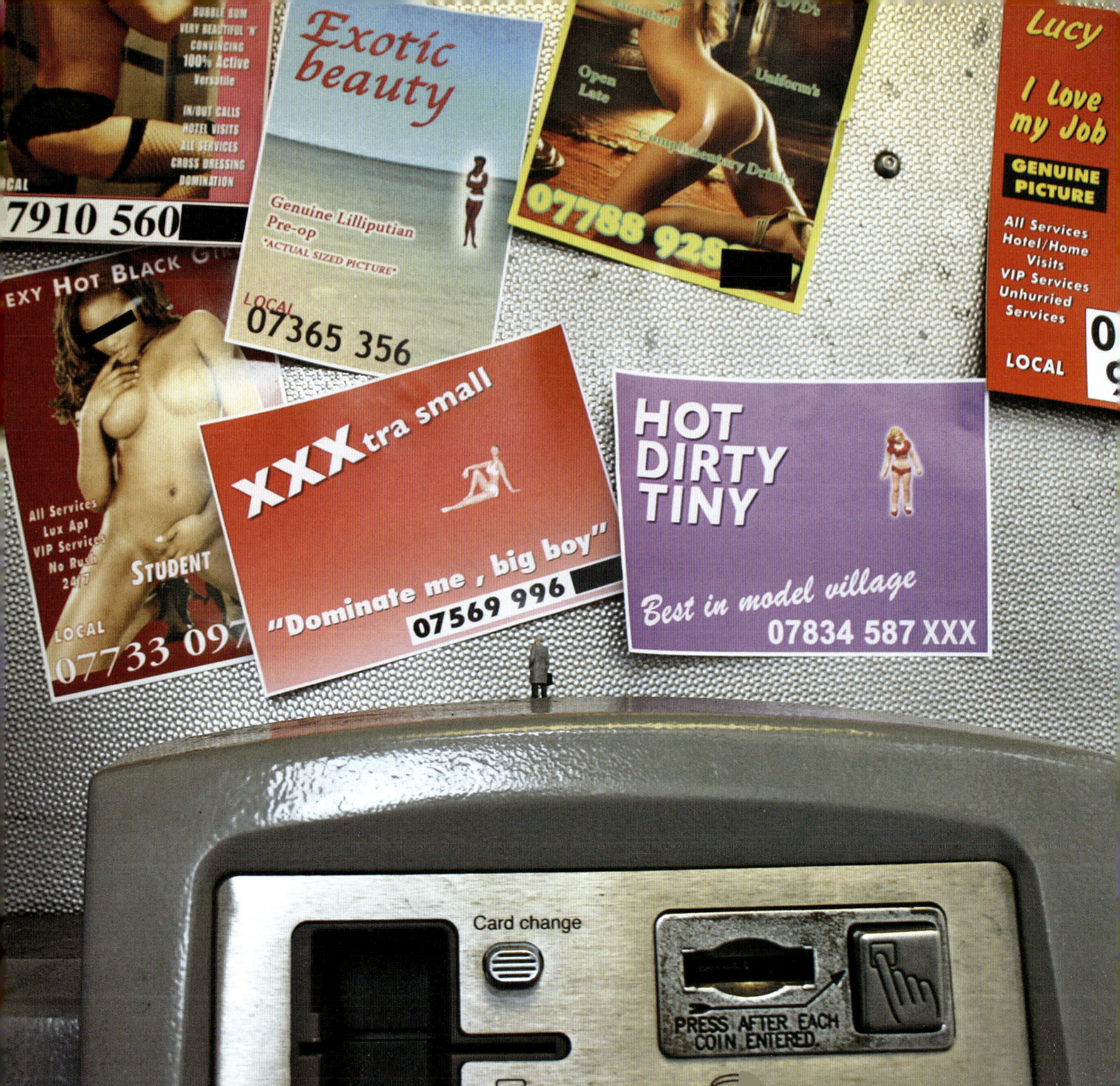

100% Active
Versatile
IN/OUT CALLS
HOTEL VISITS
ALL SERVICES
CROSS DRESSING
DOMINATION
7910 560
Exotic beauty
Genuine Lilliputian
Pre-op
ACTUAL SIZED PICTURE
LOCAL
07365 356
Open Late
Uniform's
Complimentary Drinks
07788 928
Lucy
I love my Job
GENUINE PICTURE
All Services
Hotel/Home Visits
VIP Services
Unhurried Services
LOCAL
All Services
Lux Apt
VIP Services
24/7
STUDENT
LOCAL
07733 097
XXXtra small
"Dominate me, big boy"
07569 996
HOT DIRTY TINY
Best in model village
07834 587 XXX
Card change
PRESS AFTER EACH COIN ENTERED.

LOCAL
07365 35
XXXtra small
"Dominate me , big boy
07569 996 3
HOT
DIRTY
TINY
Best in model village
07834 587

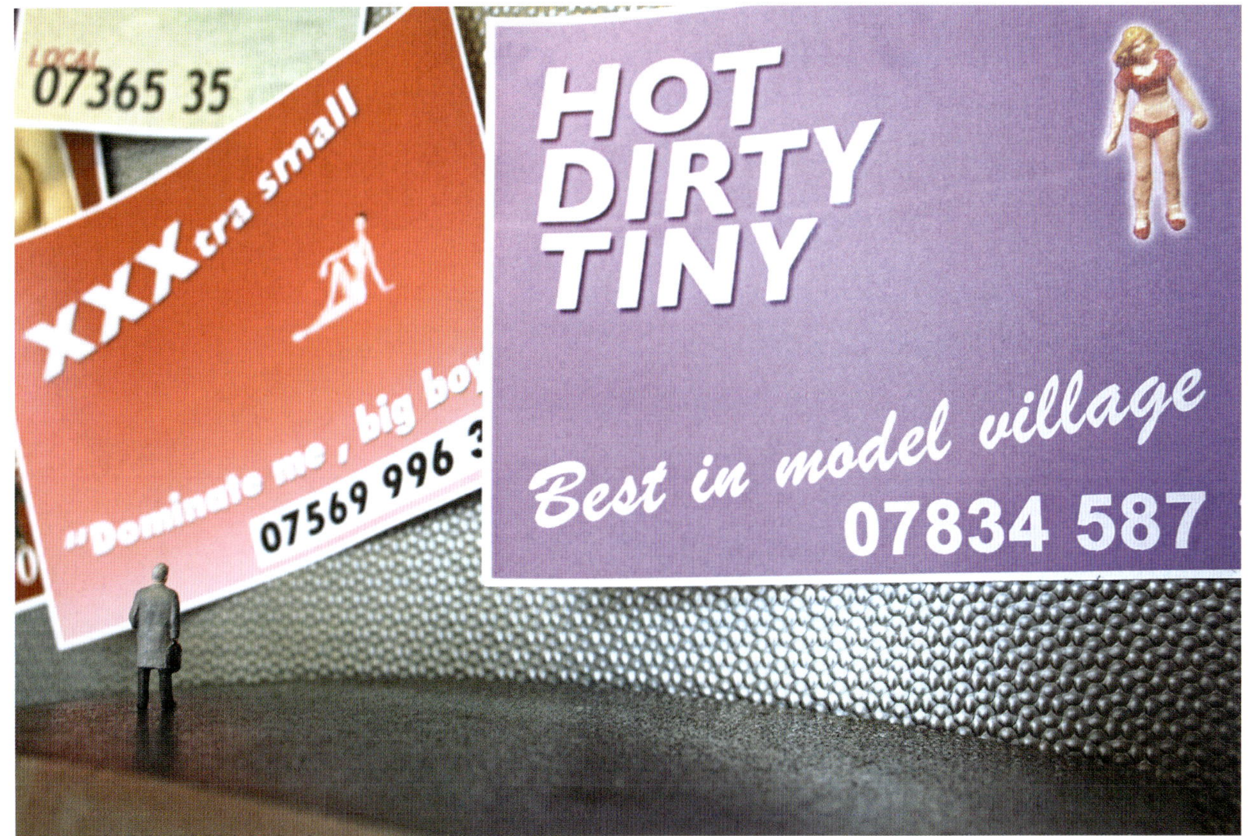

Phone Box

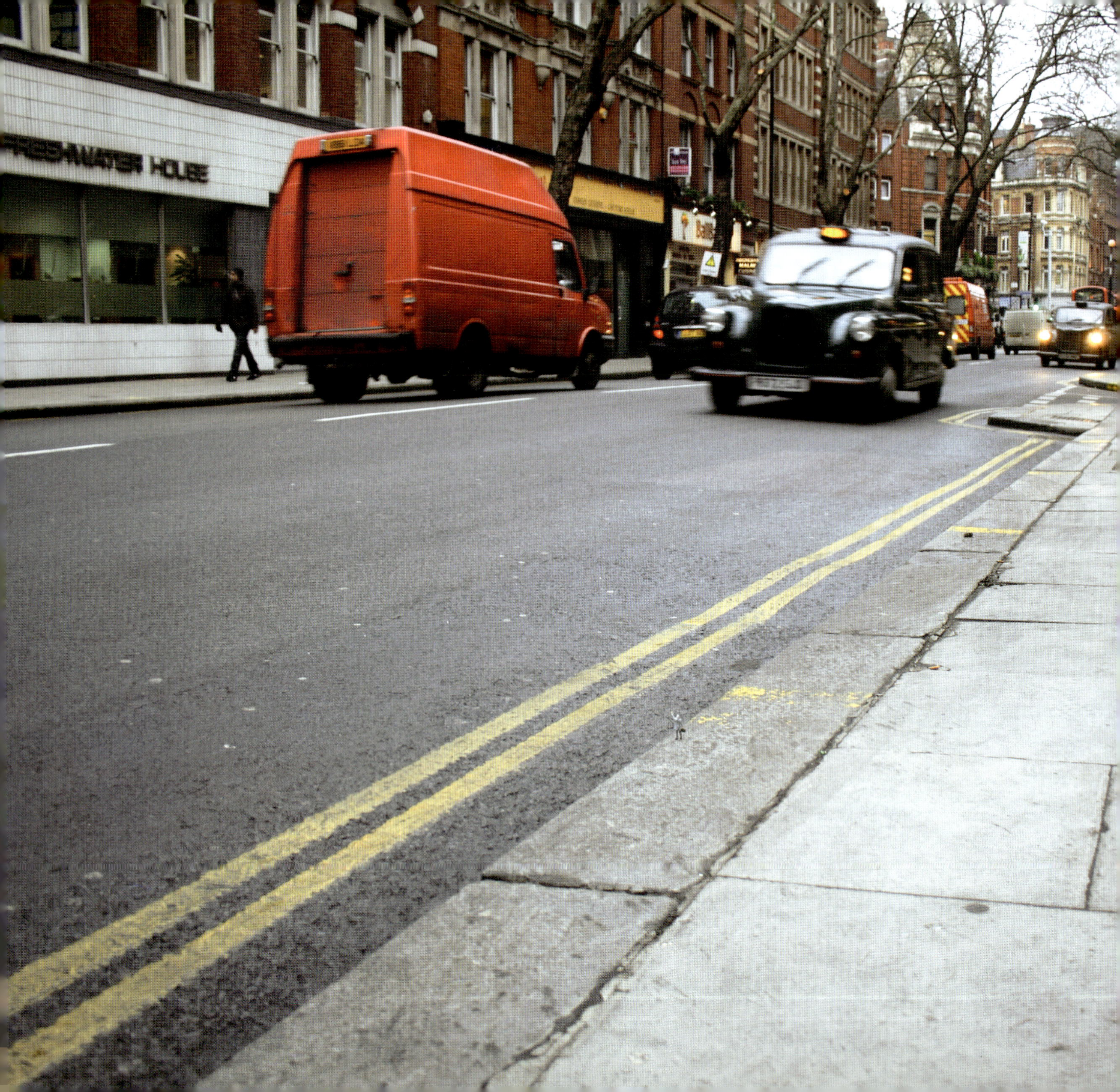
FRESHWATER HOUSE

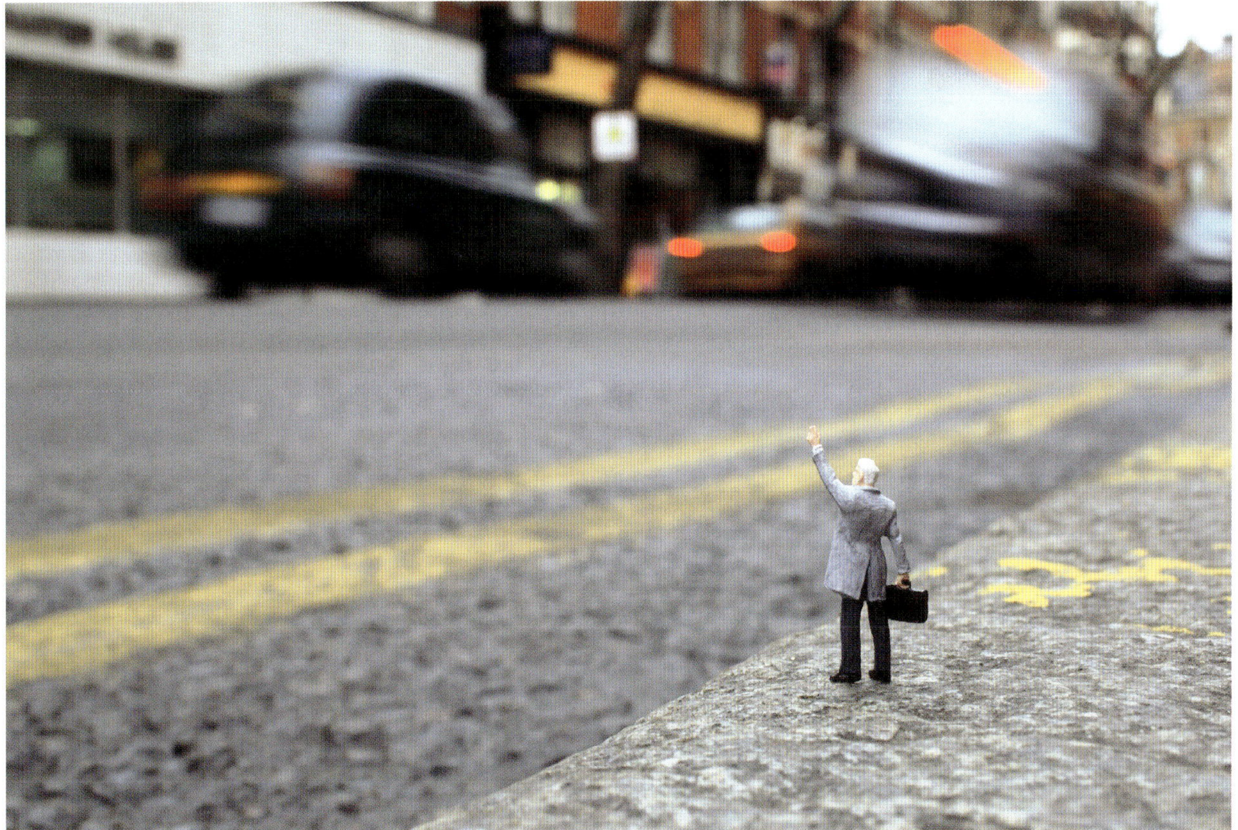

'Taxi!'

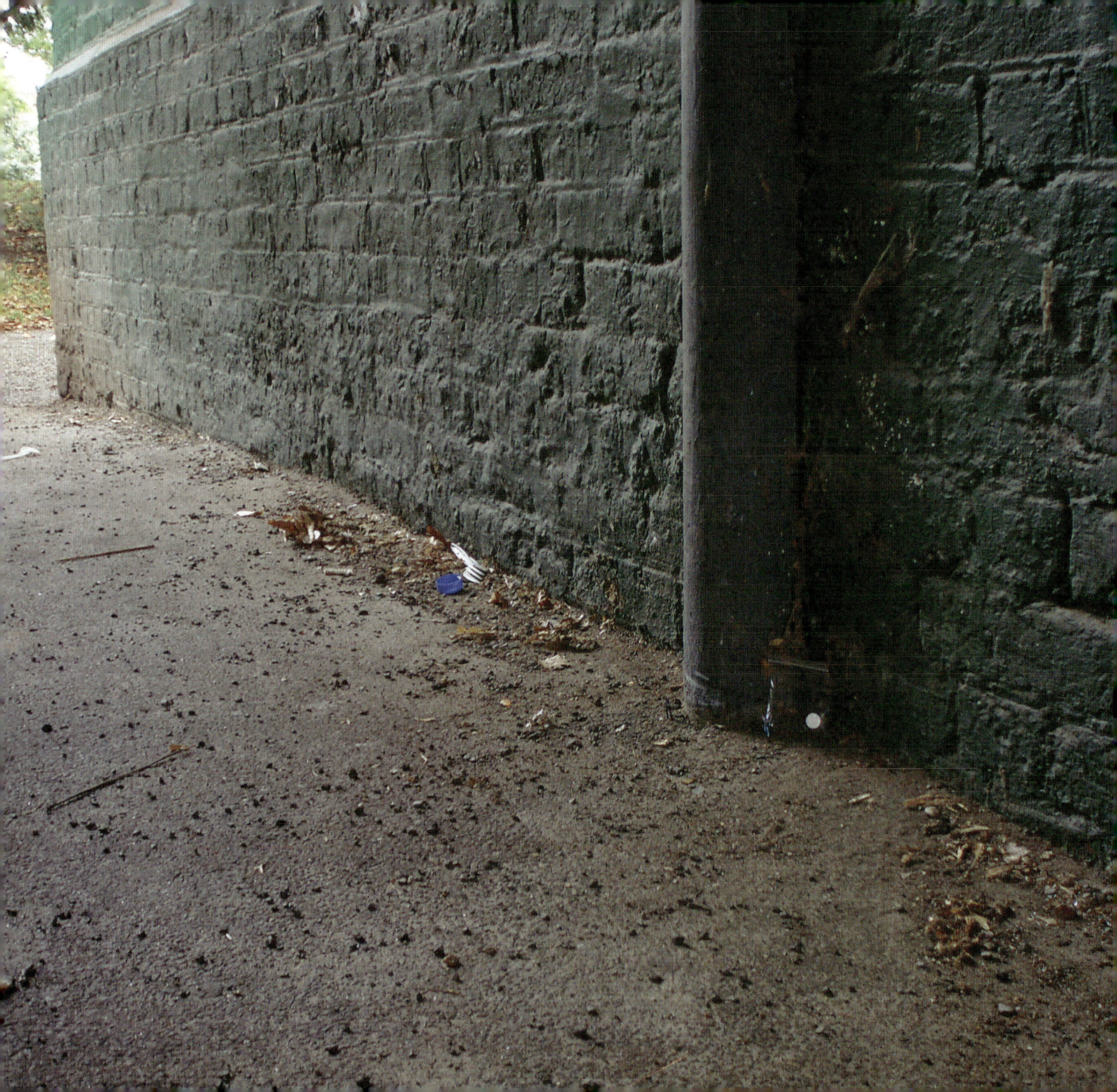

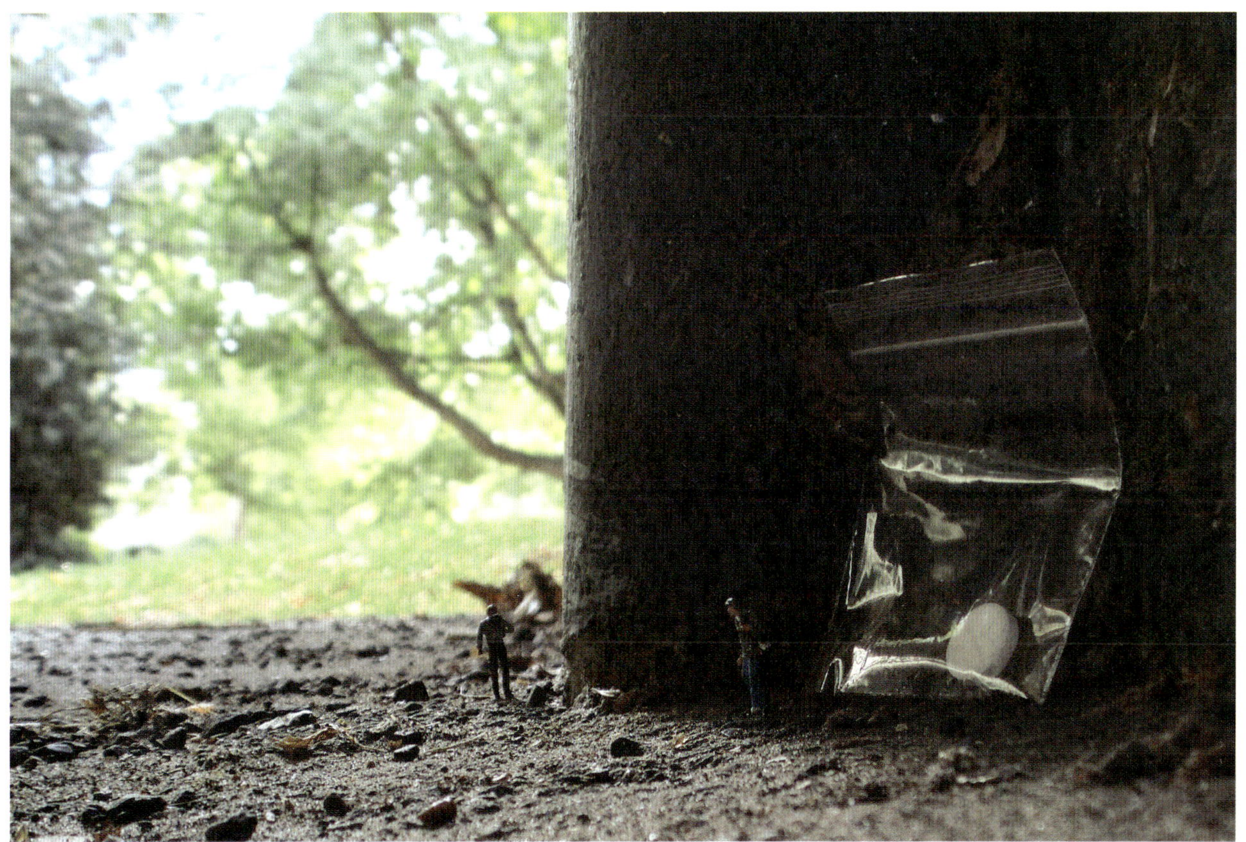

Dealer

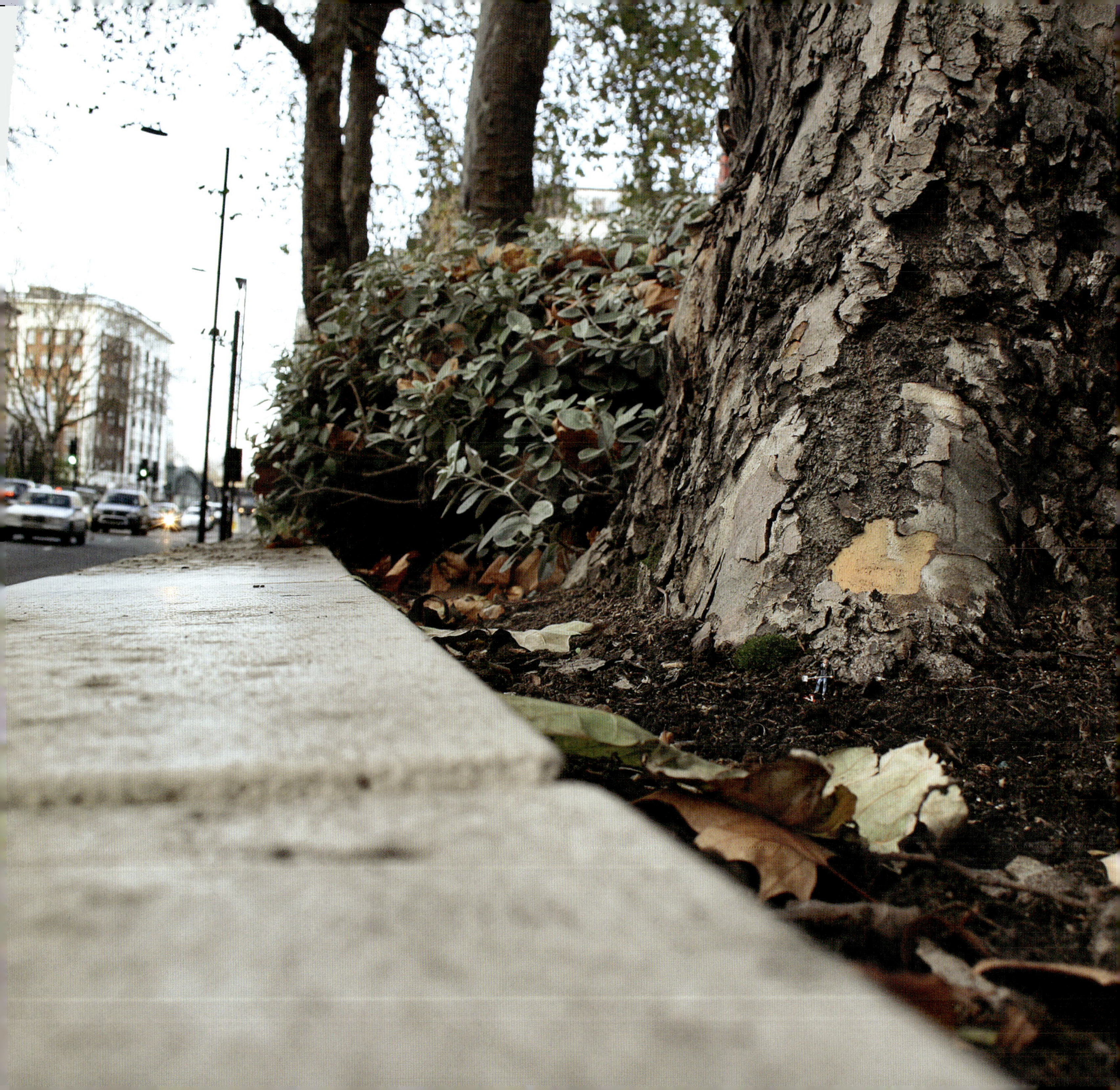

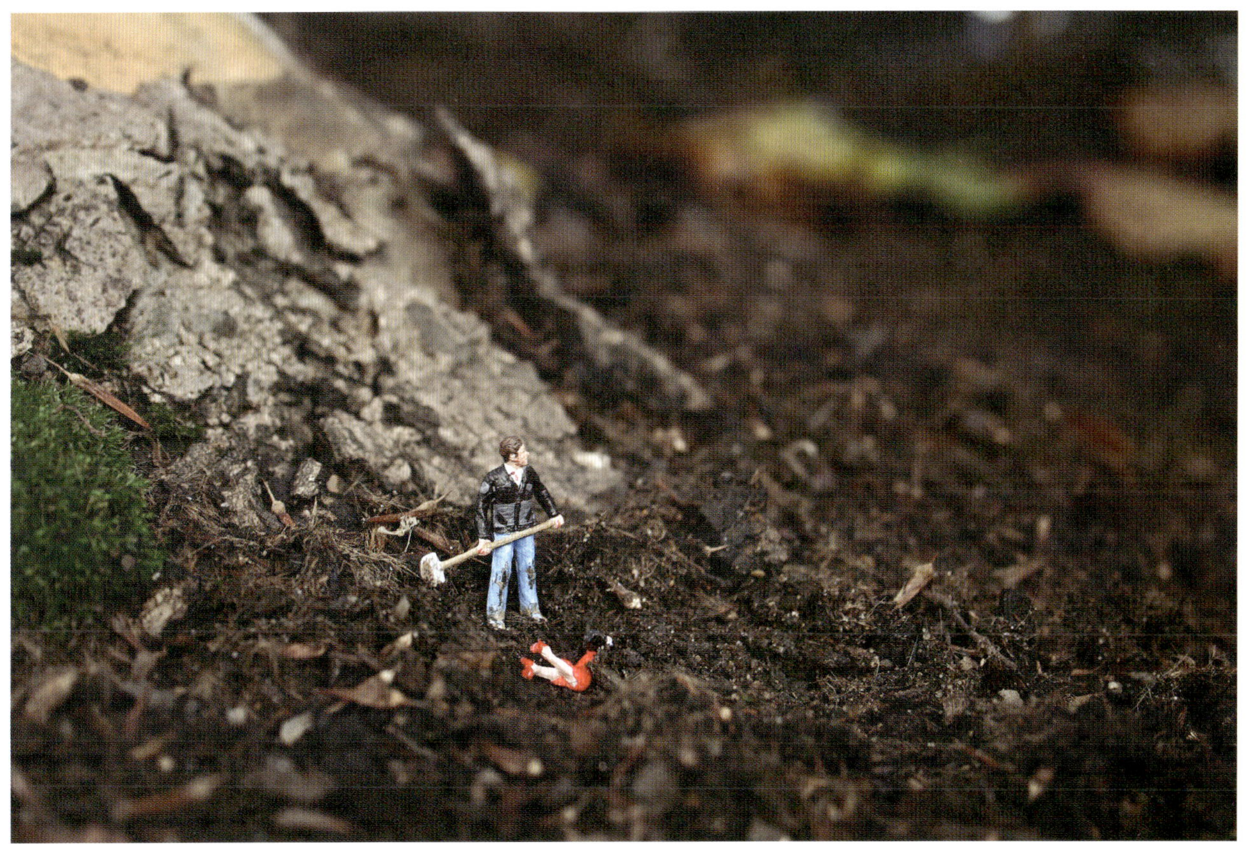

Bad First Date

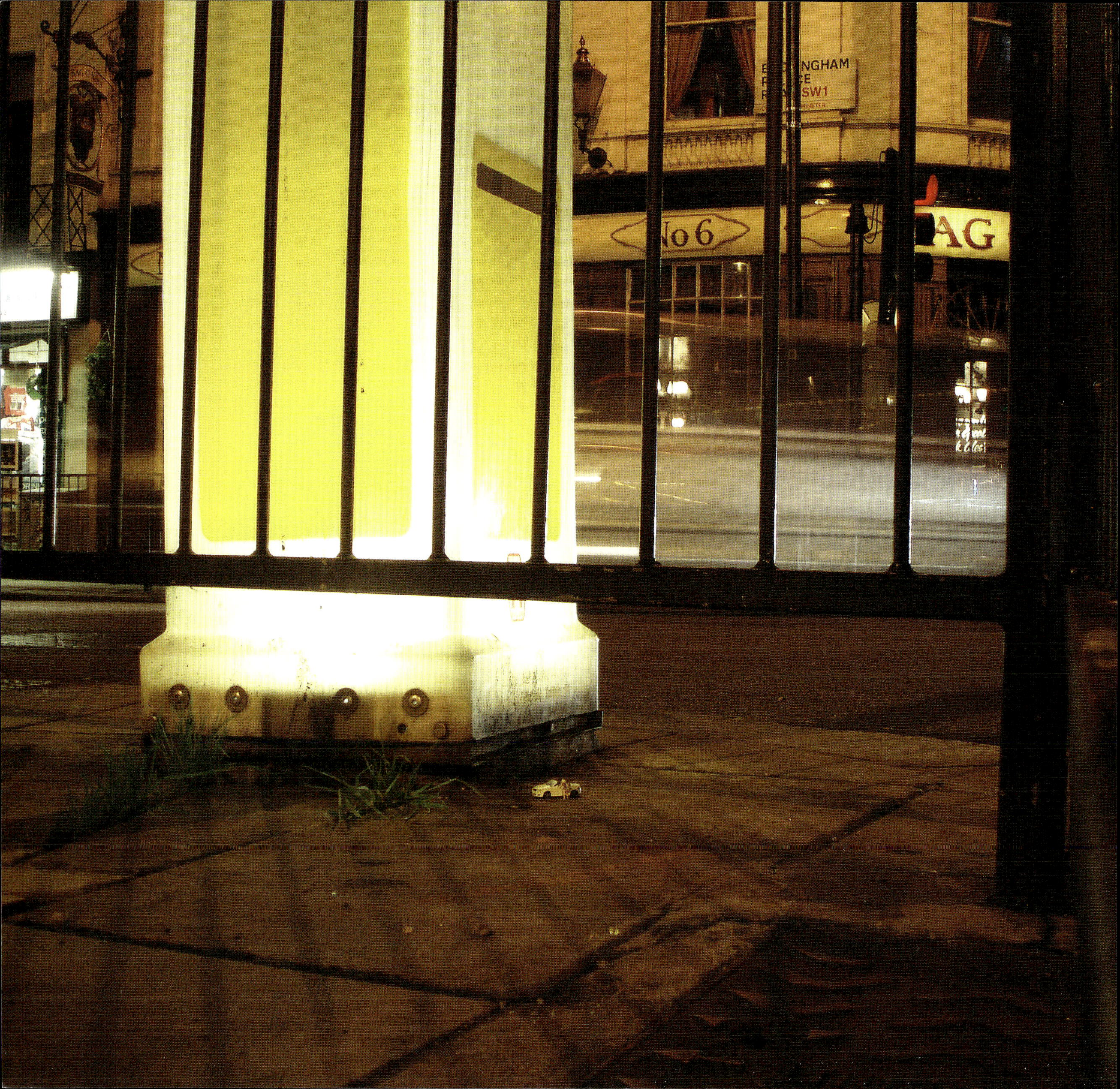
No 6

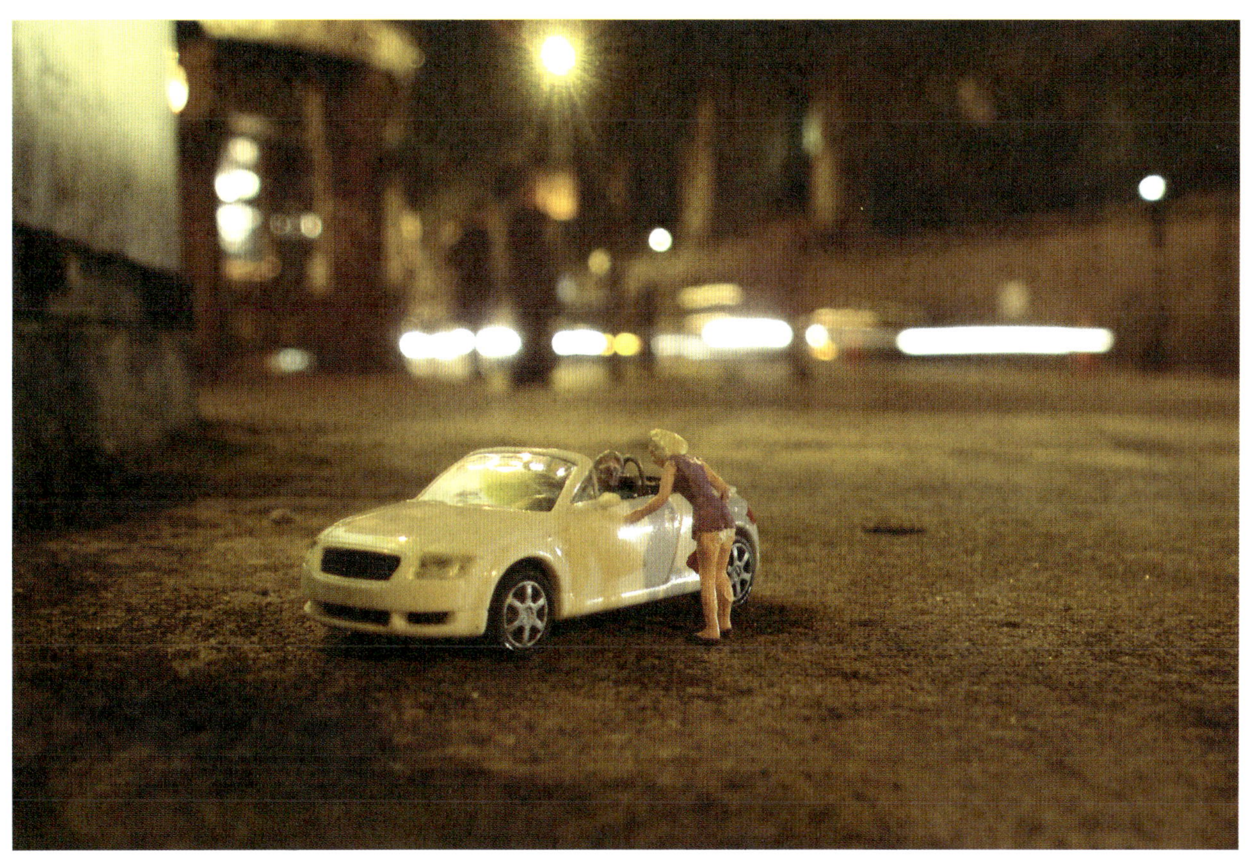

For Sale/Sold

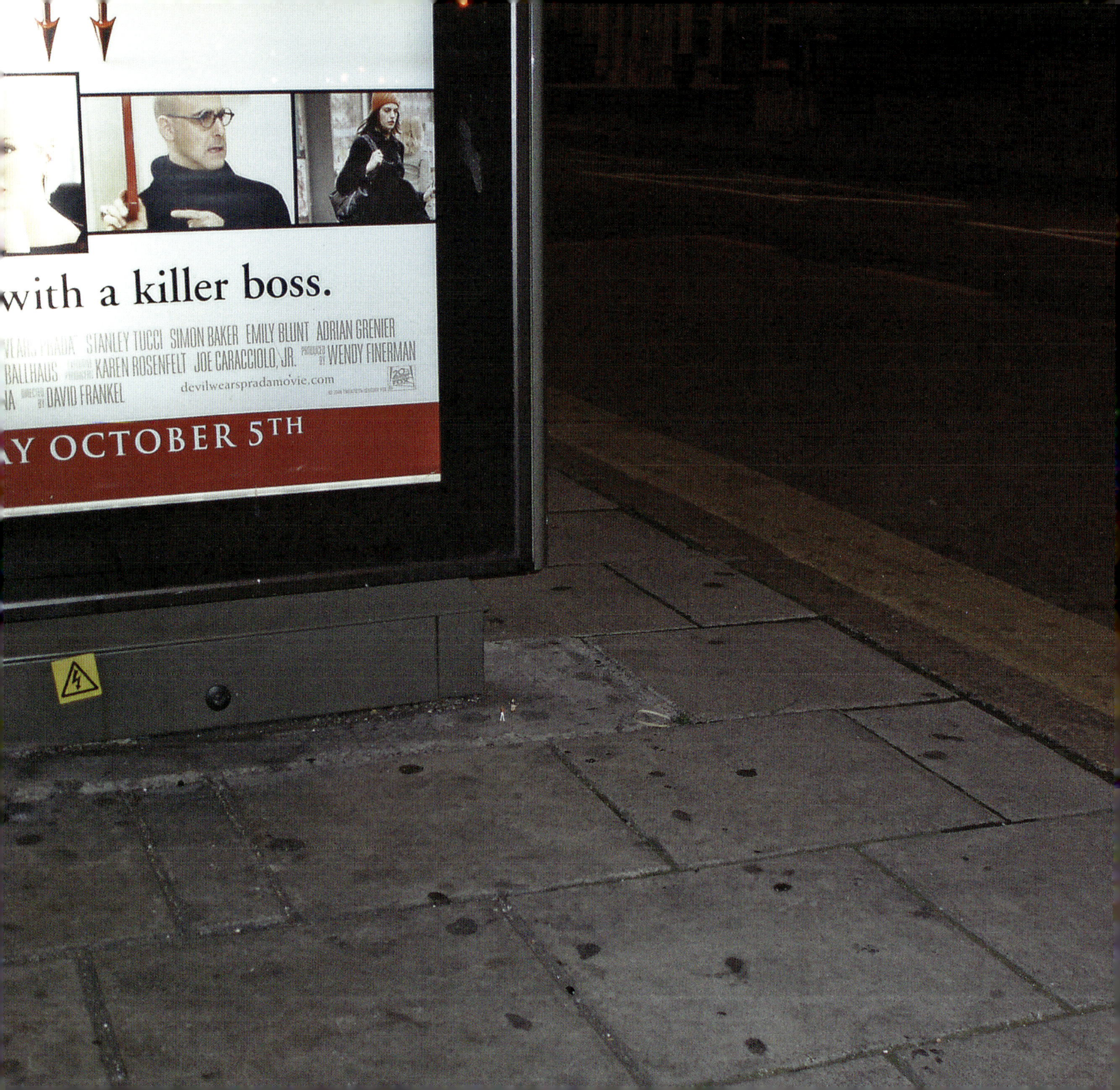

with a killer boss.
STANLEY TUCCI SIMON BAKER EMILY BLUNT ADRIAN GRENIER
BALLHAUS KAREN ROSENFELT JOE CARACCIOLO, JR. WENDY FINERMAN
DAVID FRANKEL
devilwearspradamovie.com
OCTOBER 5TH

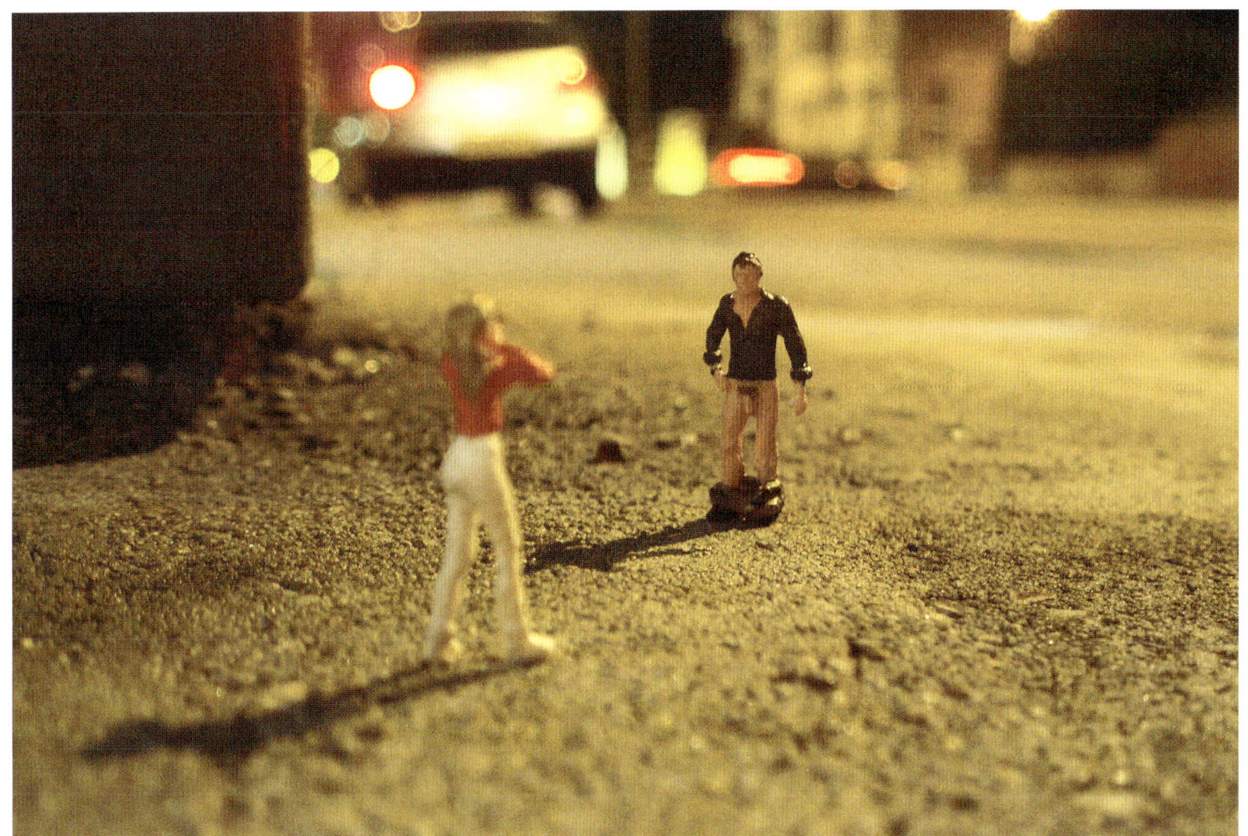

Indecent Proposal

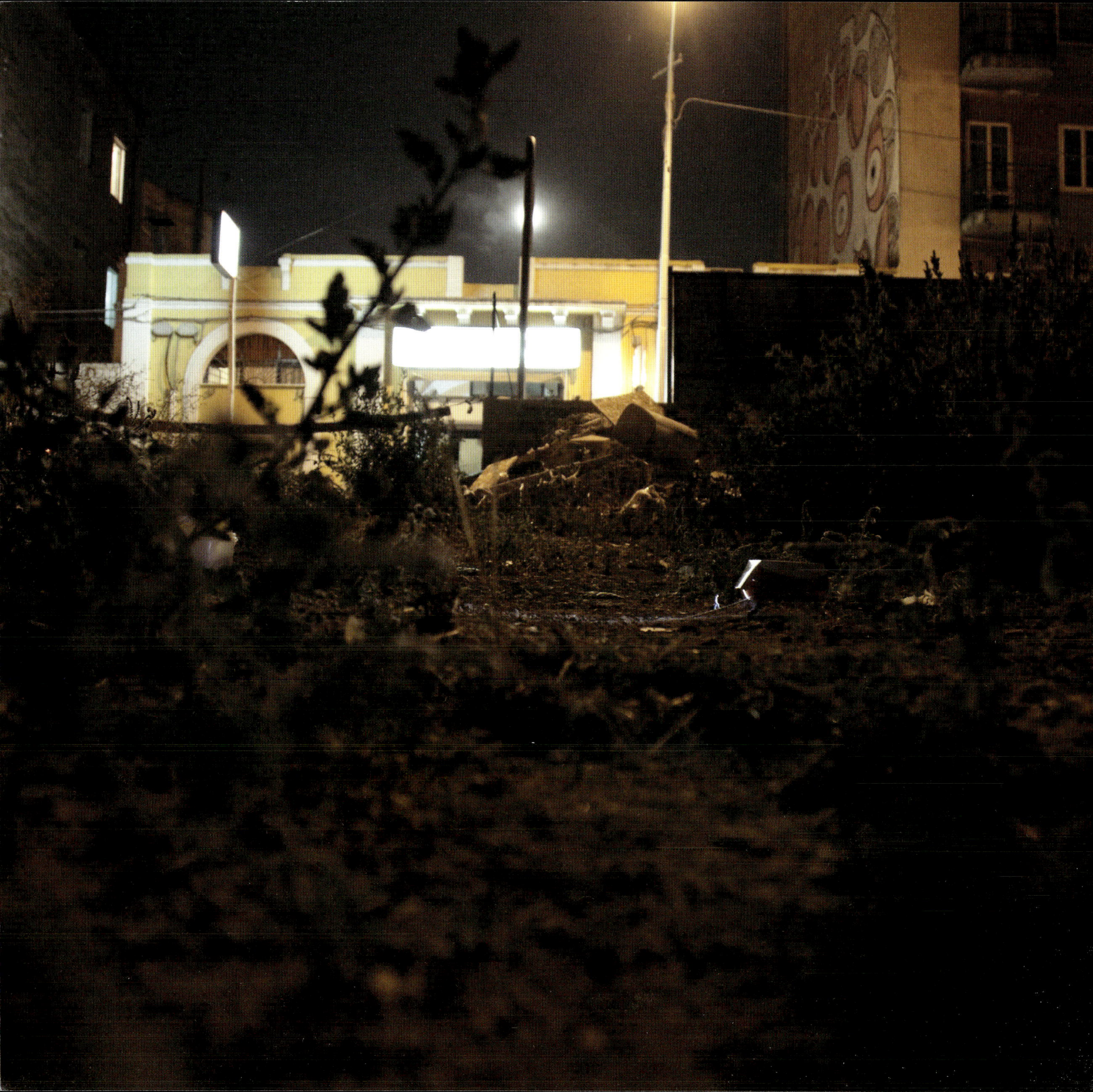

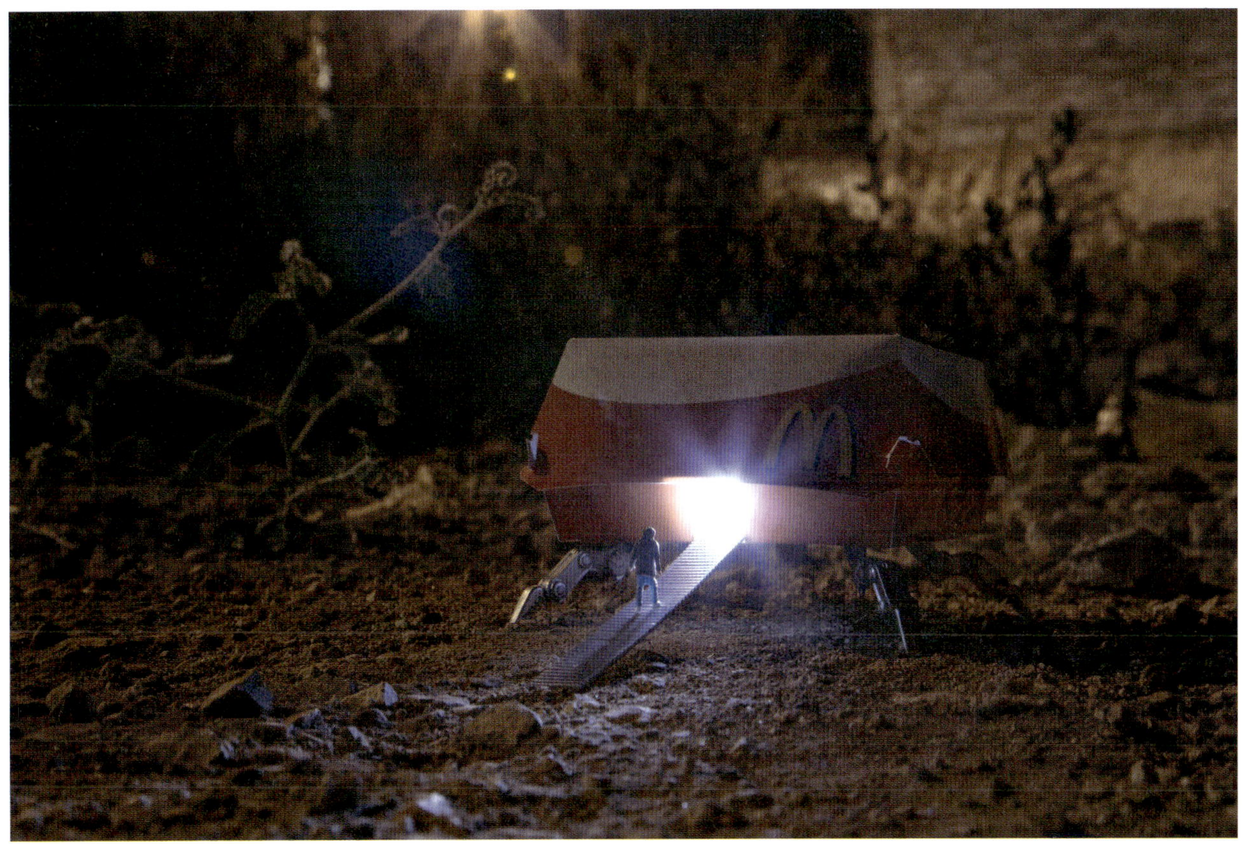

Life as We Know It

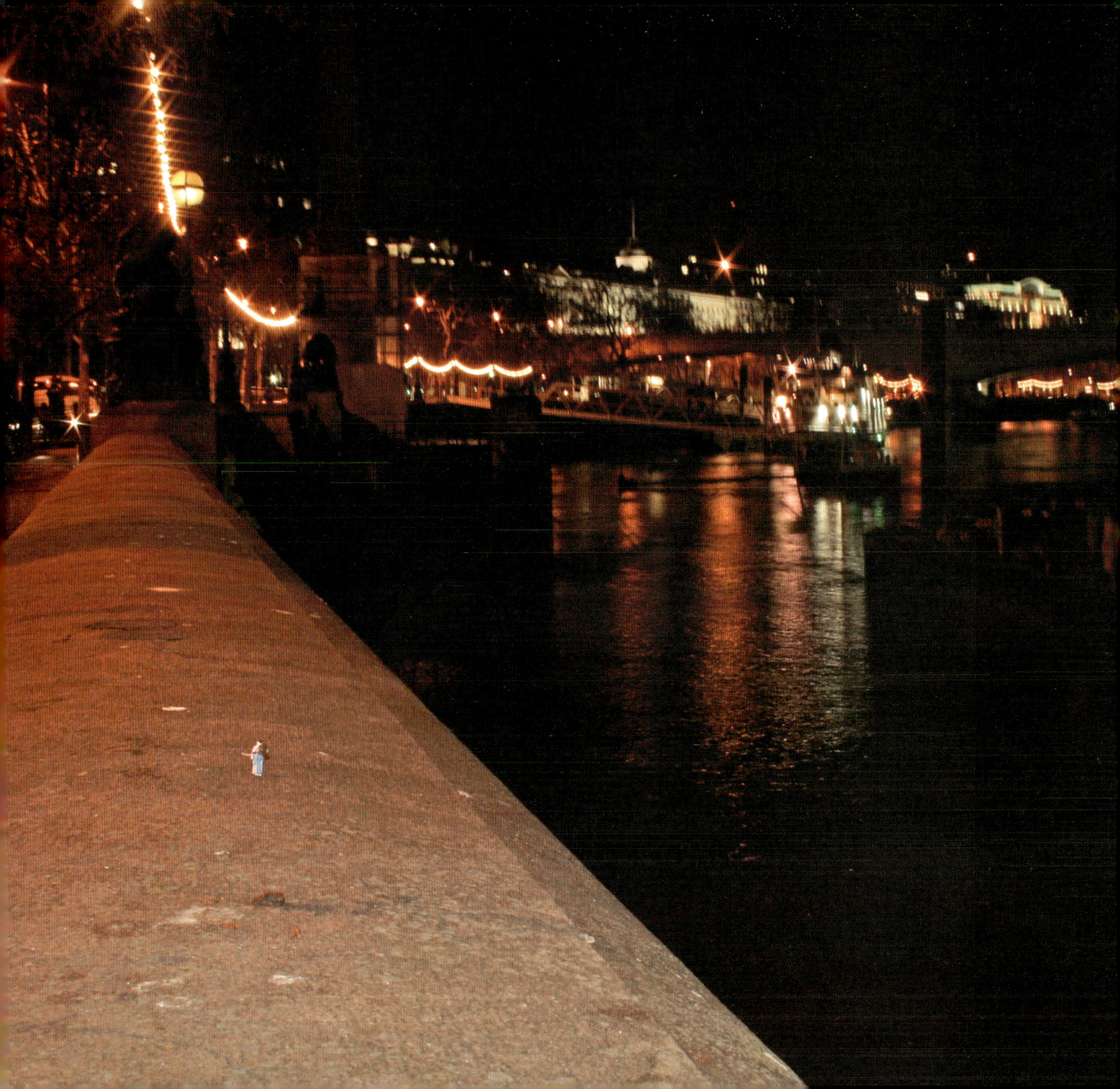

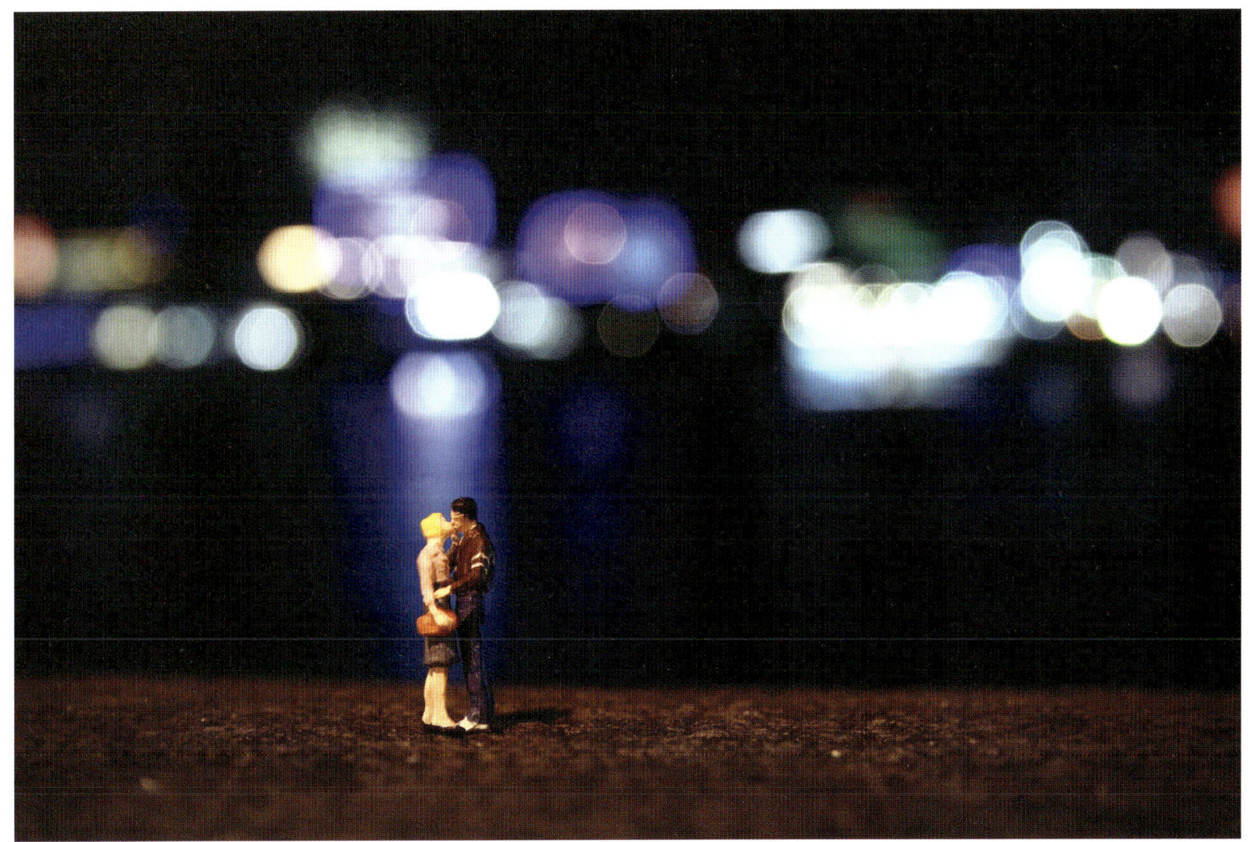
Last Kiss

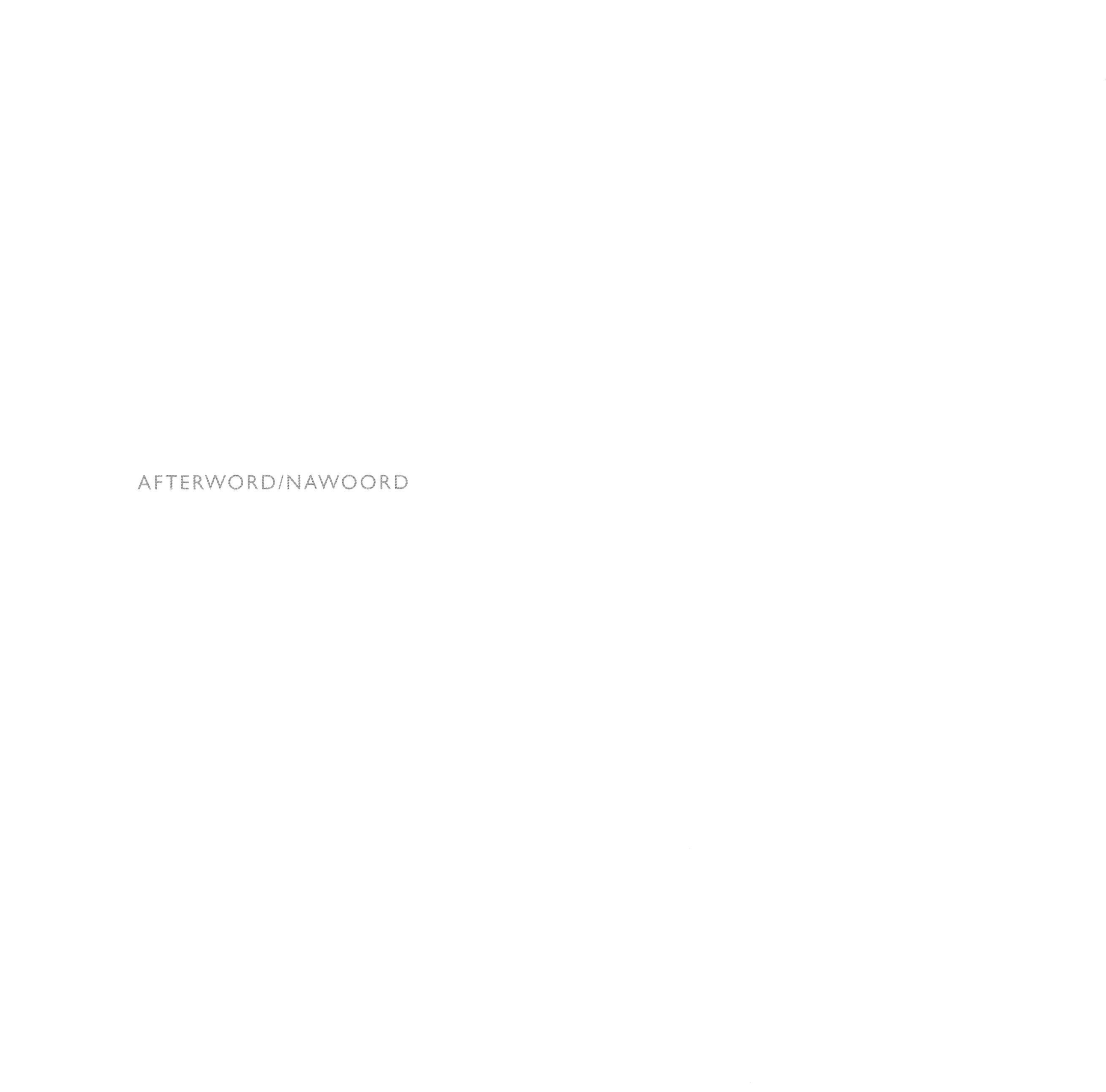

AFTERWORD/NAWOORD

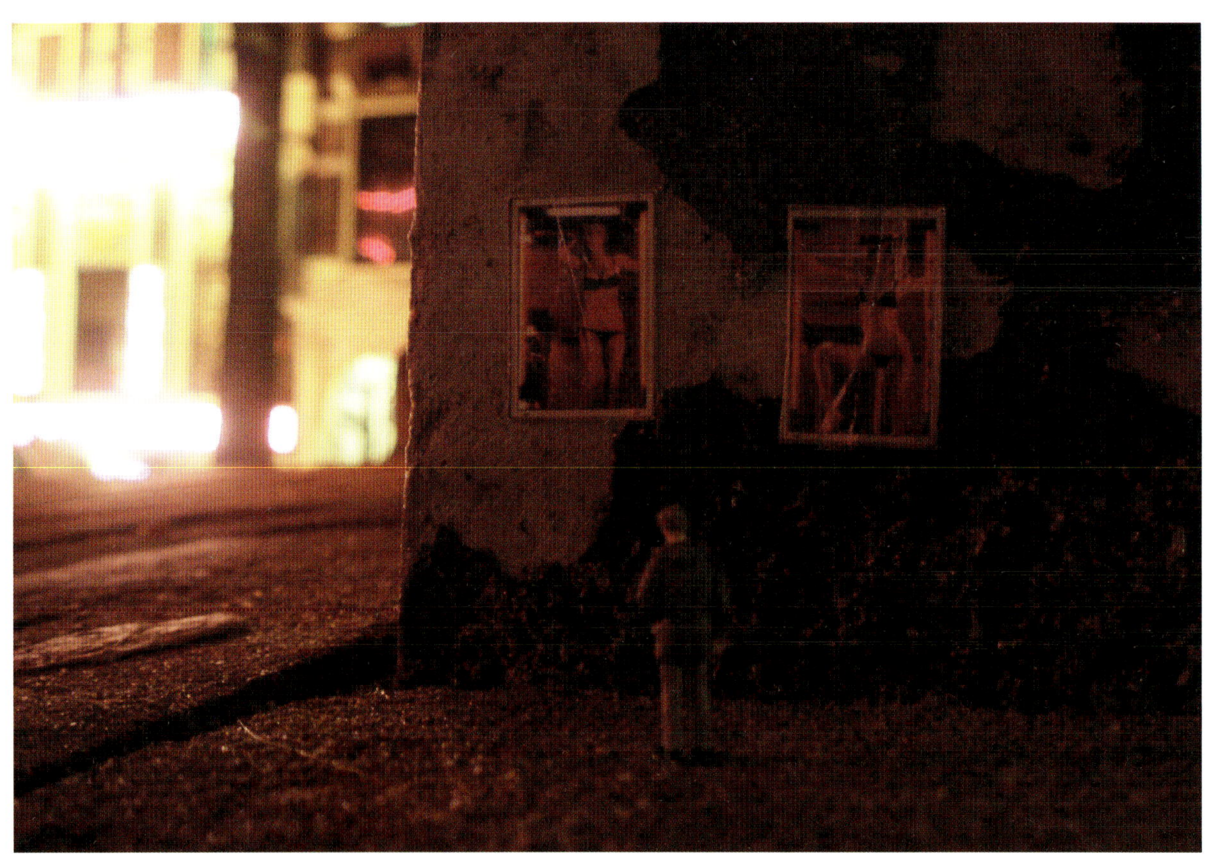

SLINKACHU'S GUIDE TO TAKING PERFECTLY FOCUSED, WELL-COMPOSED PHOTOGRAPHS IN AMSTERDAM'S NOTORIOUSLY CAMERA-ADVERSE RED LIGHT DISTRICT ON A FRIDAY NIGHT DURING THE HEIGHT OF THE TOURIST SEASON WITHOUT GETTING TRAMPLED, MUGGED OR BEATEN UP BY A PIMP.

STEP 1: Give up

STEP 2: Go get drunk

SLINKACHU'S HANDLEIDING VOOR HET MAKEN VAN HAARSCHERPE, COMPOSITORISCH STERKE FOTO'S, OP DE BERUCHTE CAMERA-ONVRIENDELIJKE AMSTERDAMSE WALLEN, OP EEN VRIJDAGAVOND, TIJDENS HET TOERISTISCH HOOGSEIZOEN, ZONDER ONDER DE VOET TE WORDEN GELOPEN, BEROOFD TE WORDEN, OF IN ELKAAR TE WORDEN GESLAGEN DOOR EEN POOIER.

STAP 1: Geef het op

STAP 2: Ga je klemzuipen

INDEX/INHOUD

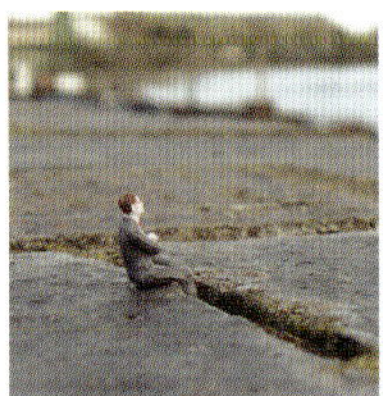

Pages 10 - 11

Dreams of Packing it All In

Hammersmith

London

2006

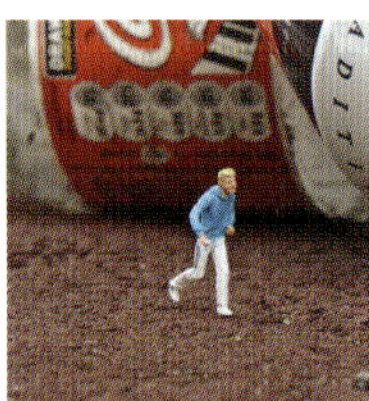

Pages 12 - 13

Scenic Route

Royal Oak area

London

2007

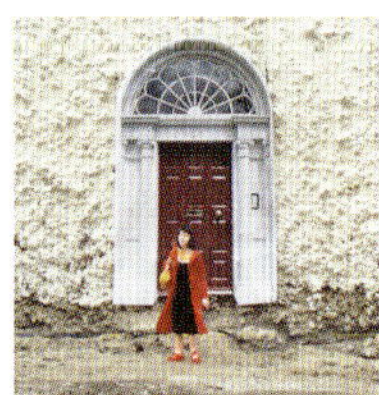

Pages 14 - 15

Paddington Doorway

Paddington

London

2006

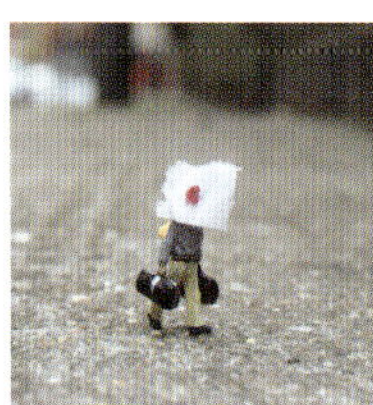

Pages 16 - 17

Close Shave

Soho

London

2009

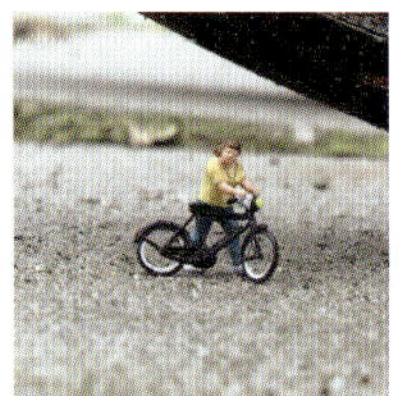

Pages 18 - 19

Living Life in the Cycle Lane

Amstel Station

Amsterdam

2009

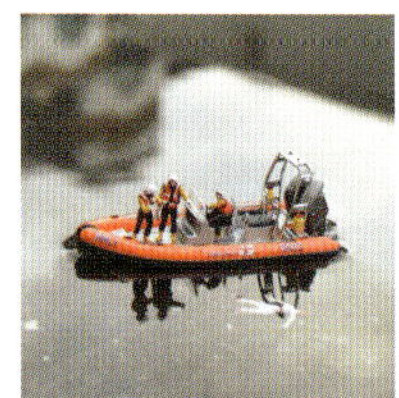

Pages 20 - 21

After the Storm

lower Hill

London

2008

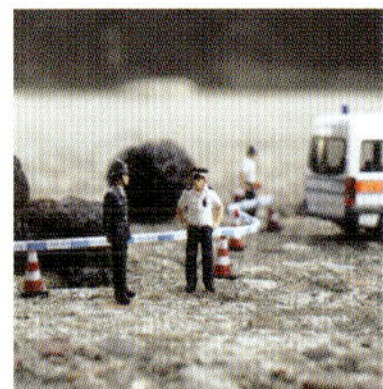

Pages 34 - 35

Terror Alert

Shoreditch

London

2007

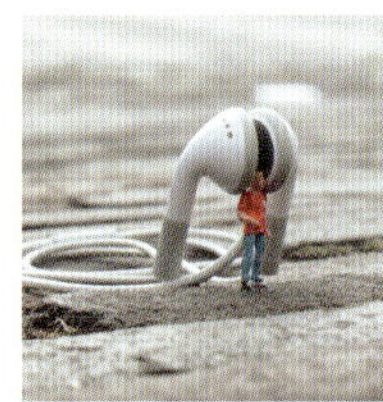

Pages 36 - 37

Background Noise

Homomonument

Amsterdam

2009

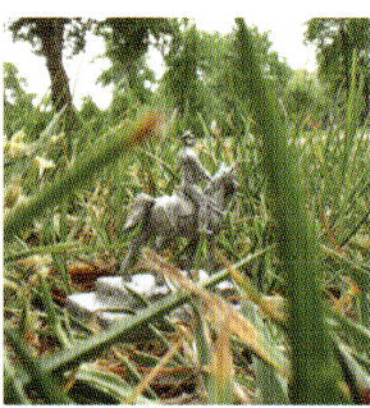

Pages 38 - 39

The Forgotten Soldier

Kensington Park

London

2007

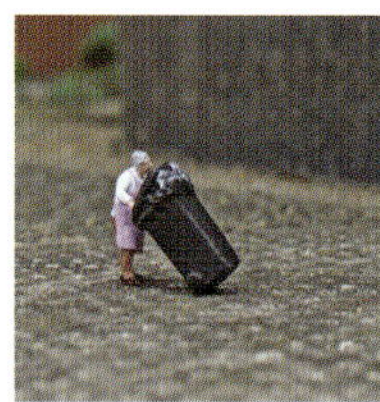

Pages 40 - 41

Bin Day

Lewisham

London

2007

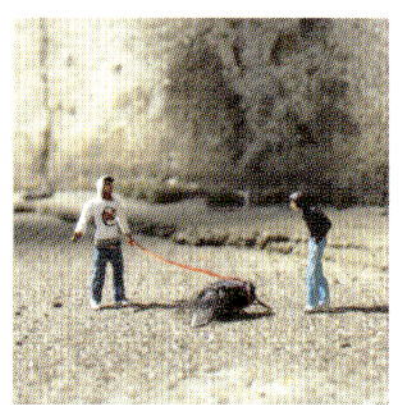

Pages 42 - 43

Banned Breed

South Kensington

London

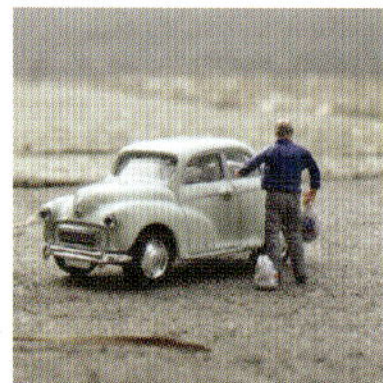

Pages 44 - 45

Shopping for One Again

Chiswick

London

2006

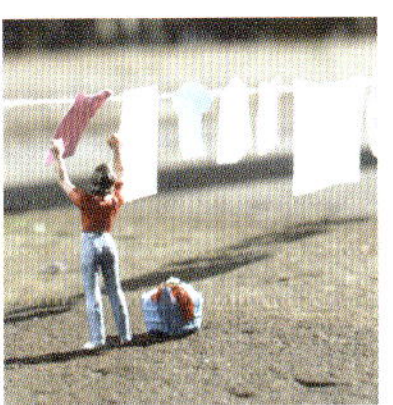

Pages 22 - 23

Hung Up

Shoreditch

London

2007

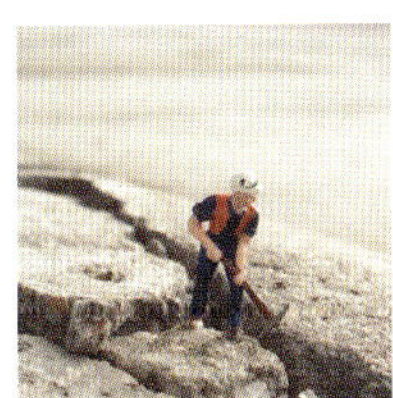

Pages 24 - 25

Roadworks

Vauxhall

London

2006

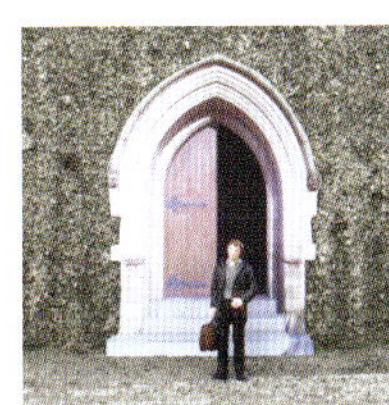

Pages 30 –31

Quiet Sunday

Mary le Bow church

Cheapside

London

2007

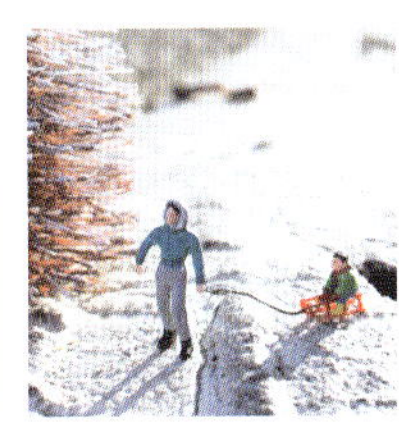

Pages 28 - 29

Wonderland

Battersea

London

2009

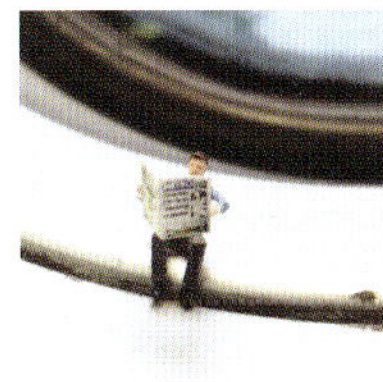

Pages 30 - 31

Commuting

District Line

London metro

2006

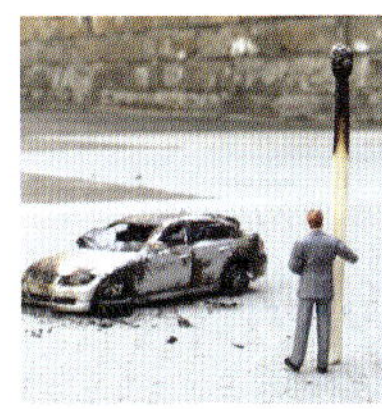

Pages 32 - 33

Company Car

Ladbroke Grove

London

2008

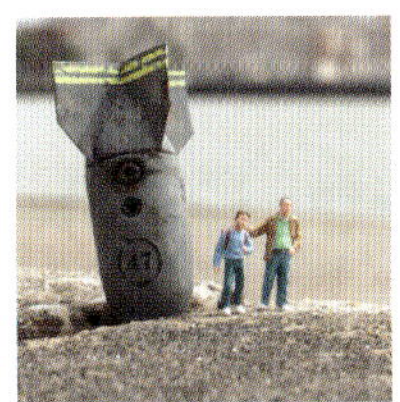

Pages 46 - 47

The Spoils of War

Boompjeskade

Rotterdam

2009

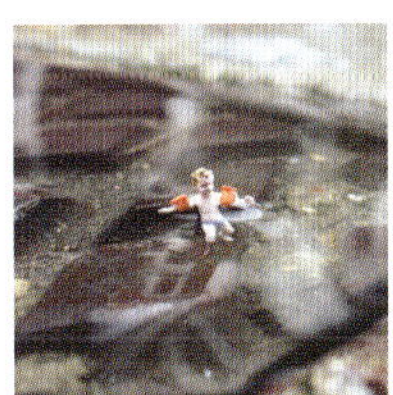

Pages 48 - 49

Manhole Swimming

Ravenscourt Park

London

2006

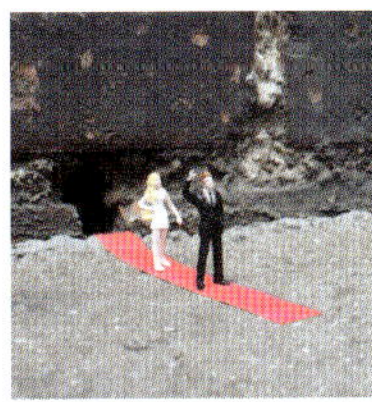

Pages 50 - 51

D-List

Westminster bridge

London

2007

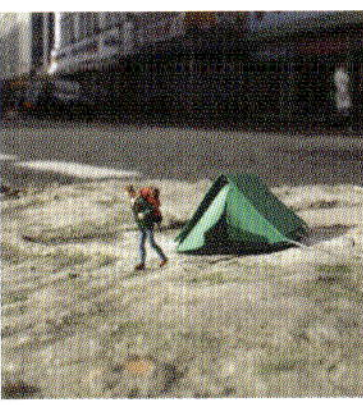

Pages 52 - 53

Urban Camping

Manchester

2007

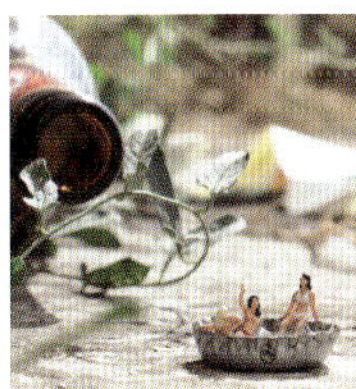

Pages 54 - 55

The High Life

Grottaglie

Italy

2009

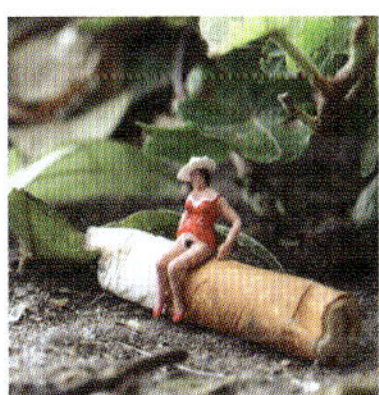

Pages 56 - 57

Exhibitionism

Hammersmith

London

2007

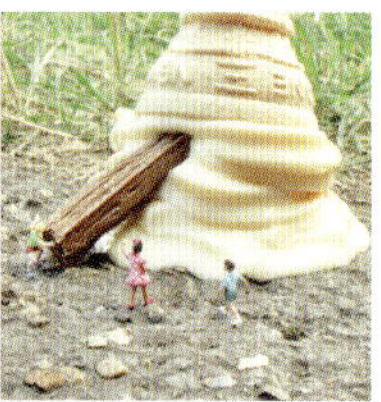

Pages 58 - 59

The Mother Lode

Hyde Park

London

2007

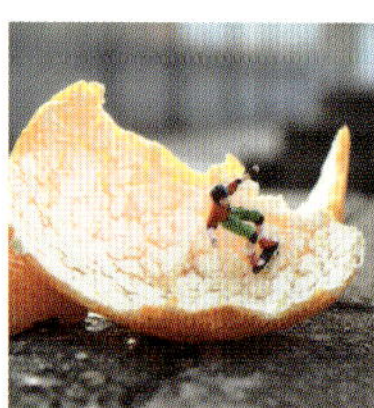

Pages 60 - 61

Local Amenities for Children

Finsbury Leisure Centre

London

2008

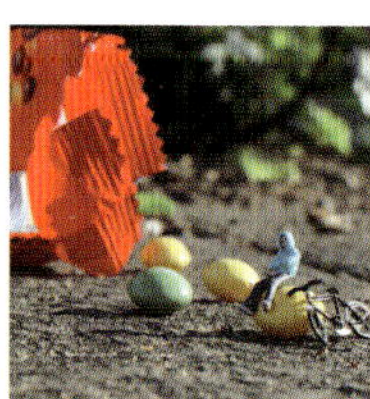

Pages 62 - 63

Unwanted Ones

Westferry

London

2008

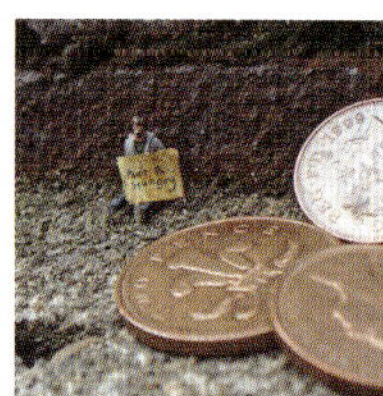

Pages 64 - 65

'Spare some change'

Hammersmith

London

2007

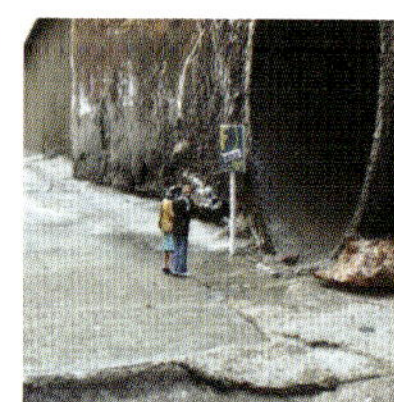

Pages 66 - 67

Our First Home

Farringdon

London

2007

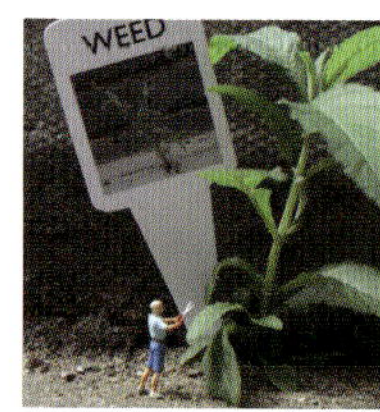

Pages 68 - 69

Britain in Bloom

Shoreditch

London

2008

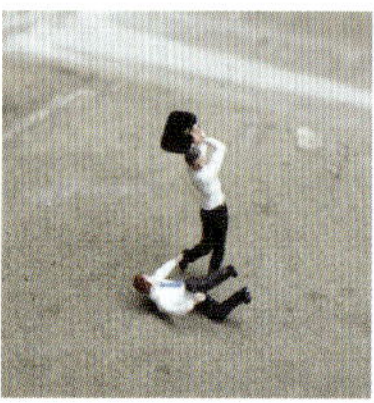

Pages 82 - 83

Office Politics

Liverpool Street area

London

2006

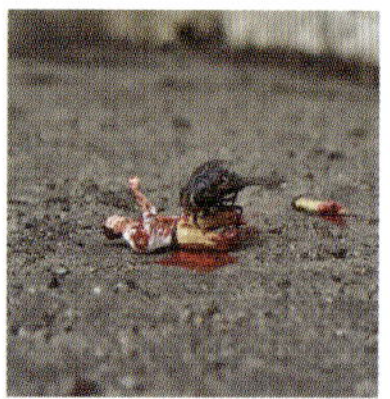

Pages 84 - 85

The Feast

London Bridge

London

2006

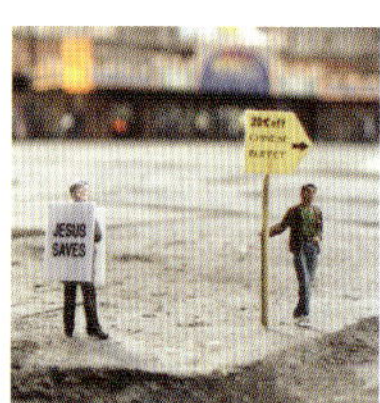

Pages 86 - 87

Jesus Saves

Cambridge Circus

London

2006

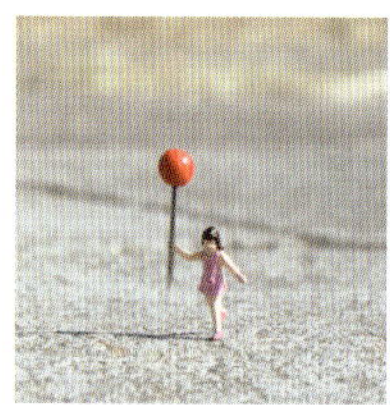

Pages 88 - 89

Concealed Weapon

Shepherds Bush

London

2008

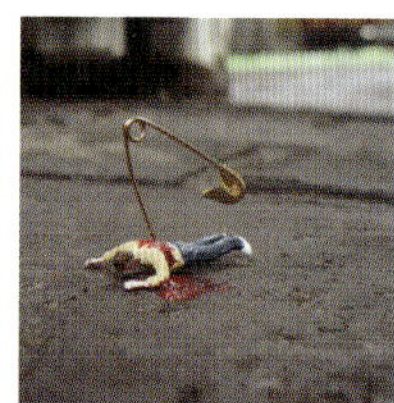

Pages 90 - 91

Pinned Down

Euston

London

2006

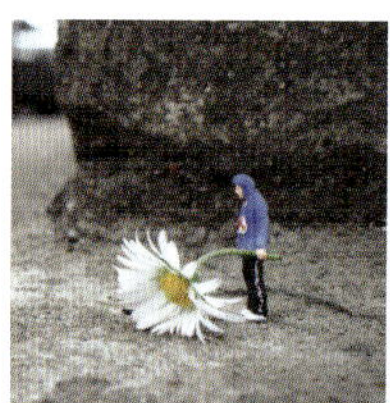

Pages 92 - 93

Ground Zero

Old Street area

London

2008

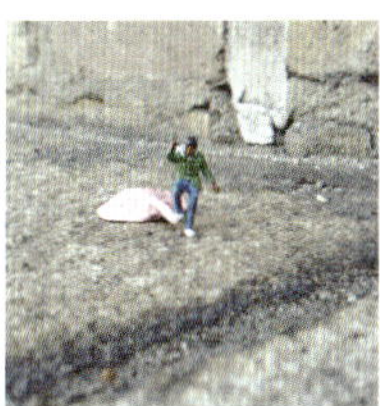

Pages 70 - 71
Gum
West India Quay
London
2006

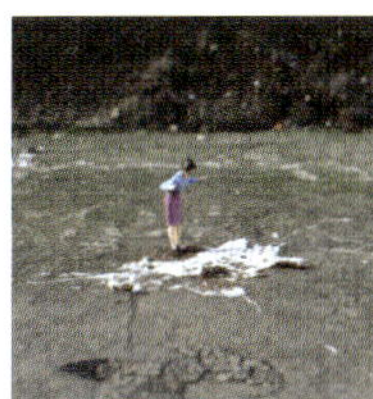

Pages 72 - 73
One False Move
Lena Street
Manchester
2007

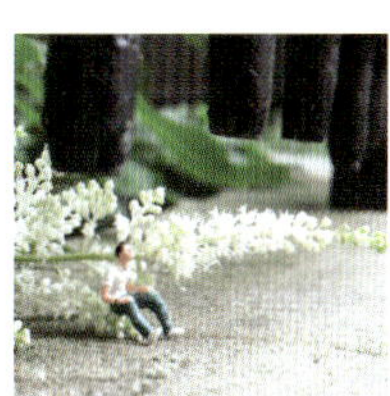

Pages 74 - 75
30 minutes
Postman's Park
London
2007

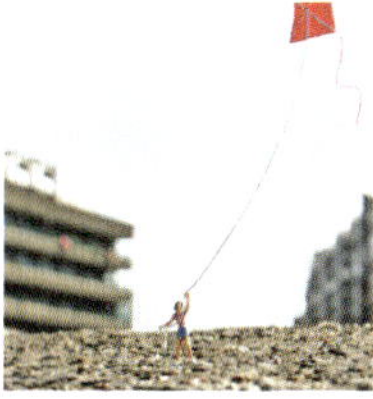

Pages 76 - 77
High as a Kite
Barbican
London
2007

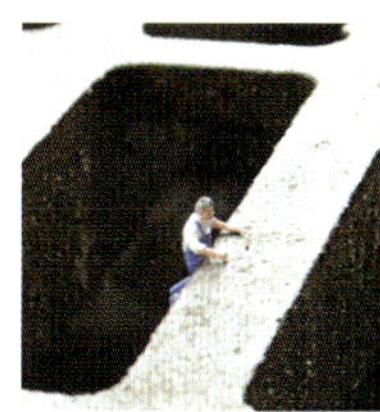

Pages 78 - 79
Drain Guy
Kings Cross area
London
2007

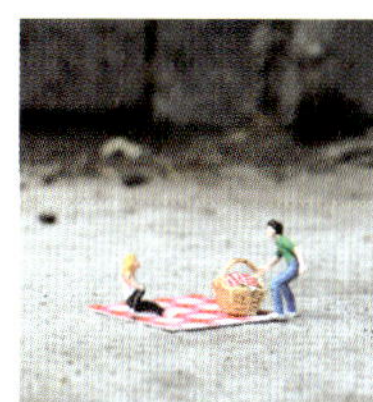

Pages 80 - 81
Last Chance to Impress
Soho
London
2008

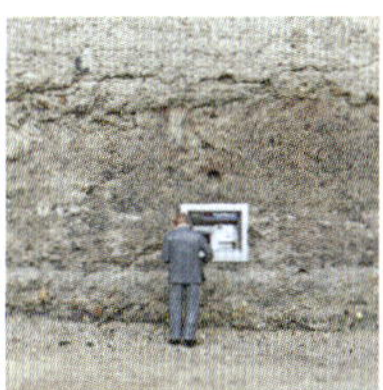

Pages 94 - 95
Cash Machine
Hammersmith
London
2007

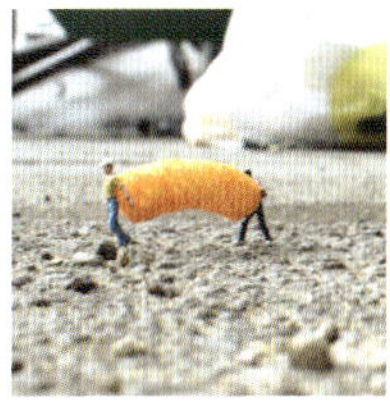

Pages 96 - 97
Scavengers
Finsbury Park
London
2008

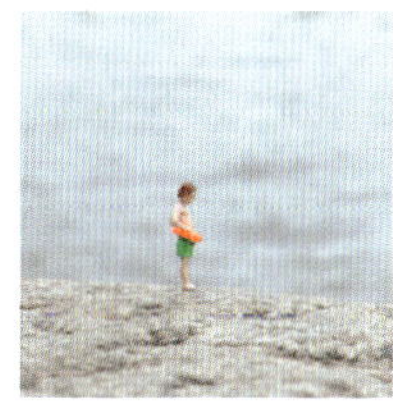

Pages 98 - 99
Flotsam
Amstelkade
Amsterdam
2009

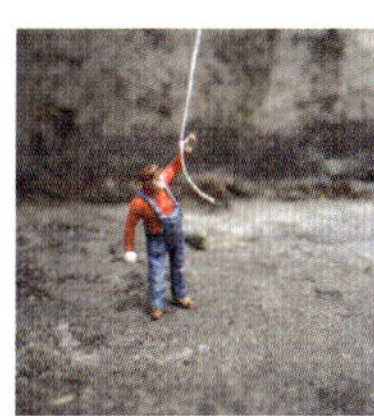

Pages 100 - 101
Balloon Man
Covent Garden area
London
2006

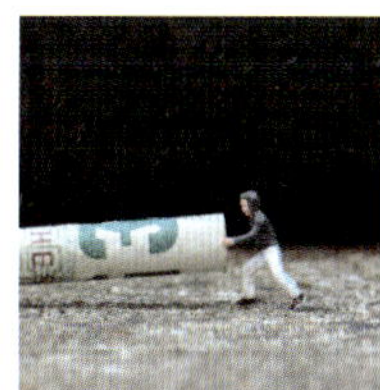

Pages 102 - 103
Pocket Money
Shoreditch
London
2008

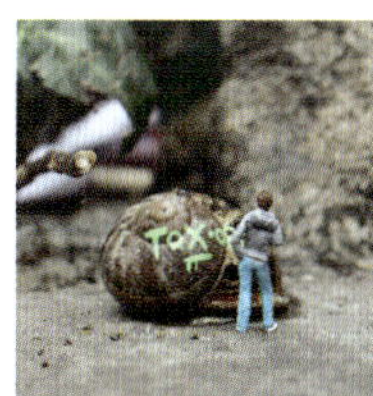

Pages 104 - 105
Tagging
Shepherds Bush
London
2008

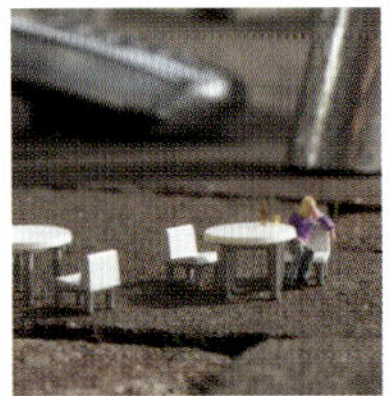

Pages 106 - 107
Spare Chair
Spui
Amsterdam
2009

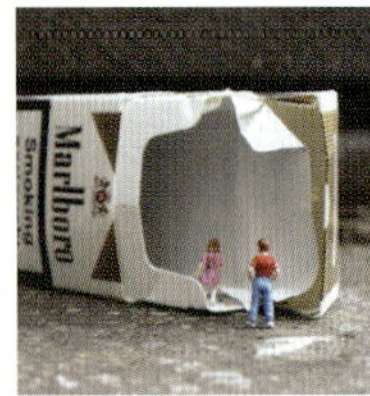

Pages 108 - 109
The Den
Manchester
2007

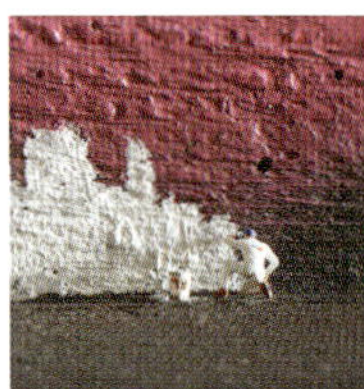

Pages 110 - 111
Buffing
Royal Festival Hall
London
2007

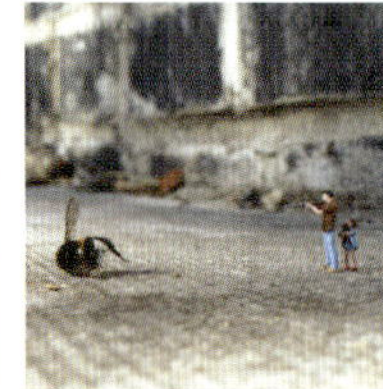

Pages 112 - 113
'They're not pets Susan'
Primrose Hill
London
2007

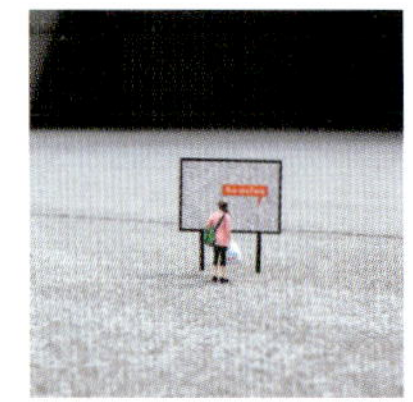

Pages 114 - 115
Tundra
Liverpool Street area
2008

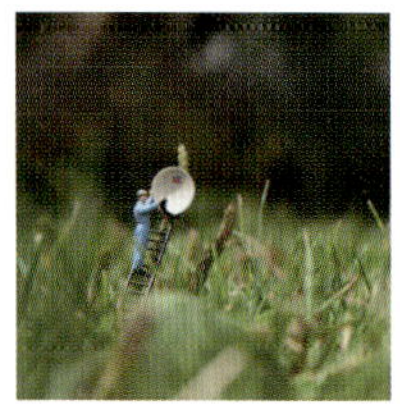

Pages 116 - 117
The Great Indoors
Vondelpark
Amsterdam
2009

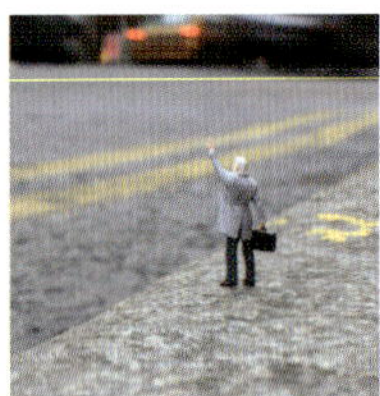

Pages 130 - 131
'Taxi!' (new version)
West End
London
2009

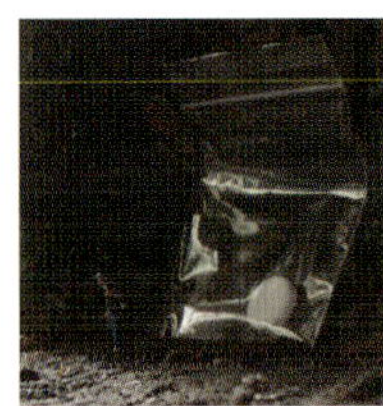

Pages 132 - 133
Dealer
Ravenscourt Park
London
2006

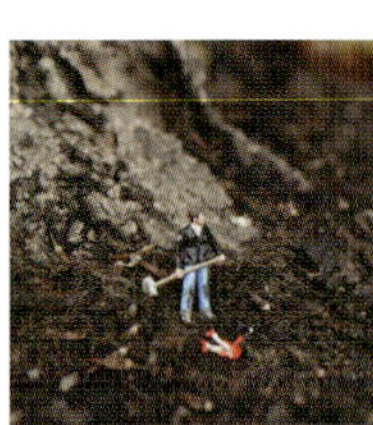

Pages 134 - 135
Bad First Date
Paddington
London
2007

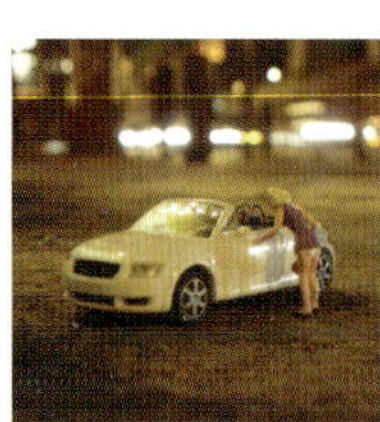

Pages 136 - 137
For Sale/Sold
Victoria
London
2006

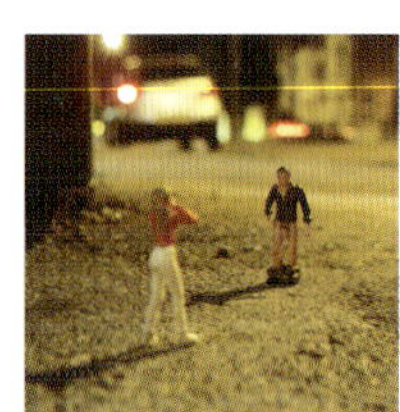

Pages 138 - 139
Indecent Proposal
Putney
London
2006

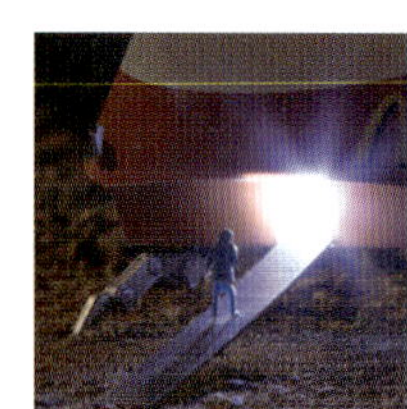

Pages 140 - 141
Life as We Know It
Grottaglie
Italy
2009

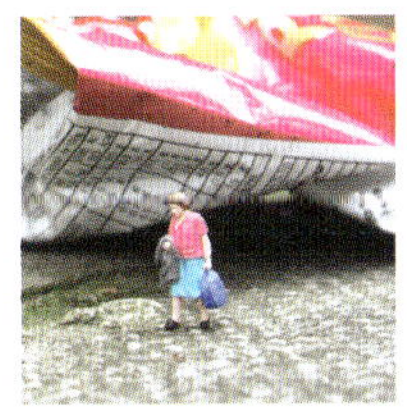

Pages 118 - 119

One Day He'll Notice Me

Notting Hill

London

2007

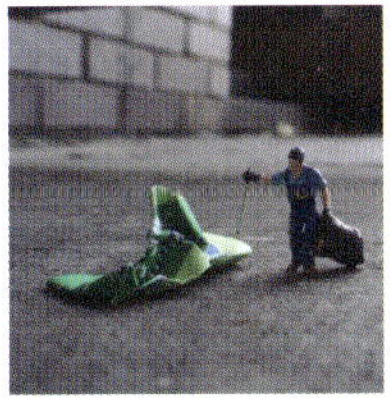

Pages 120 - 121

Rubbish

Euston

London

2006

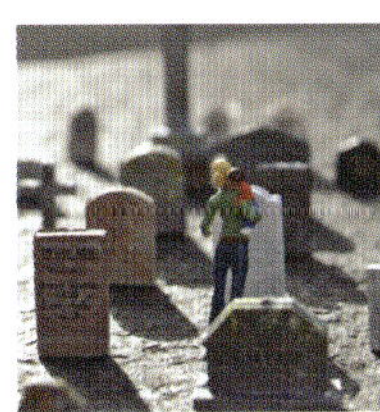

Pages 122 - 123

Twelve Months Later

Cathedral Gardens

Manchester

2007

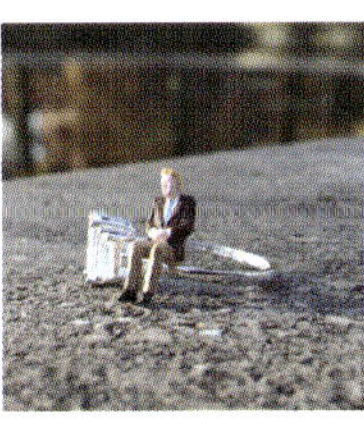

Pages 124 - 125

Plan B

Hyde Park

London

2007

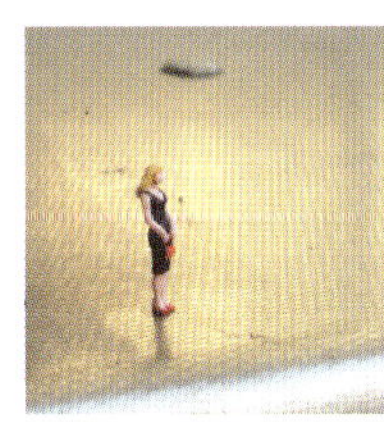

Pages 126 - 127

Stood Up Again

Southwark

London

2006

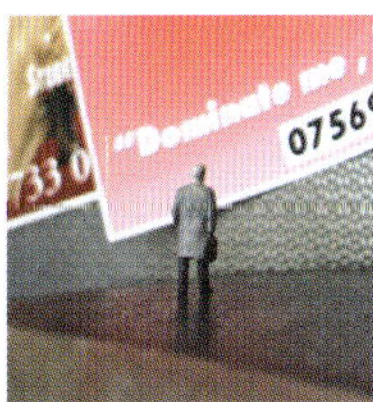

Pages 128 - 129

Phone Box

Great Marlborough Street

London

2008

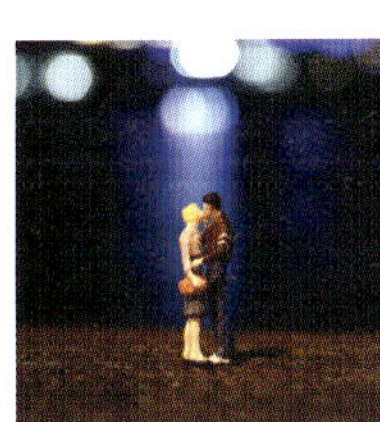

Pages 142 - 143

Last Kiss

Embankment

London

2008